JOINT TRUST PENSION PLANS

Pension Research Council

**Other Publications of the
PENSION RESEARCH COUNCIL**

JOINT TRUST PENSION PLANS

Understanding and Administering Collectively Bargained Multiemployer Plans under ERISA

DANIEL F. McGINN, F.S.A., F.C.I.A.
President, Dan McGinn & Associates Inc.
Los Angeles

Published for the

Pension Research Council
Wharton School
University of Pennsylvania

by

RICHARD D. IRWIN, INC.   Homewood, Illinois   60430
Irwin-Dorsey Limited   Georgetown, Ontario   L7G 4B3

PURPOSE OF THE COUNCIL

The Pension Research Council was formed in 1952 in response to an urgent need for a better understanding of the private pension mechanism. It is composed of nationally recognized pension experts representing leadership in every phase of private pensions. It sponsors academic research into the problems and issues surrounding the private pension institution and publishes the findings in a series of books and monographs. The studies are conducted by mature scholars drawn from both the academic and business spheres.

FOREWORD

Collectively-bargained multiemployer pension plans account for about one fifth of the total coverage of private pension plans. By and large they cover segments of the labor force where the employment relationship with a single employer is tenuous or of temporary duration; consequently, coverage under a conventional corporate pension plan would generally be ineffective. To provide protection against old-age penury, collectively bargained multiemployer pension plans, herein called *joint trust pension plans,* utilize concepts and techniques not found among plans with single employer sponsorship. Some of these features are at once the strength and weakness of the joint trust approach to plan sponsorship and administration.

Despite the great importance of these plans and their challenging characteristics, there is a paucity of literature about them. There have been scattered articles in professional journals and the trade press, and the International Foundation of Employee Benefit Plans has published materials on special aspects of their operations. However, prior to the preparation of this book there was no comprehensive, up-to-date treatise that treated the entire subject in a systematic and balanced manner. The professionals who administer and provide technical services to these plans seem to have been understandably too preoccupied with their day-to-day responsibilities to describe their operations. Unfortunately, there also has been a reluctance on the part of some individuals and firms to share the special insights that they have gained over the years.

With the establishment of the Certified Employee Benefit Specialist (CEBS) program by the International Foundation of Employee Benefit Plans and the Wharton School, the need for an authoritative treatment of joint trust pension plans became imperative. A thorough understanding of the legal, actuarial, and administrative structure of these plans is essential for anyone who holds himself out as a professional in this field. This book meets that need admirably. It is authoritative, pragmatic, up-to-the-minute, and highly readable. It deals with all the major facets of plan operation, with special emphasis on the actuarial function.

Dan McGinn is eminently well-qualified to write on the subject. A Fellow of the Society of Actuaries, he heads a rapidly growing firm of consulting actuaries that serves both joint trust and corporate benefit clients. His clientele includes several of the nation's largest joint trust plans. While he is located on the West Coast, and the bulk of his practice is there, he has clients in many parts of this country and in Canada. Moreover, he has professional ties with other organizations that have given him a truly national exposure to joint trust practices and operations. The manuscript was read by a large body of practitioners whose comments and suggestions reflected their broad experience in the field.

The Pension Research Council is deeply indebted to Dan McGinn for undertaking this prodigious task. Already heavily burdened with responsibilities flowing from ERISA and the management of his firm, he somehow found the time to organize and write this massive tome. Despite the pressures on his time and the very natural desire to get the job over with, he was extremely meticulous in his research and in his exposition. He rewrote and reorganized until the product measured up to his high standards. He can take justifiable pride in his accomplishment. The book makes a unique contribution to pension literature.

As with all Council publications, the views expressed herein are those of the author and should not be imputed to any member or members of the Council.

May 1978   DAN M. McGILL

PREFACE

Although there is general public awareness of the existence of so-called union pension funds, there is little understanding of the ramifications of these pension plans into the lives of millions of employees. Also, there is practically a total lack of public knowledge of the conditions under which these pension funds operate, the rules and regulations governing pension fund investments, and the rights of beneficiaries.

As the reader will learn in this text, the so-called union pension funds result from collective bargaining between unions and employers and must, by law, be under the joint control of an equal number of union *and* employer trustees. These plans are, therefore, collectively bargained multiemployer pension plans jointly administered by union and management trustees, and throughout this text will be referred to as "joint trust pension plans."

This book is intended to provide trustees, employers, plan participants, employees, governmental agencies, students, and the public with practical insight into the operations of these pension plans and to create an awareness of the complicated conditions under which they were created and have grown—primarily during the last quarter century. I hope the readers of the book will be able to develop an understanding of how these pension plans have been established, are being administered, and may grow in the future. As a result, perhaps the readers will recognize the importance of the continued success of these pension plans in the lives of millions of union-represented employees throughout the United States.

The text of this book has been developed with a great deal of outside technical and editorial assistance. The viewpoints, opinions, suggestions, and commentaries provided by experts in the field of employee benefits, and especially pensions, have been invaluable in assisting me to develop the initial manuscript and in making numerous technical revisions and modifications.

The members of the Pension Research Council were very help-ful in providing valuable insights and viewpoints. The editorial and technical assistance provided by Dan McGill, chairman of the Council, was outstanding. In addition, the following Council members contributed generously: Donald S. Grubbs, F.S.A., E.A., Consulting Actuary with George B. Buck, Consulting Actuaries; Howard E. Winklevoss, E.A., Consulting Actuary, Winklevoss & Associates, Inc.; and Robert Tilove, Senior Vice President, Martin E. Segal Company.

The actuarial commentaries and criticisms of Raymond Bend-er, F.S.A., E.A., Vice President and Actuary of Prudential In-surance Company, were remarkable. This text reflects a great reservoir of knowledge I accumulated while working jointly with Mr. Bender on a very large joint trust pension plan for over six years.

Two other individuals who generously offered assistance were Marc Gertner, Attorney, Shumaker, Loop & Kendrick and Warren Saltzman, Attorney, Saltzman and Johnson. Each law-yer's counsel on numerous legal aspects of ERISA were exceed-ingly helpful.

Finally, I wish to thank my own actuarial staff. Three actuaries acted as technical critics and editors. They are: Martin Stempel, F.S.A., E.A., Vice President and Actuary; Steven A. Eisenberg, F.S.A., E.A., Actuary; and J. Thomas Bolen, E.A., Associate Actuary. Their contributions remarkably improved the value of the ideas expressed and concepts explained.

In addition, the assistance of my secretarial staff during the lengthy development of the manuscript was outstanding. I espe-cially salute my long-time secretary, Anita Rosales, and her secre-tarial assistant, Julia Gossett, for their cheerful, thoughtful, energetic and cooperative efforts.

May 1978   DANIEL F. McGINN

CONTENTS

CHAPTER 1

INTRODUCTION

The subject of pension plans is a most complex topic—both for professionals in the field to explain and for laypersons to understand. Pensions involve numerous aspects of benefit design, tax consequences, actuarial calculations, public concerns regarding benefit equity between different generations of employees, and problems of plan investments and funding. The subject has always been difficult because of the diverse concerns of employers, employees, and the government. However, though the discussion of pensions in general is complicated, the several additional factors which influence joint trust pension plans makes the discussion of their establishment and maintenance even more difficult.

Joint trust pension plans are established when employers negotiate with unions to make contributions under collective bargaining agreements to pension plans. The Labor-Management Relations Act of 1947 (popularly known as the Taft-Hartley Act) sets out the conditions for negotiating such employee benefits and provides particular constraints on the operation of the resulting benefit plans. Most significantly, the act requires that employer contributions cannot be made to a union or its representative but must be made to a trust jointly and equally administered by union and employer representatives (or to a life insurance company under an insurance contract issued to the employer as contractholder). The fact that such a plan results from collective bargaining between employers and unions and is supported by contributions made to a trust, an entity separate from both parties but

1

jointly managed by representatives of both, is the dominant characteristic which distinguishes joint trust pension plans from other types of pension programs—notably corporate pension plans. A corporate pension plan may be subject, in whole or in part, to the collective bargaining process, but the plan and its fund are generally established and managed by the corporation alone.

In addition to the Taft-Hartley Act, the Employee Retirement Income Security Act of 1974 (known as ERISA) has had a significant impact on the operation of joint trust pension plans. ERISA imposes certain fiduciary duties and standards of conduct and minimum participation, vesting and funding requirements on all plans subject to the act, in addition to numerous other requirements and conditions, many of which have different provisions for joint trust plans—making even more intricate any discussion of joint trust pension plans.

The purpose of this text is to set forth for the reader both a comprehensive explanation of the structure of joint trust pension plans and a description of the environment in which they operate. It will be helpful, at the outset, for the reader to have a general understanding of the framework within which joint trust pension plans are established and maintained.

STEPS IN DEVELOPING THE PLAN

The first step in the development of a joint trust pension plan occurs when a union negotiates with an employer for contributions for pension benefits to be made under a written document, generally a collective bargaining agreement. The bargaining parties then retain legal counsel to prepare a trust agreement for execution by the collective bargaining parties. The trust agreement will provide for the establishment, continuation, and termination of the plan; the appointment of trustees; the receipt, investment, and use of employer contributions; and the delineation of the powers and duties of the trustees with respect to investment of fund assets and plan administration. After the trust agreement is signed and the bargaining parties have designated the trustees, the trustees are empowered to establish and administer a pension plan.

The next steps which the trustees must take include:

1. Arranging to have a pension plan designed and a plan document prepared. The trustees usually retain an actuary to design, within broad guidelines established by the trustees, alternate benefit structures that the bargained contributions can support, including the types of benefits and the conditions governing entitlement to those benefits. In order to perform the necessary actuarial cost calculations, the actuary must establish assumptions as to future experience of the plan by analyzing available employee census data, the economic factors which affect the trade or industry, and the provisions of the trust and collective bargaining agreements. After the trustees decide on the level of pension benefits and other plan features they wish to include, the actuary (or other consultant) prepares an initial plan document draft to ensure that the provisions are consistent with the basis used to develop costs. The pension plan's legal counsel then revises the plan draft, as required, so that the plan provisions will be in proper legal form and will meet the conditions of the Internal Revenue Code necessary for the tax qualification of the plan.

2. Establishing administrative procedures and practices for the plan. To manage the day-to-day affairs of the trust, the trustees will retain a contract administrator or employ a salaried administrator to establish all administrative procedures and practices required for the proper operation of the plan; that is, the preparation of necessary information relating to the plan for distribution to participants, the billing and collection of employer contributions, the payment of benefits, the gathering of census data required for benefit calculation purposes and the actuary's periodic cost studies, and the preparation of forms for timely filings with governmental authorities. The trustees will also retain an accountant to ensure that practices and procedures are established correctly, all governmental requirements are properly met, and independent reports of plan operations are prepared for the trustees.

3. Selecting an investment manager who will invest the accumulated employer contributions not currently required for benefit payments and expenses. (The trustees are responsible under law for the investment of trust assets; however, ERISA specifically allows for the delegation of this responsibility to a

professional investment manager, and most trustees do dele-gate investment responsibility.) The trustees, together with the investment manager, then will establish an investment pol-icy to carry out their investment objectives. The investment income earned on such invested funds, together with future employer contributions not required for then current benefit payments and expenses, should be sufficient to pay for all future benefits and expenses of the trust during its lifetime.

Thus, it may be seen that the framework for the operation of a joint trust pension plan involves five basic elements; the collective bargaining agreement, the trust agreement, the pension plan, administrative procedures, and investment practices.

In some areas of operation, administration of a joint trust pen-sion plan requires an interface between the bargaining parties and the plan's board of trustees. In numerous other situations, the board of trustees is frequently involved with the plan's partici-pants, professional advisors (attorney, actuary, accountant, invest-ment manager, and administrator), and governmental authorities. The text of this book will address the concerns of the joint trust pension plan from its inception through its requirements to suc-cessfully meet the demands of the plan participants, the govern-ment, the union, and the contributing employers.

As a starting point, it will be helpful to provide a brief overview of the legal background in which joint trust and other benefit plans developed. With this information, the reader will more read-ily understand why Congress believed that ERISA was necessary and will understand the environment in which the joint trust pen-sion plans exist today.

LEGAL AND REGULATORY FRAMEWORK

The historical background of joint trust pension plans probably looks—at first glance—like a patchwork quilt of conflicting and confusing law. This is perhaps due to the evolution of the activities of labor unions. The present legal foundation of a labor union was laid by the National Labor Relations Act of 1935, better known as the Wagner Act. This act gave employees the right to organize, making the right legally enforceable by requiring employers to bargain collectively with employees through representatives chosen by the employees. The act also established the National Labor Relations Board and gave it jurisdiction over questions of representation and unfair labor practices. The act required employers to bargain with union representatives for the "wages" and "conditions of employment" of the employees they represented. After many years it was established by court decision that benefit plans, especially pensions, were a mandatory subject for collective bargaining.

In 1947 the Labor-Management Relations Act (Taft-Hartley Act) became law and established an independent federal agency for mediation and conciliation of labor disputes. With respect to employee benefit plans, the law requires that plans be nondiscriminatory with regard to union and nonunion members. Also, Section 302 of the act established a formal set of conditions under which collectively bargained, jointly administered benefit plans must be operated and provided the legal framework for "joint trust pension plans." (The act, of course, also governs the establishment and maintenance of other forms of joint trust benefit plans.) The act provided, inter alia, that (1) payments by employers must be made to a separate trust fund; (2) payments must be held in trust for the exclusive benefit of employees and dependents; (3) payments must be made according to a written agreement; (4) the board of trustees must have equal representation from management and labor; and (5) an annual audit of the fund must be conducted by an independent accountant. The act also mandated that each plan establish a procedure for resolving deadlocks between union and employer trustees. Although the act prohibits employers from making payments to a union or its representative for employee benefits, the employer can make contributions to either a trust fund established pursuant to a trust agreement or a life insurance company under an insurance contract issued to the employer as the contractholder. As mentioned above, by requiring the joint management of joint trust pension plans, the Taft-Hartley Act became the legal foundation for these plans.

More than ten years after the passage of the Taft-Hartley Act, the federal Welfare and Pension Plans Disclosure Act of 1958 became law. This legislation was aimed at the rights of individual participants in benefit plans and attempted to provide some measure of protection against mismanagement of plan assets. It was thought that with sufficient information about the nature and operations of a plan, participants could detect malpractice or wrongdoing and seek relief under state and federal law. The Disclosure Act as amended in 1962 granted the Secretary of Labor authority to prescribe forms, enforce compliance, and conduct investigations—shifting the burden of protecting plan assets from participants to governmental agencies. Under this act, a description of the plan and an annual financial statement had to be published for the benefit of participants.

The financial statements had to provide information concerning plan contributions, benefits paid, employees covered, assets, and liabilities, together with information concerning salaries, fees, and commissions charged to the fund and the persons to whom these latter amounts were paid. In addition, the identity of all trustees, the sources of plan financing, the procedures for presenting claims, and the remedies for denial of claims had to be set forth. All of this information had to be made available to participants upon request. Finally, those who handled the plan's funds had to be bonded according to specific rules and conditions.

In spite of this elaborate legal framework that had evolved in connection with benefit plans, some trustees neglected their responsibilities to protect the rights of plan beneficiaries. There were no established standards for the vesting of plan benefits or the funding of those benefits. Under the Internal Revenue Code, the Internal Revenue Service was not given responsibility for assuring the actuarial soundness of pension plans; rather, it was preoccupied with the prevention of tax avoidance by employers that might make excessive contributions (and obtain corresponding tax deductions) to employee benefit plans. Also, if plans terminated and the trust fund assets were not sufficient to provide the benefits promised, participants could lose the benefits on which they had relied for retirement income.

In its sweeping revision of pension regulations, the Employee Retirement Income Security Act of 1974 (ERISA) attempted to cure all of these ills. The Department of Labor was made legally responsible for portions of pension regulation previously controlled by the Treasury Department, especially areas involving the protection of the rights of the plan's participants and beneficiaries. Under ERISA, the Treasury Department was given a new responsibility to monitor the funding of pension plans to ensure adequate funding, not merely to prevent overfunding. Minimum vesting standards were established. The actions of actuaries who were responsible for certifying the adequacy of the funding of "defined benefit plans" came under a degree of control by a Joint Board for the Enrollment of Actuaries, and actuaries had to meet minimum education, experience, and examination requirements to become "enrolled" to provide their services to plans. Finally, the Pension Benefit Guaranty Corporation (PBGC) was established to provide a minimum floor of protection for all plans that provide defined benefits. (Mandatory coverage of joint trust pension plans by the PBGC was postponed until January 1978 and later extended to July 1, 1979.) If a PBGC-covered defined benefit pension plan terminates and the plan's assets are not sufficient to provide the vested accrued pension benefits, the PBGC guarantees that the vested participant will receive the lesser of the plan's vested benefits or certain minimum benefits stipulated by ERISA. ERISA superseded the Welfare and Pension Plans Disclosure Act of 1958 and made major changes in the 1954 Internal Revenue Code. In attempting to cover all of the facets of pension plans and their operations, ERISA became one of the most complex laws ever enacted by Congress.

Although ERISA has dramatically affected the attitudes of trustees, the security of participant benefits, and the administrative requirements of joint trust pension plans, the fundamental characteristics of these plans have not changed. ERISA has required a substantial increase in legal, administrative, actuarial, and accounting activities and has increased trustee awareness of fiduciary responsibilities, but the basic operations of joint trust pension plans retain their original structure.

CHAPTER 2

ESTABLISHMENT AND OPERATION

COLLECTIVE BARGAINING PROCESS

The collective bargaining process is the method used by a union and an employer or association of employers to negotiate wages, hours, and conditions of employment for the employees in a collective bargaining unit represented by the union. A joint trust pension plan is established through the bargaining process pursuant to which the union and the employer agree to establish a trust and the employer agrees to make specified contributions to that trust for the purpose of providing pension benefits. Sometimes only a single local union and a single employer are involved, but many times several local unions associated with an international union negotiate with several individual employers, with an employer association representing a large number of employers, or with a combination of both individual employers and one or more employer associations. Consequently, there will be included in the collective bargaining agreement a clause specifying a certain level of contributions to the plan in terms of cents per hour, dollars per-week worked, or some unit of production. An actuarial determination is required to assist the trustees in establishing the level of benefits that can be supported by the anticipated flow of contributions to the plan.

Alternatively, the union and the employers can negotiate for the employers to make contributions to a pension trust which will be jointly managed by union and employer trustees, with the pension benefits, not the level of employer contributions, being negotiated. For example, the pension benefit to be provided might be $250 per month payable to all employees who retire at age 65. Usually, before the union will agree to the level of benefits or the employers will agree to make the contributions, the bargaining parties will retain an actuary to assist them in determining the required contributions to support a desired benefit level. Under this latter approach the employers commit themselves to maintenance of plan benefits, and future negotiations (through the bargaining process) will involve changes in levels of benefits or other plan provisions, not contribution levels. In other words, the benefit levels are established through the bargaining process, subject to approval by the board of trustees. Since labor and management have conflicting objectives, each side often employs its own actuary who becomes a party to the basic bargaining procedures.

On the surface, these two alternatives (i.e., whether collective bargaining establishes employer *contributions* to a plan or *benefits* provided by a plan) may appear to be quite similar, but the philosophies involved are radically different. If the union and the employers limit their direct involvement to the negotiation of contributions, it is the board of trustees of the pension trust who will set the benefit levels. This practice is used most often where there is an area-wide pension plan being established to cover a geographical region, a specific trade or craft in a region, and so forth. Contributions may vary significantly by bargaining unit because of the different economic circumstances governing the different areas of the region. On the other hand, the negotiation of employer-paid benefits through a jointly managed pension trust often involves a single employer and a single union local where all of the employees are to receive the same level of benefits and all of the employers are essentially in the same economic situation; that is, the employers can pay approximately the same pension contributions.

A decision as to the approach to be taken by the negotiating parties can have a dramatic impact on the language to be included in the pension clause of the bargaining agreement with respect to the funding of the plan. For example, if an employer and a union agree to provide a specific group of employees with a monthly pension of $250 payable at age 65, the employers undertake to make the required contributions irrespective of changes in the covered group that would have an effect on the cost of the benefits. Depending upon their age and sex, new entrants to the plan may increase or decrease its cost. It is possible that the cost may remain reasonably stable.

Different considerations are involved if the union and the employers negotiate the level of contributions rather than the benefit amounts. When employer contribution amounts or rates are negotiated and the level of pensions provided is established by a joint board of trustees, it is important that the pension clause of the bargaining agreement be consistent with the actuary's assumptions. For example, if the actuary makes calculations based on the assumption that a contribution will be made for every hour worked by all employees in the bargaining unit, the benefit that can be supported by a specified contribution rate is quite different from the benefit that could be supported by contributions made only for employees who have worked at least three months, or six months, and so forth. Usually, this consideration is well recognized at the inception of the plan, but problems can arise as newly organized groups of employees enter the plan unless the trustees establish a policy concerning acceptable bases for employer contributions. For example, the following provisions in a bargaining agreement might well create financial selection against the pension plan and be inconsistent with the actuary's assumptions in addition to creating inequities among different groups of contributing employers:

1. Provisions that call for contributions with respect to only those employees—
    a. Who are above a specified age; or
    b. Who will be eligible for retirement within a specified period; or
    c. Who have satisfied a specific minimum period of employment or seniority greater than the period, if any, which was the basis used initially by the actuary when the plan was designed and established (e.g., if the plan was designed to anticipate contributions for every hour

worked, then the minimum period should be the first compensable hour earned by the employee and there should be no waiting period); or

d. Who have worked more than a specified minimum number of hours in a particular period.

2. Provisions that limit the number of compensable hours for which contributions are made for an employee to a number of hours less than, say, the typical expected number of hours worked by the average employee.

3. Provisions that impose a requirement that contributions be made on account of a certain bargaining unit's employees who meet specified minimum work requirements even though such contributions are made by employers for other larger groups of employees without the same requirements.

4. Provisions that permit or require pension contributions for persons who are not members of the bargaining unit.

5. Provisions that provide for a reduction in contribution rates below a previously established level.

All of these conditions can result in financial selection by the bargaining unit involved because the effect is to change the flow of employer contributions and the level of benefit forfeitures by very short-service employees which the actuary had anticipated when the cost of the plan's benefits were estimated. Although the board of trustees cannot and should not interfere with the normal bargaining process, the trustees have an obligation to establish rules that will govern the acceptability of employer contributions. Not to do so could jeopardize both the financial soundness of the plan and the equitable treatment of different bargaining units and the employers whose contributions support the plan's benefits. Experience has demonstrated that the greatest degree of potential selection against a plan occurs in small bargaining units—and often when a closely held corporation's key employees are covered by the plan pursuant to a subscription agreement.

Employer/Employee Contributions

There are numerous ways in which contributions can be negotiated to provide pension benefits under a joint trust plan.

For example, contributions may be based on the exact number of hours worked, shifts worked, or units of coal mined. Another approach provides that a full weekly contribution be made for any week that an employee works one or more hours in that week. Alternatively, contributions may be required only for employees who work at least 20 hours in a given week. In the culinary field, contributions might be made monthly on behalf of any employee who works at least 50 hours.

In establishing the benefit level that can be provided, the actuary must have objective statistical information so that a reasonable forecast of expected contributions can be made. This consideration has always been important; but because of certain requirements of ERISA, it is imperative that the actuary fully understand the nature and effect of the language in the bargaining agreement before giving a board of trustees, the union, or the employer any advice as to the level of pension which can be established by a specified rate of employer contributions.

Very few bargaining agreements require employee contributions because unions have generally taken the position that if a pension plan is to be established the employer should make all of the contributions to support the plan. However, there are some plans that do require employee contributions, and the existence of that requirement changes the provisions of the plan governing participation. If employee contributions are made simultaneously when employer contributions are made, participation must be immediate since the plan cannot feasibly require contributions without providing for corresponding plan participation. Under ERISA-revised joint trust plans, often a minimum number of contributory hours (e.g., 500 or 1,000 hours) are required before participation commences. This requirement defers the need to communicate the plan to transitory employees and reduces administrative and record-keeping expenses but is impractical in contributory plans.

Employee contributions to a joint trust fund complicate administration since employee contributions must be accumulated with a minimum rate of interest for purposes of determining the portion of the pension to be provided by such employee contributions. Also, if an employee withdraws from participation, the value of the employee's contribution account must provide a nonforfeitable pension if he or she is not otherwise vested. If the employee's contribution account value is withdrawn upon termination of coverage, the employee may have to be granted the right to reinstate earned benefits within two years of plan reentry by returning the value distributed to him or her, adjusted with interest to the date of reinstatement. Contributory plans have always been rare in the joint trust field; and with the complexities introduced by ERISA, such plans may eventually disappear altogether.

Effect of ERISA on the Bargaining Process

The typical collective bargaining agreement stipulates that the liability of employers is limited to specified contributions. If the joint trust pension is a "defined benefit" plan under ERISA, then Title IV of the act imposes a *contingent liability* on contributing employers should the plan terminate, or should a "substantial employer" withdraw from participation and the plan terminates within five years of the employer's withdrawal.[1] ERISA also imposes certain tax liabilities on contributing employers if a funding deficiency accumulates in the ERISA-mandated funding standard account and the deficiency is not quickly eliminated.

If a defined benefit joint trust pension plan terminates for any reason on or after July 1, 1979, the termination insurance provisions of ERISA will guarantee the payment of vested benefits of the plan up to a certain maximum dollar limit (and subject to certain other restrictions) *if* the fund's assets are not sufficient to provide the benefits.[2] The Pension Benefit Guaranty Corporation has the right to take legal action against the contributing employers to recover any amounts that it pays out—up to a maximum of 30 percent of the employer's net worth. Because of this fact alone, some employers are resisting pension contribution increases and are considering negotiations to change to a defined contribution plan rather than a defined benefit plan, because defined contribution plans are not subject to termination insurance coverage. If a plan is sufficiently funded and assets are at least

---

[1] See Withdrawal of Contributing Employers, pages 181–84.

[2] Plan termination insurance for joint trust pension plans was initially scheduled to be effective on January 1, 1978. However, the Congress deferred the effective date to allow the PBGC time to evaluate proposed changes in insurance coverage and to make recommendations for legislative action.

equal to the value of insured vested benefits, there is no contingent liability. However, thousands of plans are not fortunate enough to be so well funded at this time. The reason is quite simple. In the past when an increase in contribution rates was negotiated, it was common to increase both past and future (contributory) service benefits. This practice is generally sound as long as the plan is expected to continue, but it virtually always increases unfunded actuarial liabilities. The degree of a plan's funding significantly affects the atmosphere in which the bargaining process operates.

Under the funding standards established by ERISA it is possible for funding deficiencies to arise even though the contributions are made as stipulated in the bargaining agreement(s). The Secretary of the Treasury can impose penalty taxes on the contributing employers and require such employers to eliminate any funding deficiency.

Clearly, these conditions must be recognized in the bargaining process. Therefore, it is imperative that the actuary for a plan develop reasonable and realistic forecasts of employer contributions and prospective emerging plan liabilities. These forecasts will assist both the trustees and the bargaining parties to recognize any need for adjustment in pension contributions well in advance of the expiration of outstanding labor agreements. The use of reasonable and realistic assumptions will help to avoid funding deficiencies or, alternatively, a benefit reduction which might otherwise be needed to prevent a funding deficiency.

Involvement of the Actuary

When a single employer is considering the establishment of a pension plan, it generally retains a consulting actuary to provide advice concerning the plan design, the plan's benefit goals, and the costs of alternative benefit levels. This approach is rarely, if ever, used in connection with a joint trust pension plan. A joint trust pension plan most often comes into existence after the bargaining parties have agreed to a specified contribution rate. For example, the union generally decides to negotiate for contributions to a pension plan when the number of older employees in a bargaining unit becomes substantial. Often, it is only when the demands of older employees become significant that a union begins to negotiate for pension contributions. This is to be expected because the majority of employees in a bargaining unit usually are young and concerned principally with their family's financial requirements for cash wages, immediate health care benefits, and disability or death benefits, not deferred wages. Consequently, the level of contributions negotiated initially is the amount that the union leaders believe can be deducted from the total wage package without unduly reducing the cash wages. The pension contributions at the beginning most often have no relationship to a goal of providing an "adequate retirement income."

Once contributions have been negotiated, the bargaining parties will set about establishing the pension plan. Generally, one of the earliest steps involves selection of an actuary to design the plan and to recommend alternative benefit levels. Because actuarial determinations are based on so many unknown future occurrences and a great number of assumptions, trustees often feel a lack of confidence in making judgments which involve actuarial matters. The calculations of actuaries are based on their mathematical skills, but their assumptions are founded on their experience and knowledge of an industry. In addition, actuaries have to understand numerous governmental rules and regulations and have a reasonable grasp of investment matters to develop estimated costs which will satisfy minimum federal funding standards. As indicated, actuaries have to make numerous assumptions—they do not know the future number of deaths, disability retirements, age retirements, or the future life expectancy of an industry, trade, or craft. They certainly do not know future investment experience. Until the experience with a plan develops, actuaries must rely on their knowledge and experience to devise a benefit structure that can be supported by negotiated contributions.

Therefore, the retention of an actuary for the design of a plan requires a high degree of trust in the actuary's professional expertise in a very complex and little understood field. Sometimes in the past, there has been an inherent lack of confidence by management and labor in a single actuary's ability to be totally objective, and a board of trustees has retained joint actuaries—one actuary for labor and one actuary for management. Each actuary developed separate estimates of future benefit costs, usually after the broad guidelines of a plan's design have been agreed upon. In this environment, one actuary was a management advocate and the other a labor advocate, and each became a party to the bargaining process. The actuaries had to agree to the rate or rates of contributions needed to support specified benefit levels.

The retention of a labor advocate actuary and a management advocate actuary by a joint trust pension plan—at the expense of the trust fund—is no longer permissible. ERISA recognizes only òne enrolled actuary for a plan, and the enrolled actuary must certify periodically that the actuarial assumptions employed are his or her "best estimate" of probable future experience. Advocate actuaries cannot operate without a conflict of interest under ERISA. How can actuarial assumptions be negotiated without the resulting assumptions being other than each actuary's "best estimate"? The enrolled actuary must be retained by a board of trustees "on behalf of all plan participants," not on behalf of either employer trustees or union trustees. In the future, if advocate actuaries are to be retained, the union will have to retain an actuary at its expense and the employers will have to retain an actuary at their expense. Thus, a single enrolled actuary would be retained by the trust as the formal trust advisor and to provide necessary certifications. Under some circumstances, however, one actuary could be the plan's enrolled actuary, and another actuary might act as a consultant. In any event, if a trust retains two actuaries, the trustees should be careful to ensure that their responsibilities do not overlap.

During a plan's lifetime, numerous actuarial valuations must be performed, and some professional actuaries believe that under ERISA annual actuarial valuations should be made to provide the certifications required. Also, there exists a significant new influence that affects the actuary, the trustees, and the bargaining parties. This influence is the funding standard account, mandated by ERISA to measure the accumulated funding deficiencies or surpluses of a pension fund. Funding deficiencies can occur because the aggregate experience of a plan does not conform to the actuary's assumptions. For example, the employer contributions may be less than expected because of declining employment, reduced overtime, temporary layoff, strikes, and so forth. Equity asset values must reflect market values, and this requirement can contribute to funding deficiencies in a period of declining equity values. Again, the actuary's assumptions may prove inconsistent with the aggregate experience resulting from the patterns of age and disability retirements, employee terminations, deaths, or administrative expenses. If the actuary has understated the costs of future benefits and expenses because of these factors, they can contribute to funding deficiencies. The funding standard account is intended to monitor these possibilities, and deficiencies must be eliminated by the trustees' action to reduce benefits or by the bargaining parties' agreement to increase contributions by the date of a bargaining agreement's expiration. Consequently, the actuary now is involved indirectly with the basic bargaining process related to a joint trust pension plan because ERISA's funding standards may require benefit and/or employer contribution adjustments from time to time.

THE TRUST AND THE TRUSTEES

The trust agreement is the legal document that provides for the election or appointment of trustees and defines the duties and powers of the trustees who are responsible for the operation of the joint trust pension plan, for example, the collection of contributions, investment of assets, determination of benefit entitlement, and payment of benefits and administrative expenses. The board of trustees includes equal representation from both labor and management. With the enactment of ERISA, a great deal of interest has been focused on the duties of the trustees—especially from the viewpoint of fiduciary responsibilities, including trustee responsibilities for plan administration, investments, and the proper funding of plan benefits.

Structure of the Trust Agreement

The powers and duties are delineated in the trust agreement which becomes effective when it is executed by union representatives and representatives of individual employers and employer associations, where applicable. The trust agreement often designates the initial trustees and also provides for the future election or appointment of trustees when trustees resign, retire, die, or are terminated by the appointing union or employer(s) or employer association(s). The board of trustees has the basic duty, among others, of investing plan assets; but it may choose to delegate this duty to an investment manager, that is, a bank corporate co-trustee, an insurance company, or a registered investment advisor. If a bank (or trust company) corporate co-trustee is designated, there will be a co-trustee agreement setting forth the duties and responsibilities of the corporate co-trustee, and that document will be executed by the board of trustees and the corporate co-trustee. If a bank or trust company has no investment management responsibilities, it generally will act as the custodian of trust funds under a custodial agreement.

Several sections of the trust agreement define the powers and responsibilities of the trustees, along with the essential legal restrictions on the operations of the trust. A typical trust agreement contains provisions, among others, regarding (1) nondiversion of trust assets; (2) the investment powers of the trustees; (3) the payment of reasonable and necessary fees for legal, trustee, and other expenses of the plan; (4) the records, accounts, and reports to be maintained by the trustees; (5) the payment of benefits under the plan; and (6) the rights and duties of the trustees in case of amendment or termination of the plan. (Appendix A contains a specimen trust agreement for a joint trust pension plan.)

The trust agreement, then, is primarily concerned with the receipt, investment, and disbursement of funds under a pension plan. The plan provisions may be incorporated in the trust agreement, but they are more frequently set forth in a separate plan document. The advantage of a separate plan document is that the plan can be amended by the trustees without amending the trust agreement, which may require approval of the original signatories to the trust agreement or their successors.

The Custodian of Trust Funds

Under a joint trust pension plan, employer contributions and employee contributions, if any, are generally collected directly by the custodian of plan assets under the terms of the custodial agreement. Often, the administrator collects the contributions with the reports remitted by employers, and payments are transferred to the custodian only after the hours worked and contributions are reconciled. The accumulated funds, to the extent that they are not required for benefit and expense payments, are invested pursuant to an investment policy adopted by the board. Usually, the investment fund is managed by a professional investment advisor, by an insurance company, a bank corporate co-trustee, or a combination of two or more of these organizations. At the direction of the board of trustees, the corporate co-trustee or insurance company may make the benefit payments to eligible participants under the plan, and the operating expenses generally will be paid out of a trust checking account. Generally, the administrator will draw the checks for authorized benefits and expenses against accounts held by the custodian.

The custodian is subject to the basic principle of trust law that the assets of a trust for which it acts as custodian must be segregated from both the assets of all other trusts administered under its jurisdiction and from its own assets. However, if the custodian has investment responsibilities under a co-trustee agreement, this principle of trust law does not prevent the custodian from investing part or all of a trust fund's assets in one or more of its bank pooled funds. The requirement to segregate trust assets stems from the fact that the relationship among the parties to a trust is essentially fiduciary rather than contractual in nature. The very essence of this trust concept is that the trustee holds legal title to and possession of specifically identifiable securities, real property, and so forth, for whose safeguarding and (possibly) management the custodian is held strictly accountable. Although the custodian may have legal right of ownership, all beneficial rights belong to the plan's participants and beneficiaries.

Trustee Obligations and Responsibilities

The obligations and responsibilities of trustees are well defined in common law. A trustee is held to a high standard of conduct. Under ERISA, trustees of Taft-Hartley funds (exclusive of a corporate co-trustee who acts as an investment manager) generally are not paid for services rendered (ERISA prohibits the compensation of a trustee for services if the trustee already receives full-time pay from an employer or union whose employees or members are plan participants). However, the lack of compensation neither diminishes trustee duties nor reduces the level of competency required.

The conduct which makes an individual an ERISA fiduciary is outlined in Section 3(21)A of ERISA which provides that a person is a fiduciary with respect to an employee benefit plan to the extent that:

(i)   he exercises any discretionary authority or discretionary control respecting management of such plan or exercises any authority or control respecting management or disposition of its assets,

(ii) he renders investment advice for a fee or other compensation, direct or indirect, with respect to any moneys or other property of such plan, or has any authority or responsibility to do so, or

(iii) he has any discretionary authority or discretionary responsibility in the administration of such plan.

Normally, only the trustees, the investment manager and sometimes the administrative manager are fiduciaries.

The fiduciary responsibility provisions of ERISA (Section 404) require all fiduciaries:

a.   To discharge their duties with respect to the plan *solely in the interest of participants and beneficiaries;*

b.   To act for the *exclusive purpose of providing benefits* to participants and beneficiaries and *defraying reasonable costs* of administering the plan;

c.   To exercise care, skill, prudence, and diligence under the circumstances then prevailing, that a *prudent man acting in like capacity and familiar with such matters would use* in the conduct of an enterprise of like character with like aims;

d.   To *diversify investments* of the plan so as to minimize the risk of large losses unless under the circumstances it is clearly prudent not to do so; and

e.   To act *in accordance with the documents and instruments governing the plan* insofar as such documents are consistent with the provisions of ERISA.

The specification of fiduciary responsibilities requires that the trustee act as a "prudent man." Under these criteria professionals, for example, investment managers, appear to be subject to a "prudent expert" rule and trustees, when they carry out their regular administrative duties, seem to be governed by a not-so-stringent prudent man requirement.

The act indicates that a fiduciary is liable and responsible for acts and omissions committed within the fiduciary context. ERISA also goes one step further and states, in Section 405, that a fiduciary is liable for breach of fiduciary responsibilities by a cofiduciary:

a. If the fiduciary *participates* knowingly in an act or omission by another fiduciary;

b. If a fiduciary knowingly undertakes to *conceal* an act or omission of another fiduciary;

c. If a fiduciary's failure to comply with the exclusive benefit rule in the administration of the fiduciary's specific responsibility *enables* another fiduciary to commit a breach; and

d. If a fiduciary has knowledge of a breach of fiduciary responsibility by a co-fiduciary and does not make *reasonable efforts to remedy the breach.*

When trustees of joint trust pension plans have only periodic involvement with trust operations, they can suffer from a lack of sufficient knowledge to properly control trust operations and may be especially vulnerable to fiduciary abuses and resultant co-fiduciary liability. To date, however, few cases of co-fiduciary complaints have come to light.

Protection against Fiduciary Liability

Trustees, acting individually or as a board, can best protect themselves from problems of fiduciary liability by accepting the position of trustee only with an understanding of the responsibilities involved and the skills required to fulfill those duties, and by utilizing professional advisors who are carefully chosen and periodically monitored in the performance of *their* duties.

The best vehicle for specific delineation of trustee duties and responsibilities is the trust agreement. All trust agreements should be reviewed in light of the fiduciary provisions of ERISA to ensure that the trustees can establish rules and regulations for trust operations that are sufficiently flexible to permit routine administration without a formal meeting of the board of trustees. The authority of the trustees to delegate duties to an investment manager and other advisors should be set forth in detail. The trust agreement should state that trustees are to be reimbursed only for reasonable expenses properly and actually incurred. (As indicated above, ERISA prohibits a trust from compensating a trustee for services if the trustee is already receiving full-time compensation from a participating employer or union.) If necessary, the trustees should be empowered specifically to enter into reciprocity or merger agreements. More important, however, than the adoption of an organized set of rules and regulations, or the retention of qualified professional advisors, or active participation in regular trustee meetings, is the continuing obligation of the individual trustee to act prudently and in the interests of the plan participants and beneficiaries.

The Trustee and Fund Investments

As a basic rule, the duty to manage plan assets is vested solely in the board of trustees. Section 402(a)(1) of ERISA requires that a plan be established and maintained *pursuant to a written instrument* which shall provide for one or more named fiduciaries who have the authority to control and manage the plan. Section 402(b)(1) stipulates that a plan must have a procedure for establishing and carrying out a funding policy and method. (In general, a funding policy is used by investment managers to predict the plan's cash flow so they can establish an investment policy.) Also, Section 403(a) emphasizes the trustee responsibility for plan assets through its requirement that the assets of the plan be held in trust by the trustees who have the exclusive authority to manage the plan assets.

In general, trustees will provide themselves protection from allegations of improper investment decisions by selecting one or more professional investment managers to carry out their investment responsibilities. ERISA Sections 402(c)(3) and 405(c) allow the trustees to delegate their investment authority and responsibility to certain types of investment managers—generally banks, insurance companies, and registered investment advisors. There can be no effective delegation of investment responsibility unless made to one of these classes of investment managers. In addition, the plan may secure error and omissions insurance to provide the plan some protection from potential legal suits which may be brought by participants and/or beneficiaries. Under Section 410(b)(1), a policy secured by a plan to cover liability for acts of a fiduciary must provide for recourse by the insurer against the fiduciary. Generally, the trustees personally will purchase insurance to protect themselves from recourse by the insurance carrier if a claim of misconduct is perfected.

Establishment of Investment Objectives. To achieve a long term successful investment program and to be in compliance with ERISA, a board of trustees should set both short-term and long-term objectives, establish an investment policy to meet those objectives, and communicate both to the investment manager. Once communicated, the trustees should periodically monitor the investment advisor's performance to ensure that the policy is being carried out. To establish investment objectives, the trustees must understand the liquidity needs of the plan in both the near and distant future. Consequently, unless it is clearly evident that there will be a positive cash flow for many years in the future, trustees should obtain cash flow projections from the plan actuary to get a "picture" of the plan's potential growth and to recognize the extent to which funds may be available for investment from time to time.

Investment Policy.[3] The investment objective must be communicated to the investment manager in clear and unambiguous terms. The investment policy, in general, is a written statement by which the trustees communicate to the investment manager their objectives; for example, maximum long-term total investment return within acceptable levels of risk with sufficient liquidity to avoid having to liquidate assets at a loss. The investment policy should, to the extent practicable, also express the trustees' desires concerning such items as the types of investments to be made for the fund, minimum standards as to the relative quality of securities to be held in the fund, and portfolio diversification.

It is only through the establishment of a realistic investment

---

[3] A comprehensive discussion of investment policy is included in Chapter 11 of this text.

objective and by a regular evaluation of the resultant investment policy that the trustees can expect to achieve satisfactory portfolio results and most effectively discharge their fiduciary responsibilities.

Delegation of Trustee Duties

The trustees can and usually do delegate ministerial or clerical duties. It is customary for the board of trustees to retain an administrator and authorize him or her to handle the day-to-day operations of the trust. Unless the administrator is a professional contract administrator, he or she will generally be authorized to decide on routine purchases, internal practices and procedures, and to seek assistance from trust advisors as necessary. A decision to use trust fund money to purchase data processing equipment or to completely refurbish an office would not be authorized. Such decisions remain with the joint board of trustees.

In joint trust pension plans, the board of trustees, rather than the individual employers, is responsible for the maintenance of plan records. The record-keeping function is usually performed by the administration office under the direction of the board of trustees. In recent years, there has been a significant growth of contract administration, principally to service multiemployer plans. Such a professional administrator keeps all the specific records of service and contributions on behalf of individual participants of the plan and handles all routine administrative transactions. Usually the compensation of contract administrators includes provision for reimbursement of their routine expenses.

Authorization of benefit payments is also the responsibility of the board of trustees or a committee of its members appointed by the board. However, in some cases, this function is delegated to the administrator, subject to review by the trustees. Although trustees under ERISA probably cannot delegate to anyone the decision whether or not to sue a delinquent employer, they can establish a specific policy under which the fund administrator can take such actions.

Relationship with Professional Advisors

Trustees have always worked within the parameters of fiduciary responsibility; but with the advent of ERISA, there has been a greater awareness of the need for a close working relationship between themselves and the professional advisors retained by the trust. Specifically, additional legal and actuarial advice has been necessary to redraft plan documents to conform with ERISA. Actuaries and accountants have been faced with difficult decisions regarding funding policies and asset valuation. The administrator has been confronted with increased reporting requirements. Finally, the relationship with the investment manager who, like the trustees, has a specifically *fiduciary* role, has taken on added significance. ERISA permits trustees and other fiduciaries to obtain assistance in the performance of their duties through delegation of trustee and other fiduciary duties and through the seeking of advice on how the trustees themselves can best carry out their duties.[4]

ERISA sets up a basic framework for controlling the delegation of trustee and nontrustee fiduciary duties and the selection of delegates. Through the prudent man rule, ERISA also governs the selection of legal counsel, plan consultants, actuaries, and other advisors to whom no delegation takes place. The prudent man rule requires the trustees to act with care and prudence in the selection and continued use of their fund advisors. Furthermore, the Report of the Congressional Conference Committee on ERISA and Department of Labor informational bulletins indicate that to the extent that legal counsel and plan consultants move from a purely advisory role to one where they are exercising discretion and, in effect, making trustee decisions, they will be deemed fiduciaries and subject to the fiduciary duties and responsibilities imposed by the act.

Trustee Operations

The best way to ensure effective trustee performance is to improve the quality of trustees through the use of formal and objec-

---

[4] The process and criteria for the selection of professional advisors by the joint trust pension plan are discussed on pages 31–39 and 204–9.

tive selection and participation guidelines. As a matter of business policy, effective employer participation in trust fund management can and will result in greater fund economies and, in the long run, in the saving of money for the contributing employers. From a union viewpoint, good administration of a trust fund and the attendant improvement in a plan's funding posture will inevitably serve to strengthen the membership support of the union which has negotiated the contributions and which is active in the management of the fund. At the present time, most trustees are becoming more aware of the scope of their obligations under the law and are devoting greater effort to the performance of their duties. As important and demanding as trustee duties were before passage of ERISA, they have been highlighted and more sharply focused under the act. In a time of increasing awareness of trustee responsibility, both labor and management recognize that it is imperative to select trustees who are qualified to perform duties as trustees by virtue of interest, ability, experience, and integrity.

The union trustee must not only represent through the board of trustees the needs and desires of the participants represented, but also must understand and appreciate the requirement of the trust to maintain an actuarially sound relationship between the benefit costs, available employer contributions, and plan assets. The trustee should, therefore, be familiar with the administrative, legal, actuarial, and investment factors involved in maximizing the services and benefits provided to the participants.

Management trustees frequently had a less direct interest in performing as trustees. In the past, they viewed the obligations of contributing employers as limited to the agreed-upon contributions set forth in the collective bargaining agreement. With the introduction of contingent employer liability in the event of plan termination and with concern for avoiding funding deficiencies (and resultant penalty taxes on contributing employers), management trustees now recognize that they need to play a more active, vital role in trust operations to better serve the plan participants. Like union trustees, once the level of contributions has been negotiated, employer trustees retain the obligation to maximize worker satisfaction through the prudent exercise of their duties as trustees because they too must act exclusively on behalf of the plan's beneficiaries. Management trustees are often chosen from the personnel or industrial relations staff of participating corporations. In plans where a large number of smaller employers participate, such as those of construction or craft trades, representatives of a trade group or employer association may be chosen as management trustees.

Under the terms of the trust agreement, a formal meeting, requiring a specified quorum, is the usual means for transacting trust business. Regular and active participation by all of the trustees is desirable for efficient and harmonious actions by the board and is mandatory in the exercise of the individual trustee's fiduciary responsibilities under ERISA. Various techniques can be employed to encourage and improve trustee participation. For example, a quorum can be set at a fairly high percentage before the actions of trustees can have a binding effect on benefit levels, funding or investment policies, and so forth. A more forthright device is to incorporate in the trust agreement the rule that any trustee who misses a specified number of meetings within a given period without a valid reason is deemed automatically to have resigned from the board and is to be replaced.

The trust agreement's provisions governing trustee voting are extremely important, but there is no uniform voting procedure that applies to all joint trust plans. Essentially, there are two general approaches to trustee voting employed which maintain the equal voting power of both labor and management representatives. In either instance the requirements for a quorum under the trust agreement must be met.

It is generally provided that if a trustee on one side (the union side or employer side) is absent from a meeting, then the remaining trustees on that side in attendance share the absent vote, unless the absent trustee gives his or her proxy to some particular trustee. For example, if there are five labor trustees and five management trustees and only three labor trustees are in attendance at a meeting, each labor trustee can cast one and two thirds votes. This means that each side's full voting power is always present.

There are two general methods of voting—majority vote and unit vote. When majority vote is used, in the example given above six votes would be required to decide any matter. A decision on a subject before the trustees could, therefore, be reached even if there is a split in the voting of each side.

Another method used often is referred to as *unit voting*. Under this method, a majority of the trustees on one side controls the entire voting for that side, and a block vote is then cast by the union trustees and a block vote is similarly cast by the employer trustees. In all situations, a quorum of trustees must be present to transact trust business.

If there is a deadlock between management and union trustees concerning the administration of the plan, the deadlocked issue often must be resolved by arbitration. The trust agreement usually makes specific provision for arbitration of deadlocks.

Perhaps the operation of ERISA's funding standard account requirements should be specifically reflected in certain provisions of the trust agreement. If the funding standard account produces a funding deficiency, it is possible for the contributing employers to be subject to penalty taxes merely because of the inaction of the trustees. For example, if both the management trustees and union trustees deadlock on the necessity of revising plan benefits (or the need for increasing contributions to maintain existing benefits) to eliminate a deficiency and, consequently, rely on a possibly lengthy arbitration, the contributing employers may be assessed penalty taxes if the deficiency is not eliminated on a timely basis. In this area, it may be preferable to provide a specific obligation under the trust agreement for the trustees to reduce benefits to eliminate the deficiency, instead of relying on arbitration. When the maintenance of existing benefits for plan participants would be jeopardized by trustee action to eliminate a funding deficiency, it may be difficult for the union trustees to vote for a benefit decrease to eliminate the deficiency and still believe that they are acting strictly "on behalf of all plan participants."

Some duties of the trustees can generally be delegated, although it is difficult to draw a clear dividing line. Trustees cannot delegate policy-making duties or decisions involving broad discretion other than as set forth in ERISA.

CHAPTER 3

ESTABLISHMENT AND OPERATION (CONTINUED)

SELECTING PROFESSIONAL ADVISORS[1]

There is no board of trustees of a joint trust pension plan which has all the expertise required to administer the program properly. Professionals are needed to provide accounting, actuarial, administrative, investment, and legal services.

Certain fundamental principles apply to the selection of professionals. For example, the reputation of the person or the firm is extremely important because the advisor should be recognized by peers as an expert in his or her field. There should be objective evidence of the expert's formal training as a professional—whether it be in legal, actuarial, accounting, investment, or administrative matters.

Even though trustees may retain a firm, they always deal with individuals; and it is essential that the individuals have the type of experience that justifies the trustees' reliance on their advice as that of an expert and as appropriate for their plan's unique requirements. An expert cannot be properly selected in a vacuum: it is imperative that the trustees meet the prospective advisor and interrogate this person to obtain his or her views, opinions, and attitudes. With a joint trust pension plan, the most significant

---

[1] Selection of the investment manager is discussed in a separate chapter because of the importance and complexity of that function (see Chapter 11 "Investment of Plan Assets").

issues are usually long range in nature and many problems can take a long time before they will surface. It is important that the actuary retained on behalf of the plan participants be experienced in the operations of joint trust pension plans in order that future problems may be minimized. The attorney must ensure that the plan and trust documents not include provisions that may impose severe legal problems for the plan many years in the future. The administrator must establish practices and procedures for record maintenance so that the information required by the actuary can be supplied and so that the administrator can correctly calculate plan benefits 10, 20, 30, or 40 years into the future.

Whenever a professional advisor is retained, it is important to ensure professional backup; that is, the firm should be sufficient in size to guarantee continuity of advice and it should also have industry-wide recognition as the professional organization it is supposed to be. Another consideration in the selection of a professional is evidence of original work in the field of the advisor's specialty. This can be extremely important if a plan is complex or involves an industry or trade with difficult economic characteristics. For example, the industry may be one characterized by seasonal activity or by cyclical fluctuations. Finally, the cost of services of the advisor must be considered. Before the cost can be evaluated, it is essential to have an understanding of the scope of work for which the advisor is being retained, the frequency of meeting attendance, the basis of the advisor's charges, and so forth. Clearly, the functions of each professional should be reasonably understood and delineated before the professional is requested to estimate the cost of services.

Regardless of the type of advisor retained by the board of trustees, the trustees should realize that retention of an advisor does not relieve them of their fiduciary responsibility to use common sense in evaluating recommendations. To the extent possible, trustees should independently examine all factors which form the basis of the advice of any expert. The trustees should also be careful to seek advice from experts in subject areas in which they have true expertise. The trustees should be sure that the basis for selecting an advisor and relying on the advisor's advice has ample support in the technical provisions of their trust agreements.

The Administrator

In selecting an administrator, the trustees should evaluate whether or not they wish to employ a salaried administrator or retain a contract administrator.[2] Usually, if a plan is small in size, the only practical alternative is the contract administrator. On the other hand, if a plan involves many thousands of covered employees and substantial pension contributions, a salaried administrator may be a feasible alternative.

A salaried administrator, as the employee of the board of trustees, directly controls the details of trust fund administration. Under this arrangement, it is possible that the administrative organization can more closely identify with the employees that the union represents. This can improve communications and the general satisfaction of participants with the plan. Since the organization is by its nature nonprofit, theoretically the cost of administration can be lower and perhaps of a higher quality than under contract administration because the benefit technicians are responsible only for the administration of a single pension plan. However, involvement of a board of trustees in the day-to-day operation of the administrative office can create its own problems because of the board's lack of understanding of the technical requirements of an efficiently administered plan.

Sometimes, since the financial success of a salaried administrator is under the direct control of the board of trustees, the administrator does not feel free to exercise decision-making responsibilities. Also, if the salaried administrator is young and proves to be very capable, the administrator's potential for future financial advancement may not match his or her capabilities. It may be practically impossible to compensate such an individual at the same level and in the same manner that the individual could be compensated by a contract administrator; for example, by making management perquisites available, such as a bonus arrangement or participation in a profit sharing plan.

Contract administrators usually perform the same functions as salaried administrators but administer numerous jointly managed

---

[2] See Chapter 7 for description of each type of administrator and explanation of general and specific duties.

trust funds, have a staff of trained benefit technicians, and often have their own computer operations. One of the advantages of selecting a contract administrator is that the organization is exposed to various types of boards of trustees, industries, trades, and crafts and their unique problems. Contract administrators are often acquainted with a wide variety of collective bargaining agreements and their interpretation with respect to employee benefit plans. They are familiar with different benefit forms and have an opportunity to evaluate the costs and quality of several trust advisors in the same field of activity. From the point of view of the board of trustees, a contract administrator can provide a continuity of management that may not be available from a salaried administrator. For example, since contract administrators are continuously involved with numerous trusts funds, they can and must retain the best available talent to maintain an effective administrative operation. If a member of a contract administrator's staff should leave the organization, there is usually sufficient backup to guarantee the continued efficient administration of the plan. Often, an administrator's clerical staff is represented by a union, for example, an office and professional workers union. Contract administrators, as employers, may be better able than salaried administrators to take a management position in dealing with the union that represents their clerical staff in periodic negotiations. The contract administrator *is* management whereas the salaried administrator *represents* management, the joint board of trustees. Consequently, the union trustees may find it difficult to allow a salaried administrator to take a management viewpoint in dealing with the union that represents the clerical staff when the services to their members are at stake. The union trustees may be more willing to allow liberal settlements to avoid threatened clerical staff strikes or slowdowns which would disrupt plan administration.

One of the disadvantages of a contract administrator is that the trustees give up direct control over the administrative procedures and systems. As a result, if the trustees become dissatisfied with the contract administrator, they may find it difficult to change to a new administrator because of essentially different systems, procedures, and practices. A changeover can be cumbersome, expensive and time-consuming—producing delays in claim processing and difficulties in communications with plan participants.

The Actuary

As previously indicated, the selection of an actuary can be one of the more difficult jobs for a board of trustees. Generally, the actuary is the "architectural engineer" of a joint trust pension plan. In order to evaluate an actuary, a board of trustees should assure itself that the actuary is, first of all, an enrolled actuary so that he or she can meet the requirements of ERISA in certifying the funding status of the plan from time to time. The actuary should have professional credentials, and usually these will involve membership in the Society of Actuaries and the American Academy of Actuaries. Fellowship in the Society of Actuaries is achieved after many years of rigorous examinations and is generally thought to represent the highest degree of qualification in technical actuarial matters.

The trustees should be concerned with whether or not the actuarial organization from which the actuary is to be selected has substantial years of experience in the field of joint trust pension plans. A personal interview is necessary so that the trustees can assess the actuary's breadth of knowledge of the industry or trade for which the plan was established, the operation of reciprocal agreements, and the requirements of ERISA. The board of trustees must evaluate the actuary's capability of meeting the plan's needs. For example, the trustees may need an actuary only for periodic studies and cost calculations if they already retain a benefits consultant. If the trustees desire an actuary that has benefit consulting expertise in addition to cost calculation capability, the actuary should be versed in plan design and drafting, and in administrative procedures and practices. The actuary should be capable of effectively cooperating with the administrator, attorney, accountant, and investment manager. The actuary's organization should have the facilities to provide the trustees with appropriate cash flow projections for the plan so that he or she can assist the plan's investment advisor in formulating an investment policy.

The Attorney

It is of little value for a board of trustees to select an attorney with meager experience in the field of industrial relations and joint trust pension plans. There are about as many fields of expertise in legal areas as there are in medical areas. Expertise with Taft-Hartley plans and trusts is imperative. Once again, as with the actuary, it is important to determine whether an attorney has experience with plans of a similar size and nature. The attorney should be completely conversant with the collective bargaining process, the implications of the Labor-Management Relations Act of 1947, and the details of ERISA. There should be an understanding between the trustees and the attorney as to how the attorney will work with the plan's administrator and actuary because their responsibilities so often intertwine. For example, the plan's actuary often will prepare the first draft of the plan document to provide the plan's attorney with a foundation of actuarial rules and practices, together with administrative procedures necessary to operate the plan on a sound basis. Then, the attorney, in consultation with the actuary and the trustees, puts the document into final legal form. It is important for the actuary to be intimately involved with the development of plan language for at least one basic reason: plans have rarely become insolvent because of poor legal construction, but they have become bankrupt because of inadequate actuarial advice and funding.

As with other advisors, the trustees may wish to investigate the opinions of a prospective attorney's peers to reach an opinion as to his or her proficiency in the complex field of Taft-Hartley trusts.

The Accountant

In certain respects, the selection of an accountant for a joint trust pension plan is easier than the selection of an actuary or an attorney. The accountant must, of course, be a "qualified public accountant" in order to prepare the certifications required under ERISA, but the accountant's role will be similar in substance to his or her role in other commercial enterprises. Usually, the qualified public accountant selected by a board of trustees will be a certified public accountant since such status provides the trustees assurance of competence in basic accounting knowledge.

The administrator of an employee benefit plan covering 100 or more participants must retain an independent public accountant on behalf of all plan participants. The accountant's responsibilities include the examination of the books and records of the plan, and the rendering of an opinion as to whether or not the financial statements and supplemental schedules have been prepared in conformity with generally accepted accounting principles. The accountant's duties also relate to the summary annual report that must be distributed to the participants. In spite of the accountant's required involvement with many aspects of ERISA, there are no special legal requirements under ERISA for the accountant to be familiar with employee benefit plans. "Qualified public accountant" is simply defined in the law as a public accountant certified or licensed by a state, or by the Secretary of Labor in states where there are no state licensing procedures.

Each year the accountant must prepare audited financial statements for the plan, including the statements of income and disbursements and the financial balance sheet. However, special detailed information must be examined which is unlike information prepared for a common commercial enterprise. The accountant who conducts the required examination of pension plans and prepares the specified reports should be conversant with specific provisions of ERISA, pension plan financing in general, and the details of the plan's provisions and operations. For example, the accountant must be prepared to examine the schedule of transactions between the trust fund and a "party-in-interest" as defined in the act. The accountant must also comment in the notes to financial statements on the funding policy of the plan and on any changes in that policy during the year. The accountant must also be reasonably familiar with the plan so that he or she can describe the plan and any significant amendments made during the period examined.

In addition, to adequately serve a joint trust pension plan, the accountant must cope with (1) special financial control problems of joint trusts (e.g., when employers remit contributions by a single check for employees covered under multiple trust funds); (2) the need to ensure through payroll audit procedures that contributions are being properly made pursuant to the collective bargaining agreements; and (3) the requirement to audit administrative procedures and practices for conformity to a plan's and trust's rules and regulations—according to both these technical legal documents as well as the rules and regulations stipulated in the minutes of the trustees' meetings.

As in selecting any professional person, the trustees should consider the reputation of the accountant in the joint trust pension field so that (1) they have a basic assurance of the accountant's full understanding of the impact of ERISA on financial reporting and (2) the accountant can efficiently operate with the trust's other professionals. For example, in preparing the required opinion of the financial condition of the plan for the annual report, the accountant may rely on correctness of any actuarial matter certified to by the enrolled actuary, but is not obliged to do so. The accountant should be able to effectively communicate with the actuary so that there can be an adequate understanding by the accountant of fundamental actuarial matters; otherwise, the accountant may feel compelled to retain an actuarial consultant in order to reach an informed opinion concerning the plan's financial condition. Then, again, the accountant will be the key individual in the trust's preparation of the summary annual report for the participants. In this matter, the accountant must deal with the administrator as well as the actuary and the plan's attorney.

Finally, the knowledgeable accountant can provide continuing protection for the trustees as the functions of the qualified public accountant are performed for the trust. Accountants who are truly experts in the joint trust field will be fully capable of—

1. Performing payroll audits to ensure adequate compliance by employers with the provisions of collective bargaining agreements.
2. Monitoring procedures followed in connection with benefit claim awards/denials to assure adherence to rules and regulations of the plan and the Department of Labor.
3. Advising on the maintenance of employee benefit records so that correct benefit calculations and actuarial studies can be performed on a timely basis—allowing proper communication of benefit rights to participants and providing a means by which ERISA's funding standard account requirements can be met.

In performing these exceedingly important functions on a cooperative basis with the plan's other professionals, the trustees can reasonably expect an unqualified opinion to be issued by the accountant when the IRS/DOL/PBGC Form 5500 financial statements are filed with the government. Important by-products of an unqualified opinion include (1) avoiding unnecessary government examination of trust activities and (2) maintaining the ability of the trust to secure or renew fiduciary liability insurance protection on an economical basis. Of course, maintenance of such insurance is of paramount importance to the trust fund itself and to the trustees who have personal fiduciary responsibilities.

Naturally, before reaching a decision concerning the retention of an accountant, the trustees must also evaluate his or her ability to understand and communicate personally with the trustees, the extent of accounting staff backup, the ability to prepare the required reports on a timely basis, the reasonableness of the fees for the service to be rendered, and the geographical location of the accounting firm.

DESIGNING THE PLAN

At the outset of a pension plan, the trustees' most important responsibility is to solve the problem that prompted negotiations for pension plan contributions. In general, the trustees will wish to provide a reasonable level of pension benefits for older employees to allow them to retire from active employment and thereby create more work opportunities for younger employees. Depending upon the level of contributions negotiated, the trustees will usually give recognition to the seniority of covered employees by recognizing past service in the benefit structure. On the other hand, pension benefits for future service should be as high as feasible in order to satisfy younger, active employees.

The determination of the level of benefits to be granted is only one aspect of plan design. Consideration must be given to the practical administration of the plan, the legal issues which affect plan operations, and the effect of collective bargaining agreements. Impinging on all these matters will be the actuarial considerations.

As mentioned previously, actuaries, when they provide both actuarial and related consulting service for a board of trustees, are the architectural engineers of a joint trust pension plan. The industry or trade can be considered to be the structural foundation on which the plan is built. (The trust agreement is the legal foundation of the plan.) The consulting actuary will adopt considerably different procedures in establishing benefit levels and funding practices depending upon whether the foundation is a thriving, growing industry or trade, or one that is likely to decline. The actuary must be aware of provisions in the collective bargaining agreement (or other written agreements) to make certain that all employee groups to be covered by the plan will be treated consistently, that is, to ensure that different groups do not exercise financial selection against the plan because of different conditions governing the payment of employer contributions.

Also, the plan and trust agreement must reserve to the trustees the right to require additional bargaining units to meet certain actuarial criteria before they enter the plan so that accumulated plan assets will not be diluted by addition of groups with age-sex-service characteristics that generate high cost.

In developing the pension plan document, actuaries analyze the available employee census data, the economic factors that affect the trade or industry, and the provisions of the trust and collective bargaining agreements to set the actuarial assumptions needed to make cost calculations. Usually, they then present to the board of trustees alternative types of benefits, different benefit levels, and conditions governing entitlement to benefits that the bargained employer contributions can support.

In the process of developing alternative forms and levels of benefits, the actuary must keep in mind the unique characteristics of joint trust pension plans. For example, the employer contributions are fixed in advance by the collective bargaining agreement and, consequently, the plan could be considered a "defined contribution" arrangement. On the other hand, the benefits generally are also established by a formula, such as $10 per year of service or 2 percent of employer contributions. In the latter respect, the plan has the characteristic of a "defined benefit" plan. Clearly, the actuaries cannot guarantee that their assumptions will be perfectly fulfilled so that there is no *certainty* that the bargained contributions, in fact, will indefinitely support the recommended benefits. After all, the industry might decline; investment earnings may be less than expected; the covered employees, as a group, might live longer than anticipated; and so on. With knowledge of the many variables and their potential financial effects, the actuary generally will recommend benefit levels which can be supported by the bargained employer contributions if experience conforms in the aggregate to his or her actuarial assumptions.

In addition to the actuarial assumptions, there is another important factor which influences the level of benefits that the actuary proposes—the amortization period. In general, the amortization period is the number of years required to fully fund all unfunded liabilities for past service benefits created when a plan is established or benefit improvements when the plan is amended. ERISA mandates that the period should not exceed 40 years for a plan's initial unfunded liability or for the liability created by a plan improvement. The actuary will often select a 30-year, or shorter, amortization period—to allow a contingency margin in actuarial assumptions. This element of conservatism should protect the trustees from having to require increased contributions to maintain benefits if actual experience does not match actuarial assumptions. The selection of a conservative amortization period should also protect the plan from having an experience deficiency which could expose employers to a liability for increased contributions or penalty taxes because of deficiencies.

QUALIFYING THE PLAN WITH THE IRS

In order for a pension plan to enjoy the tax advantages provided by the Internal Revenue Code, the plan must meet extensive requirements of the Code. All existing qualified plans have had to be amended to meet ERISA's numerous new requirements. In addition, plans have to be requalified by the IRS each time the plan is amended for a change in the level of benefits, conditions of entitlement to plan benefits, or any other substantial feature of the plan. Briefly, the primary advantages of a qualified plan are the tax deductions for the contributions paid by employers, the tax deferral of amounts contributed for plan participants, and the tax exemption of investment income attributable to the investments of the plan. It is extremely important for a plan to apply for and receive an "advance determination" by the Internal Revenue Service of the qualification of the plan to have reasonable assurance of these several advantages instead of risking a possible adverse finding, with retroactive penalties upon audit by the IRS. However, the IRS will look to the plan's actual operation in determining whether or not a plan retains its qualified status.

In addition to the above, the timely filing with the IRS of a request for an advance determination assures an extension of time for making retroactive amendments, if necessary. In general, a multiemployer plan is granted time to meet IRS qualification requirements—until the end of the tenth month following the plan year in which the qualification requirements became effective. (This is referred to as the "remedial amendment period.") If an application for IRS determination is filed before the end of this remedial amendment period, the trustees are given additional time to amend the plan to continue its qualification if the IRS requires plan modifications.

Almost every item of plan design is related to IRS qualification. The following comments set forth some significant areas which must be considered before filing for IRS approval.

"Hours of Service" Definition

The final regulations by the Department of Labor (DOL) on hours of service have been especially bothersome for joint trust pension plans. Until regulations were issued there was a virtual paralysis in plan redrafting and making changes in administrative procedures. Joint trust pension plans have almost always based benefit determinations and eligibility on "hours worked" (or related contributions); consequently, the hours counted have been those hours reported and for which contributions have been actually required or paid to the trust. The DOL hours of service regulations have imposed a major change in the definition of an "hour" for benefit and/or vesting service, resulting in great administrative complications.[3]

The rigorous hours of service requirements, or acceptable

---

[3] See Chapter 4 for a discussion of the hours of service requirements for participation.

alternatives established by the Department of Labor, must be incorporated into an ERISA conformed plan, or the IRS will not determine the plan to be "qualified." The IRS considers the determination of hours of service to be the absolute domain of the Department of Labor because of the explicit language of Title II of ERISA.

Employees of Withdrawn Employers

Because of the liberalization of vesting provisions under ERISA, it is especially important for a joint trust pension plan to protect itself against the financial selection of the employers who withdraw from the plan by termination of the bargaining agreement which requires contributions to the plan. Without specific protection, it is possible for an employer unit which has participated in the plan and has been granted substantial past service credits to leave the plan with a significant unfunded past service liability. The degree can vary—depending upon the extent to which (1) the employees are vested at the time of the employer's withdrawal, and (2) past service benefits may have been improved since the time that the employer unit entered plan coverage.

ERISA provides that pension benefits originally granted before the employer "maintained the plan" (i.e., past service benefits) can be forfeited if an employer in a joint trust pension plan withdraws. There have been questions covering whether or not a portion or all "improved past service benefits" can be likewise canceled upon an employer unit's withdrawal. For example, when an employer joined a plan, the benefit unit may have been $4 per year of past service. If that benefit unit were later increased to, say, $7 per year of past service, can the $3 increase in benefit unit be forfeited if the employer withdraws from the plan? The IRS has issued a letter ruling[4] which cites a specific set of circumstances under which a reduction of past service benefits would be allowed upon withdrawal of an employer from a plan. Consequently, there is reason to believe that a plan may be able to cancel or reduce all past service benefits when an employer withdraws. In any event,

---

[4] The IRS ruling is designated "Letter Ruling 7751002," dated September 17, 1977. The ruling carries a stamped legend that "This document may not be used or cited as precedent. Section 6110 (j)(3) of the Internal Revenue Code."

the construction of the plan provisions governing this matter has an important impact on employees covered by plans of the construction trades and plans involved with seasonal industries. Often, such employees have very short periods of employment with a single employer in an industry, and equity considerations require careful definition of the conditions governing the cancellation of past service benefits when an employer unit withdraws. It is possible that an employee's past service benefits are primarily attributable to industry service rendered with employers who continue plan participation, not to service with the employer with which an employee was employed when the employer joined the plan.

Owner-Operator Coverage

Another area of continuing concern to joint trust pension plans involves employees who are "owner-operators." These employees are individuals who in many respects appear to be self-employed because they own or lease the equipment that is used to perform the work required by a contracting employer. If such employees are truly self-employed individuals, federal laws require that they be excluded from coverage under a joint trust pension plan or any qualified corporate pension plan. Their service, in the capacity of self-employed individuals (or sole proprietors or partners), cannot be counted for benefit or vesting purposes under a regular qualified pension plan. To the extent that these owner-operators wish to be covered by a pension plan, they must establish a so-called Keogh (or HR-10) plan and follow the rules and regulations governing contributions to a Keogh plan, usually a defined contribution pension plan.

In the construction trades and many other commercial enterprises covered by joint trust pension plans, however, there are many times when an apparently self-employed individual is self-employed only in a very narrow, technical sense; that is, the individual owns or leases equipment and enters into a contract with an employer to render services. The employer pays this individual on the basis of jobs performed or hours worked, and the individual must provide insurance and pay for maintenance of equipment, general operating expenses, and so on. However, the question of whether or not that individual is covered by a joint trust plan does not depend solely on these features of the contractual relationship. There have been court decisions which have construed such individuals to be legitimately covered as common law employees under a joint trust pension plan, if control over their conditions of employment and timing of performance of services is governed solely and rigorously by the employer with whom the individuals have a contract.[5]

If such individuals are to be covered by a joint trust pension plan, great care must be taken in the drafting and administration of the plan so that the appropriateness of the coverage of such owner-operators is sufficiently clear to allow not only an initial IRS approval of the plan but the continuing approval of the plan by the IRS upon review and/or audit.

Union Employee Coverage

ERISA limitations on benefits cause some concern for joint trust pension plans which cover the employees of the union locals which participate in the plan. Under ERISA, the aggregate annual pension benefits provided to any employee as a result of the contributions of any one employer may not exceed the lesser of—

The average of an employee's highest three consecutive years of compensation, or

$75,000, adjusted to reflect cost-of-living changes as published annually under federal regulation.

These limitations do not apply if the aggregate annual pension benefit is $10,000 or less.

In its capacity as an employer, a local union may be contributing on behalf of its employees to more than one joint trust pension plan and also may be contributing, via a monthly capitation on union members (or a portion of the monthly dues), to a pension plan or other qualified defined benefit or savings plan sponsored by its international union or by a conference of affiliated local unions. In order to achieve IRS qualification of a

---

[5] The courts have ruled that these individuals in such situations are only "self-employed" individuals for the convenience of the employer: the control over the employees' methods of work, time and conditions of employment, in fact, allows the owner-operators to be covered under a joint trust pension plan.

pension plan, the plan should include language that limits benefits to be paid from the joint trust pension plan. When combined with the pension benefits of any other plan for which the employer contributes, the plan's benefits should not exceed the maximum benefits allowable under ERISA, according to regulations published by the Internal Revenue Service. Although, if the limits are exceeded, the benefits payable under nonnegotiated pension plans may be reduced first according to issued IRS regulations, it is possible that a joint trust pension plan will be involved even though the IRS regulations allow such plan's benefits to be considered for reduction "as a last resort."

Because of the complexity in achieving compliance with ERISA's provisions governing the aggregation of pension benefits under all plans maintained by one employer for limitation purposes, the IRS regulations allow compliance to be achieved primarily by employer-sponsored plans. This regulation should provide substantial relief for most joint trust pension plans. However, when the same employer contributes to two separate joint trust plans, the plans are not exempted from the aggregation rules. In order to obtain IRS approval of a joint trust pension plan which covers local unions that contribute to one or more other joint trust pension plans, the IRS may require the separate boards of trustees of such plans to enter into a "treaty" by which an agreement is reached to limit the pension coverage of the two plans in a manner which is equitable and achieves ERISA compliance.

Defined contribution plans are also involved in this problem, although few realize the involvement. Even if a union does not have a benefit limitation problem because of regular defined benefit pension plan coverage, it may have a problem if it sponsors or participates in a form of thrift plan or money-purchase pension plan. ERISA establishes limits on contributions to such plans, and they are affected by the limits imposed on defined benefit plans. For example, when maximum coverage is being provided under a regular pension plan, the maximum annual contribution under a thrift, profit sharing, or money-purchase plan is reduced to the lesser of 10 percent of compensation or $10,000, adjusted to reflect cost-of-living changes under federal regulation.

Experience will demonstrate to what extent joint trust pension plans become enmeshed in IRS qualification problems because of the benefit limitations of ERISA. Certainly these matters require careful consideration at the time the joint trust pension plan is being readied for IRS filing because the continued qualification of a plan is imperative to both the contributing employers and to the covered participants.

CHAPTER 4

ELIGIBILITY REQUIREMENTS FOR PARTICIPATION

PLAN COVERAGE CHARACTERISTICS

A joint trust pension plan may cover any type of employee group such as hourly employees, part time, or seasonal employees and employees in many sectors of the economy. The particular type of employee group covered will—to the extent required or allowed under ERISA—be reflected in the plan's eligibility requirements for participation. This chapter will discuss the general philosophy of trustees regarding plan coverage, the service requirements for participation, and the general and specific treatment accorded certain employee groups.

A joint trust pension plan must at least meet the same participation requirements as a corporate pension plan. However, because of the unique characteristics of joint trust plans, the eligibility provisions are very often different from and more liberal than corporate pension plans. ERISA generally requires that a plan maintained by an employer include all employees who have reached the age of 25 and have completed one year of service and, for a defined benefit plan, are not within five years of the plan's normal retirement age. Few, if any, joint trust pension plans incorporate these limits in establishing plan participation requirements. The reason is simple: the usual collective bargaining agreement between an employer and the union requires that contributions be made for all employees within a bargaining unit, regardless of age. Moreover, a majority of bargaining agreements require contributions on all hours worked. Since employer contributions to joint trust pension plans have been considered by employees to be a form of deferred wages, participation in most pre-ERISA plans normally has been either immediate or deferred only until contributions were required. In very few instances have contributions been deferred for more than six months under a bargaining agreement. Although rare, if a joint trust pension plan requires employee contributions, the plan participation would commence when the employee contributions commence—often after a three-month or other probationary employment period.

Service Requirement for Participation—General

Employees covered by joint trust pension plans may, in a single year, work for several employers who contribute to the plan. For this reason alone, service under joint trust pension plans is measured according to the number of hours, days, weeks, or months of service with *all* contributing employers in a plan year—depending on the terms of the plan and the bargaining agreements. Consequently, this combined employer service is counted in determining when an employee becomes a participant. As can be recognized, due to the nature of joint trust pension plans, the requirements for plan participation under a joint trust pension plan are quite different from the requirements of a corporate pension plan.

ERISA specifically provides that an employee who is over age 25 must be eligible to participate in a pension plan no later than the earlier of (1) the first day of the first plan year commencing after the completion of a year of service, or (2) six months after the completion of a year of service. A standard year of service is earned when an employee accumulates 1,000 hours of service within a continuous 12-month period from the date of hire. If an employee fails to earn 1,000 hours of service within this 12-month period, then the 12-month period may be measured from the anniversary of the *date of hire* or may be based on plan years for the purpose of determining eligibility for participation. If the employee then earns 1,000 hours of service during such period, he or she must become a participant no later than stated above. This rule can apply continually from one employment anniversary date to the next anniversary date or from plan year to plan year.

If the minimum participation requirements of ERISA, exclusive of the age requirement, are incorporated into a joint trust pension plan's eligibility provisions, 1,000 hours of service would be required within the 12-month period immediately following an employee's date of hire. If this tack is followed, the hours of service records of a covered employee would have to be examined for the initial 12-month period following his or her first covered hour, and an employee who satisfies this eligibility requirement would have to be allowed to commence plan participation no later than the earlier of (1) the first day of the first plan year beginning after the date on which the employee first satisfied such requirement, or (2) six months after the employee first satisfied such requirements. The record of an employee who continues in covered employment but fails initially to meet the 1,000 hours of service requirement would have to be tested in successive 12-month periods based on either anniversaries of hire date or plan years to establish whether or not the employee has met the participation requirements.

The administrative complications involved in applying the above technique to establish the effective date of a covered employee's plan participation may justify eliminating any hours of service requirement for establishing plan participation; that is, allow an employee to become a participant when the employee first has a contribution made on his or her behalf. However, one of the principal reasons why plans require a minimum number of hours of contributory service before an employee becomes a participant relates to the fact that a joint trust pension plan may otherwise be burdened with a great volume of materials to be disseminated to employees within a short time period following their employment and before the administrator has established adequate records for these newly entering employees. Usually, newly hired employees are subject to a high rate of turnover, and many trustees have established minimum participation requirements to limit the extent to which the administrator must obtain and maintain name and address files for transient employees who are hired and work a very short time but who do not remain in employment for at least 1,000 hours of service.

Administration of a participation requirement can be simplified by allowing entrance into plan participation at six-month intervals during a plan year. For example, if a plan is on a calendar-year basis, plan participation might be allowed on January 1 or July 1 of the plan year for any covered employee who met the 1,000 hours of service requirement during the immediately preceding 12-month period. Alternatively, an even more simplified approach might be adopted to reduce administrative efforts. For instance, the effective date of participation under a joint trust pension plan might be established as of the first day of the month immediately following an employee's accumulation of 1,000 hours of service with all contributing employers in any two consecutive plan years. This technique for determining the effective date of an employee's participation under the plan eliminates the complexities inherent in the literal application of ERISA's eligibility rules and will generally allow an earlier date of plan participation at little additional administrative cost.

Although joint trust pension plans may follow the precise ERISA participation rules, under the simplified participation rule previously suggested, a plan administrator need only accumulate the hours of service reported for each employee from month to month and then establish when and if the employee first participates in the plan. Using the standard year of service rule, an employee who never works 1,000 hours in any two consecutive plan years will not participate in the plan. When an employee's participation date is defined by the simplified participation rule, past service may be granted only to the extent that the employee's contributory service began within the 24-month period immediately preceding the date when the employee first meets this participation requirement. This technique controls the extent to which past service benefits are allowed under a plan by limiting past service benefits to those employees who are in substantial employment immediately following the date when an employer first contributes to the plan. For example, if an employee earns 300 hours of service in the first plan year that contributions are made on his or her behalf and 700 or more hours of service in the next plan year, the employee may be granted past service credit for unbroken service before the date of the first contributory hour. On the other hand, if 300 hours of service are earned in the first year, 500 hours of service in the second year, and 600 hours of service by the end of the third year, the employee would become a plan participant in the third plan year but may not be granted past service credits because the period of noncontributory service ended (at the time of the first contributory hour) more than 24 months before the employee became a plan participant.

Certain exceptions may be made to the regular eligibility rules for plan participation when a new employer unit is first covered under the plan. Under the latter circumstance, all bargaining unit employees may be covered immediately as plan participants with the effective date of the employer's first contribution on their behalf. One of the principal reasons for this exception to the regular eligibility rules is, when an employer unit first joins the plan, the employer adopts the plan and the plan should not require long-service existing employees to meet normal eligibility requirements. Of course, the disclosure information required to be given to plan participants under ERISA also can be readily distributed when a new employer group joins the plan.

Hours of Service for Participation

Under ERISA the standard rule is that not more than 1,000 hours of service can be required to qualify for the one year of service which, as a minimum, may be required as one of the conditions for participation in a defined benefit plan. The hours of service counted must be hours for which compensation is paid by an employer *directly or indirectly.* An hour of service must include time for which an employee was compensated while on a leave of absence, jury duty, disability, layoff, vacation, holiday, in military service (when the employee's rights are protected by law), and of course all hours worked for which compensation was actually paid. In addition, if an employee is granted a back payment award, the value of the award must be converted into an equivalent number of hours of service for which the payment was made. These requirements, which fix the determination of service on a more liberal basis than "hours for which employer contributions to the plan are required to be made," represent a significant departure from past practice for joint trust pension plans.

In recognition of the administrative complexity of these types of hours of service, the Department of Labor has published regulations which allow, among others, the following several alternatives to the standard 1,000 hours of service requirement:

a. Eight hundred seventy hours of service, in which case hours of service relating to leaves of absence, jury duty, disability, vacation, holiday, layoff, and military service may be disregarded (i.e., only hours worked for which compensation is received and certain hours for which back pay is awarded need be included); or

b. Seven hundred fifty hours of service in which case overtime hours may be disregarded in addition to the service omitted in a. above; or

c. Elapsed time, under which one year of service is granted for each 12-month period of unbroken employment; or

d. An alternative year of service may be established under which each month or partial month of employment is deemed to include 190 hours of service. Under this alternative an employee who is employed for five months and one day is deemed to have worked for six months and, therefore, achieves the 1,000 hours of service required for plan participation.

In addition to these several alternatives, special rules apply to the maritime industry because of its unique problems and the Department of Labor is to publish standards for employees covered by seasonal industry pension plans.

Thus, in order to avoid the administrative burdens of counting hours of service for periods when no contributions are required, the alternatives generally provide for more liberal conditions for participation than the basic ERISA rules. For most plans, there is little cost impact resulting from adoption of these liberal rules. This is so because even if a marginal member of a covered group of employees becomes a participant due only to the use of these more liberal participation rules, it is quite unlikely that this member will accrue sufficient service to ultimately receive a benefit.

In addition to these hours of service, employment rendered by an employee with the same employer outside of the bargaining unit covered by the plan may have to be recognized for participation purposes. If an employee is employed with an employer on or after the date the employer first contributes to a joint trust pension plan, that service must be counted for participation purposes if the employee later becomes part of a bargaining unit for which contributions to the plan are negotiated. Thus, an employee's service outside of a bargaining unit which is contiguous to the employee's bargaining unit service must be counted to the extent an employer contributes to the plan during such period. For example, assume an employer commenced contributions to a joint trust pension plan under a bargaining agreement in 1972 and a supervisory employee of that employer in 1972 was not included in a bargaining unit until 1977 when supervisory employees were first organized and represented by the union. In 1977 the employer commenced contributions to the plan for the supervisory bargaining unit. In this circumstance, the supervisory employee's service from 1972 through 1977, inclusive, must be counted for eligibility and vesting purposes under the plan as soon as the employer contributes to the plan on behalf of the supervisory employees. In other words, as soon as the first employer contribution is made on behalf of such employee, the employee may not only become a plan participant but may also have five years of vesting service on account of employment since 1972.

A similar situation can occur when an employee is employed in a division of an employer which is not represented by the union and the employee is transferred to another division of the same employer and becomes an employee in a bargaining unit for which contributions are required. The nonbargaining unit service rendered before the transfer is contiguous and must likewise be counted for participation purposes. This nonbargaining unit service does not have to apply to the calculation of benefit credits.

Both types of contiguous service create great administrative problems for a joint trust pension plan since such hours of service information is not a natural by-product of the administration of the plan. Generally, the administrator bills an employer for an employee's hours worked in covered employment, but the administrator has no knowledge of the hours of service rendered by an employee not included in the bargaining unit. In fact, the administrator generally will not know which, if any, employees are in this type of uncovered vesting employment. This is just one more complexity added by ERISA to the administration of a joint trust pension plan. This concept of counting contiguous service may make considerable sense with respect to a corporate pension plan of an employer that has many subsidiaries throughout the country under a centralized payroll system. The employer can track an employee's service which is rendered in different geographical locations. However, this tracking ability may not be available to corporations generally and, in the author's opinion, is not really possible under any circumstances for joint trust pension plans.

In addition to the numerous types of service described, hours of service rules for vesting purposes are applied retrospectively for each active participant's nonforfeited contributory service. Because many of these plans do not have adequate year-by-year records of hours of service before ERISA became law, they cannot determine yearly pre-ERISA hours of service for each employee; many plans do allow participation and vesting service during periods before the ERISA effective date to be based on either the plan's pre-ERISA rules or ERISA's elapsed time measurement of a year of service, whichever basis is more favorable to the employee.

Reestablishment of Participation after a Break in Service

ERISA allows a plan to establish a standard one-year break in service to be suffered by a participant who earns no more than one half of the hours of service specified in the law or regulations for one year of vesting service. For example, if the standard 1,000 hours of service is used to measure a year of service for participation and vesting, then an employee may suffer a one-year break in service if 500 or fewer hours of service are earned. If an employee incurs a one-year break in service, the employee no longer has to be considered an active participant in the plan and may forfeit all earned service and benefit credits unless he or she is already partially or fully vested in plan benefits. Whether or not an employee is vested, after a "one-year break in service" is incurred, a plan may again require the employee to meet its participation requirements after reemployment before again becoming an active participant. If an employee who has incurred a one-year break in service is reemployed by a contributing employer before a number of consecutive one-year breaks in service have been accumulated equal to the accumulated number of vesting service years, all of the employee's vesting service years and all earned benefit credits under the plan must be reinstated upon becoming an active participant. If such employee recommences participation after the number of consecutive one-year breaks in service has equaled or exceeded the accumulated number of vesting service years (the rule of parity), and if the employee has no vested interest in plan benefits, all accrued vesting service and benefits are permanently forfeited, and he or she becomes an active participant just as any new employee. If the employee is vested, no vested benefits can be forfeited because of a break in service.

TREATMENT OF SPECIAL EMPLOYEE GROUPS

Participation of Nonbargaining Units

A joint trust pension plan must cover all employees represented by the union, including nonunion employees, provided the employees comprise a bargaining unit acceptable to the board of trustees of the pension plan. The contributions made under the collective bargaining agreement are made on behalf of all employees in the bargaining unit. There can be no discrimination against nonunion employees. However, it is possible for certain employee groups to be covered by the plan even though there is no collective bargaining agreement. If the plan and trust permit, it is possible for the employees of the entity providing administrative services to the plan, employees of the local unions whose members are participants, and, sometimes, certain independent contractors to be covered by the plan. Under the latter category, only those independent contractors can be covered whose employment is essentially *controlled* by a contributing employer in the same manner as a regular "common law" employee. Under certain circumstances, if the plan and trust permit, corporate officers of a participating employer may also be covered by a plan if the officers are employees in full-time employment and perform work related to the industry for which the plan was established. Under no circumstances can coverage be allowed for service in the capacity of a sole proprietor, self-employed individual, or partner in an unincorporated partnership.

Groups of employees who are not covered by a collective bargaining agreement may be included by execution of a subscription agreement by which the employer agrees to be bound by the terms and conditions of the trust agreement and plan, and thereby agrees to make contributions to the trust. Whenever nonbargaining unit employee groups are covered by a joint trust pension plan, trustees must always be concerned with potential financial selection against the plan. Consequently, certain rules are often established by the trustees as conditions precedent to allowing nonbargaining unit employee participation in the plan. For example, *all* employees in a group not represented by another international union may have to be included for plan coverage. In addition, when multiple contribution rates (and benefit levels) are allowed under the plan, the contribution rate to provide plan benefits applicable to the nonbargaining unit employees of a contributing employer should not exceed the highest contribution rate of the bargaining unit employees of that employer who are covered by the plan. If a local union wishes to cover its employees, the maximum contribution rate often may be limited to the maximum rate of contribution which has been negotiated by the local union on behalf of its bargaining unit employees. However, the greatest potential for financial selection against a plan exists when corporate officers of a contributing employer are allowed to participate, since these individuals may control the participation of the employer and employee promotions to their own advantage. As a consequence, participation of corporate officers, if allowed, may be subjected to certain limits on the amount of and the manner in which past service is granted under the plan; also, the levels of contributions and future service benefits may be limited.

Participation of Certain Bargaining Units

Most joint trust pension plans have been established to cover employees who are expected to remain in the industry and generally to be employed on a full-time basis. Prior to ERISA some plans included participation, break-in-service, and vesting provisions which effectively precluded most part-time and seasonal employees from ever earning vested retirement benefits even though contributions were made on their behalf. For example, a plan may have granted a full or fractional benefit credit only if an employee had contributions made on the employee's behalf for 1,000 hours or more in a plan year. In addition, the plan may have stipulated that all earned benefit and service credits be forfeited if an employee failed to earn 1,000 hours of contributory service in two consecutive plan years.

In industries which include many part-time or seasonal employees, it was possible for employees to work many years in the same industry without earning any benefit credits or vesting rights because they only worked for a few hundred hours each year. Such industries might include retail store clerks; employees who work only in the seasons when food is harvested, canned, or frozen; and so forth. Although as of January 1978 the Department of Labor has not issued regulations which define "seasonal employees" and the applicable participation, break-in-service, and vesting rules, regulations ultimately may require special recognition of the employment characteristics of seasonal employees in the design of participation, break in service, and vesting rules. For example, if pension contributions are negotiated on behalf of a seasonal group which typically earns only 500 hours of service per year and the full-time employees covered under the same plan average about 1,500 hours of service each year, the requirements for participation, break in service, and vesting for the seasonal employees may be set at one third of the requirements established for the full-time employees. If the basic requirement for a full-time employee's participation is 1,000 hours of service, part-time or seasonal employees may, in this case, need only 333 hours of service to participate. Likewise, if the one-year break in service is based on 500 hours of service for full-time employees, the part-time or seasonal employee break in service rule may be based on 166 hours of service.

Hopefully, any special seasonal employee regulations will be simplified to merely require one half the number of hours of service required under a plan's standard participation, break in service, and vesting rules for full-time employees on the premise that employment for fewer hours of service represents merely incidental employment which need not be recognized. The principal problem with which the DOL is grappling appears to be the determination of what, in fact, constitutes a seasonal industry, so that a plan with less than some level of seasonal participants could continue to apply a single, full-time standard of hours for all participants.

CHAPTER 5

ADOPTION OF PLAN BY EMPLOYER GROUPS AFTER INCEPTION

Two fundamental, but subtle, assumptions incorporated into most actuarial valuations for joint trust pension plans are that (1) there will be an indefinite flow of contributions at a specified level to fund plan benefits, and (2) the flow of contributions, together with investment earnings, will meet all benefit payments and expense requirements of the plan. In addition, until all unfunded liabilities are amortized, the flow of contributions must also be sufficient to pay off all unfunded liabilities over time periods specified by ERISA.

There may be almost no chance for these actuarial assumptions to be fulfilled unless the rules and regulations of the plan encourage the entrance of new groups. The reason should be clear: some employers contributing to the plan may not survive in business. Some employers may move from the geographical region covered by the plan; others may leave the industry; still others may ultimately go into bankruptcy. Sometimes, the industry will become obsolete or less viable, resulting in declining numbers of employers and reducing numbers of covered employees. Therefore, the plan's benefit design and the rules for newly entering groups should be conducive to retaining a stable (or increasing) population of covered employees with favorable age, service, sex, and contribution rate characteristics. Hopefully, the characteristics of the plan participants will continue to be at least as favorable as those of the employees covered by the plan when initially established. If groups which wish to enter do not have beneficial cost characteristics, their entry into the plan may require benefit limitations which allow entry so that average benefit costs of the plan are not unduly increased.

CONDITIONS FOR ACCEPTANCE OF NEW GROUPS

To achieve reasonable controls over the relationship of benefit costs to employer contributions for newly entering groups, the rules that govern acceptability of labor agreements should require consistency in the pension clauses of all participating employer groups. For example, if the existing benefit levels were based on employer contributions bargained for every hour worked, new groups should not be allowed to enter unless the labor agreement includes this same condition. On the other hand, if the existing group's bargained contributions are based only on hours worked after a three-month probationary period, a new group should not be required to meet a more rigorous contribution standard. Other factors which should be considered when a new group is evaluated are:

1. The *level of initial contributions* and whether or not it will likely support the current level of past service benefits granted under the plan. For example, the plan's past service benefits may have been increased since the plan's inception because of an increase in contribution rates from, say, 20 cents to 50 cents per hour. Unless a newly entering group's contribution rate were also to be 50 cents per hour, the past service benefit may not be financially feasible.
2. The *average number of hours worked* by the entering group. If the average hours worked by the new group is significantly lower than the average of the existing group, the same hourly rate of contributions may not support the same level of past service benefits even though future (contributory) service benefits may be proportional to both the hourly contribution rate and the actual hours worked.

3. The *level of employee turnover of a new group.* Turnover may be considerably lower or higher than the existing group's rate of employment termination—possibly generating fewer or greater numbers of nonvested benefit forfeitures and, consequently, creating both financial and equity problems. For example, if a plan covers principally employees in a skilled trade with very low employee turnover characteristics, questions of equity can be generated by the entrance of employees who perform factory work in a related industry but who, as a group, have very high employee turnover characteristics.

PAST SERVICE BENEFITS FOR NEW GROUPS

A plan's rules governing the granting of past service benefits also can generate financial problems when new groups have an opportunity for coverage. For example, if the level of past service benefit credit is relatively high in relation to the future service credit earned for an average year of covered employment, and if past service credit can be received for 10, 20, or even 30 years of service before plan entry, numerous financial selection opportunities can arise. The degree of selection against the plan tends to depend on the size of the entering group. If the group is small, it is possible that a few very long-service employees who are close to the plan's normal retirement age can receive a virtual "windfall" of benefits from the plan after a short period of contributory service. Sometimes the small employer group may go out of existence long before it has paid even a small fraction of the value of the windfall benefits. This situation can be extremely hazardous if the plan has rules that allow corporate officers to participate in the plan and to receive past service benefits. Consequently, the plan must establish rules to guard against undue financial selection and may do so alternatively as follows:

1. Require a substantial number of years of contributory service before an individual may retire. Under ERISA, the normal retirement age can be set as the later of attainment of age 65 or the tenth anniversary of the employee's plan participation date. However, such a restrictive provision for a plan's normal retirement age may discourage new groups from entering the

plan if older employees would have to wait ten years before they had a right to retire and to receive a benefit (presumably, the early retirement provisions also would not allow retirement until an employee had at least ten years of plan participation).

2. Grant only one or two years of past service credit for each full year of future contributory service. For example, if an employee has ten years of past service and two years of past service credit are earned for each full year of future (contributory) service, an older employee would not receive all the past service credit until five years of contributory service have been completed.

3. Do not allow past service credits to be granted to corporate officers who participate in the plan.

Sometimes the selection against a plan created by its past service rules can be more financially damaging if the plan's past and future service benefits are directly related to the bargaining unit's final or final average contribution rate. In such a situation, it is possible, especially for smaller bargaining units, to commence participation at a relatively low level and bargain for contribution rate increases in such a manner that the highest practical contribution rate applies at just about the time when the older, long-service employees are scheduled to retire. When this type of plan is involved, controls in addition to those mentioned above are required. These additional controls must be applied either by limiting the extent to which a contribution rate increase can be recognized by the plan in a single year for benefit calculation purposes (e.q., a maximum hourly rate increase of 5 cents or 10 cents per year might be imposed) or by limiting the final contribution rate used for benefit calculations, expressed as a multiple of an individual's "career average" rate (e.g., the final contribution rate for an individual may be limited to 150 percent or 200 percent of his or her career average contribution rate).

Even when the above controls are applied, there are other potential past service (and sometimes contributory service) problems which can occur if two or more separately identifiable bargaining units of the same employer are covered under a single plan at different contribution rates. If the employees of one unit can move into another bargaining unit which has a higher contri- bution rate and, consequently, receive greater pension benefits for service rendered in the initial bargaining unit, it is possible for the bargaining parties to financially select against the plan unless there are objective standards governing the movement of em- ployees between bargaining units. Thus, the plan's rules on ac- ceptability of collective bargaining agreements must anticipate this potential financial hazard.

To illustrate the kind of financial hazard which a plan can expe- rience when there are two separate bargaining units participating in a single plan (or two separate employee classifications within a single bargaining unit), consider a plan that provides benefits re- lated to a final contribution rate (i.e., the contribution rate appli- cable at the time of retirement or vested termination) and allows a wide range of contribution rates. If one bargaining unit with a low contribution rate includes employees who load and unload trucks or work in a warehouse and the other unit has a high contribution rate and includes supervisors, schedulers, and truck drivers, it is possible for an employee in the first unit to be promoted into the second unit. The promotion may occur after several years of em- ployment in the first unit. If this "final rate" plan counts all service for benefit purposes, the mere promotion of an employee can increase the plan's unfunded liabilities because a type of past ser- vice benefit is effectively granted to the employee after the em- ployee has moved into the unit with a higher contribution rate. The extent of increase in liabilities is directly related to both the employee's length of service in the first unit and the differential in contribution rates between the two units.

This same type of problem could arise if one unit covered sea- sonal employees and the other unit included full-time employees, such as in the food processing industry where the food product is seasonal in nature. There are probably numerous similar types of circumstances where this situation can arise. In each situation the bargaining units may be entirely legitimate in nature and the contribution rate differentials fully justified, but the financial problems of a final rate pension plan can be significant.

Finally, a plan can be seriously damaged if the plan's provisions do not mandate the forfeiture of past service benefits upon the withdrawal of an employer unit. This is especially likely if past service of a newly entering group is counted for vesting service purposes (perhaps in conjunction with two to five years of contributory service); then, it is possible for a new group to enter the plan, have contributions made for a few years, and then to withdraw—leaving the plan responsible for substantial unfunded past service liabilities. If the withdrawn employer had increased contribution rates while the employer group participated in the plan and if past service benefits had been increased during this period, the financial burden on the plan could be extremely great.

PAST SERVICE CONSIDERATIONS: PLAN MERGERS

Before ERISA, many joint trust pension plans merged from time to time without special consideration being given to the financial effect of the merger. In some instances, petitions for merger from the trustees of a financially distressed plan were accepted by trustees of a healthy plan if the merger strengthened the union and broadened its jurisdiction. More frequently, an unhealthy plan was merged with a healthy plan if the negative financial effect on the healthy plan was nominal. For example, if an actuarially sound pension plan had a premerger unfunded actuarial liability that could be amortized in 30 years and the postmerger unfunded liability could be amortized in 31 to 32 years, the merger would probably be considered acceptable.

Since the enactment of ERISA, plan mergers should only be considered after careful analysis and evaluation by the actuary. The actuary, of course, should have a thorough knowledge of all prior and probable future experience of the groups considering merger to ensure the nondilution of assets and the continued sound funding posture of the plan serviced. Mergers may be somewhat more difficult under the rules adopted by the Pension Benefit Guarantee Corporation (PBGC) pursuant to ERISA Section 208. The PBGC merger regulations are essentially identical with the merger rules and regulations published by the IRS. That is, detailed records of earned benefits and service of a merging plan must be recorded and must be safeguarded, to the extent the earned benefits were funded at the time of merger, for a period of five years or until prior plan termination. If a plan is not terminated within the five-year period following merger, the special provisions will no longer apply, and all plan participants receive a similar degree of protection by the PBGC if the plan later terminates. The PBGC rules governing the merger of joint trust plans may require that accurate detailed census data and financial information be obtained before trustees decide to allow mergers, but, generally, such mergers should not be unduly complicated.

Before ERISA, when one plan wished to merge with another, the actuary normally would propose that past service benefits granted to the employees covered by the merging plan be limited if the relative level of the entering group's unfunded liability were very great or if the required charge for amortizing its unfunded liability were substantially greater than that of the plan with which they wished to merge. The limitation might be set so that the unfunded liability attributable to benefits earned up to the time of merger could be amortized over the same period as the existing plan's unfunded liability. In some instances, to achieve this condition at the appropriate contribution rate, the number of years of past service credits would be limited, or a smaller benefit unit for prior service would be allowed. This type of solution might have been achieved readily if the merging plan's benefit level was quite modest and particularly if the contribution rate after merger were scheduled to be significantly higher than under the plan before merger. However, most plans have merged so that the premerger benefits would not be reduced even if the actuary determined that the merger would increase the plan's amortization period.

In the atmosphere of ERISA the actuary and the trustees have keen awareness of the need to maintain the benefit security of existing plan participants, and, consequently, each contemplated merger requires careful evaluation and treatment. For example, two groups of employees, covered by separate plans that provide identical benefits and have identical contribution rates and amortization periods for their unfunded liabilities, could have substantially different proportions of earned benefits that are funded. As a matter of fact, one of the groups mentioned above could have a significantly shorter amortization period and yet have a smaller proportion of its earned benefits funded. The reason rests with the implications of the actuarial cost method. Under an entry age normal cost method, the plan's "level" normal cost and unfunded liability reflect a "going-concern" valuation technique, and the amount of annual contributions in excess of the "level" normal cost amortizes the unfunded liability.

If the entry age characteristics of a group produce a low normal cost, a great proportion of the contributions will be available to amortize the plan's unfunded liability. Consequently, when the unfunded liability is very large and the plan's normal cost is very low, the amortization period can be as moderate (i.e., 30 years) as another plan which has a relatively high normal cost and small unfunded liability. For example, if the annual employer contributions for each of two plans is $1 million, one plan may have an unfunded liability of $5.8 million, requiring an annual amortization payment over a 30-year period of $400,000, and the other plan's unfunded liability could be $12.4 million with an annual amortization payment also over a 30-year period of $850,000. Clearly, both plans have a considerably different funding status even though contributions and amortization periods are identical. Therefore, a plan's actuary may conclude that a different actuarial cost method should be employed to evaluate how two plans may be merged without diluting the funding of each plan's benefits. Even though PBGC regulations do not require "equal funding" of earned benefits before joint trust pension plans are merged, trustees may want to give serious consideration to allowing plan mergers for future service benefit purposes, while maintaining the premerger earned benefits and assets separately until all premerger earned benefits have been fully funded.

If the boards of trustees of separate plans recognize all merger problems and considerations and still wish to merge, a plan's actuary continues to have an obligation to evaluate whether or not the merger would be in the best interests of the plan participants. Since the plan's actuary is retained "on behalf of all the plan participants," he or she should determine if the funding of future service benefits for the plan's participants would be materially affected by the probable future experience of the merging group.

If the industry of the merging group is in financial distress or there has been an obvious declining trend in the number of participating employers and/or hours worked, it is possible that a merger may be harmful in the long term to the actuary's plan participants. Assuming that decisions have been satisfactorily reached concerning the disposition of existing investment portfolios and the funding of premerger earned benefits, the actuary should use costing techniques and, possibly, a benefit redesign to provide adequate protection for the plan's participants against a possible decline in the industry or obsolescence of the trade of the merging employee group.

CHAPTER 6

BENEFIT STRUCTURE

When a plan is first established, the board of trustees usually gives its attention primarily to the pension benefits for older employees who are close to retirement age. Typically, the retirement age is geared to the age when unreduced social security benefits will be payable; that is, age 65. The type of benefit formula used reflects the level of contributions that have been negotiated, and usually the trustees give recognition to the seniority of covered employees by recognizing past service in the benefit formula. With the enactment of ERISA, covered employees earn nonforfeitable rights to accrued pension benefits and certain rules now apply in determining the amount of the accrued benefits.

Whenever it is financially feasible, trustees attempt to provide some additional benefits beyond the primary pension benefit payable at the normal retirement age. For example, benefits may be allowed to commence earlier than the stated normal retirement age, say, after the attainment of a specified age with a minimum number of years of credited service. Also, benefits may be provided for participants who die before retirement, and often some type of death benefit is afforded to pensioners who die soon after retirement. Under ERISA, spouse pension protection must be allowed if a covered employee dies while eligible for early retirement within ten years of normal retirement age. Another important benefit which trustees often include in a pension plan is a disability pension for those covered employees with substantial service who become disabled before they are eligible for normal retirement benefits.

71

RETIREMENT BENEFITS

Types of Benefit Formulas

Flat Pension Benefit. When joint trust pension plans were originally established, the level of contributions was very low and a flat pension benefit was the most common form of pension. For example, the pension payable at age 65 might be $100 per month for life for any covered employee with 15 or more years of service. For a number of years, these flat pension benefit formulas were retained while contribution rate increases were negotiated. However, the benefit per year of service for employees with, say, only 15 years of service really was disproportionately high relative to longer service employees, and the amount of the flat benefit payable to employees entering at younger ages was too low. Also, trustees imposed restrictive entry age requirements in some instances to control the cost increases for newly entering groups. Consequently, as contributions to pensions continued to increase and employees nearing retirement age demanded larger pensions and more equity in the design of pension benefits, plans were modified to grant a unit of benefit for each year of service.

Unit Pension Benefit. Under this type of formula, a monthly pension unit of, say, $5 per month is earned for each year of benefit service. A year of benefit service is normally granted for a specified number of covered hours (e.g., 1,500 or 1,800 covered hours), but past service is sometimes based on elapsed time if it is difficult or impossible to get records of hours of service before the establishment of the plan. Sometimes, if a retiring employee with substantial past service and little future service would otherwise receive a monthly pension of less than $75 or $100 per month, a flat minimum benefit is provided.

Initially, the unit was often the same for both past and future service, where *past service* is service before the establishment of the plan and *future service* is subsequent service. As time elapsed and contribution rates escalated, many plans substantially increased the benefit unit for future service and did not increase the benefit unit for past service or only allowed moderate increases in the benefit unit for past service. For example, when the monthly pension benefit per year of service was at a level of $5 or some smaller amount, usually no distinction would be made between past and future service benefits. However, as contributions increased and the number of pensioners and covered participants nearing retirement age increased, trustees began to realize that future service benefits might be seriously curtailed if past service benefits were kept at the same level as future service benefits. Consequently, many pension plans today that provide a benefit unit per year of service and reflect relatively high contribution rates provide past service benefits of $5 to $10 per year of service and future service benefits of as much as $25 or even $50 per year of service. On the other hand, numerous plans have retained the concept of equal benefit rates for both past and future service even though the practice substantially limits the level of benefits which can be earned by newly entering plan participants.

As years have passed and contribution rates have been increased periodically, trustees have also realized that if the benefit unit for all future service is constantly increased, the plan's unfunded liabilities likewise increase dramatically even when the past service benefit unit has not been improved. In other words, the continual increase of all benefit credits earned after the establishment of the plan has a similar impact on unfunded liabilities as continually increasing past service benefits. In order to control the proportion of employer contributions required to amortize unfunded liabilities, some plans have decided to improve only "future" future service benefits (i.e., benefits earned for service rendered after a contribution increase), rather than all future (contributory) service benefits. Under this arrangement, there would be one benefit unit for original past service and two different benefit units for future service. For example, the past service benefit unit might be $5; the benefit unit for future service up to the plan anniversary when contributions are increased might be $20; and the future service benefit unit thereafter might be $30.

Another element considered in this type of unit benefit formula is the *number* of past service credits that are allowed and, perhaps, the total combined number of past and future service benefit credits granted under the plan. For example, a limit of 10 or 15 years of past service credit is often imposed, but some plans count all past service credits with essentially no limit. When a plan is first established, the unbroken service with all employer entities that have been parties to the union's labor agreements might be counted. Sometimes, credit will be granted only for each calendar quarter for which an employer *in the industry* made social security contributions on behalf of a covered employee. This type of approach would often be used with plans established for the construction trades since employees oftentimes would not be continually employed by any single employer. This method is sometimes used if employment records are incomplete or unavailable for service before a plan's inception. However, when plans are established for industries where employees usually work for a single employer, past service benefits may be limited to only the continuous employment of the participant with the employer who makes the first contribution on the participant's behalf to the joint trust pension plan. Occasionally, a maximum number of benefit units will be imposed under a plan so that no more than 25 or 30 benefit units, whether they are past service units or future service units, will be allowed.

"Percentage of Employer Contributions" Pension Benefit. Another formula sometimes used establishes the monthly pension benefit for an employee as a percentage of the employer contributions; for example, the formula might be 1.5 percent, 2 percent, or 2.5 percent of employer contributions. The specific percentage factor would be established according to the actuary's cost calculations which will reflect the age, service, and employer contribution rate characteristics of the covered employees. This type of formula establishes the future service benefit under a plan, and the past service benefit is usually fixed as a benefit unit of, say, $4 to $6 per year of past service credit. When a wide variety of contribution rates are payable under the plan, this "percentage of employer contributions" formula is very convenient. For example, if contributions on behalf of one group of employees could be as little as $200 per year and for other groups could be as much as $3,000 per year, this formula is convenient not only for record-keeping purposes but also for purposes of communicating benefits to employees. For a specified hourly contribution rate, this formula produces a unit pension benefit for a single plan year, and the unit benefit earned is directly proportional to the hours of service on which contributions are made. One of the great advantages of this formula is the fact that it generally does not create onerous unfunded liabilities when contribution rates are increased.

There are, however, some disadvantages to this type of formula. The benefit provided is based on an average of the contribution rates earned over the employee's working career; and in a period of rapidly escalating contribution rates, the older, long-service employees do not have an opportunity to receive substantial benefit improvements since they may have only a few years of plan coverage at the higher contribution rates. Another disadvantage is that the past service benefit may not be adequately supported by extremely low contribution rates for some of the groups. For example, if the past service benefit unit were $10 per year of past service, it might take a contribution rate of at least 20 cents or 25 cents per hour to fund both the future service benefits and the past service benefits.

Final Contribution Rate Pension Benefit. The majority of benefit formulas are established to provide specified benefit units per year of service, and increased benefits are only granted by positive trustee action from time to time as contribution rates change. However, there are formulas that gear pension benefits to the final contribution rate or final average contribution rate. The contributions may be expressed in cents per hour or in dollars per week, and sometimes the benefits are scheduled in advance according to the final or final average contribution rate. Under this type of formula, the hours worked or weeks worked are accumulated and a year of benefit service is granted for, say, 1,800 hours or 50 weeks worked, depending upon the particular plan's basis of required contributions. For example, an employee who worked 18,000 hours over a number of years would have earned ten benefit service years. Thus, under this method, the number of years of contributory service is determined and a specified benefit unit will be multiplied by that number of years. The benefit unit will be directly related to the final contribution rate or final average contribution rate. The *final contribution rate* will often be defined as the contribution rate applicable to the bargaining unit in which covered employees worked the majority of their hours or weeks during the last three to five years of covered employment. With this formula, the benefit unit for past service is frequently the same as the unit applicable to future service, but it could be a single specified benefit unit independent of the final contribution rate, such as $10 per year of past service.

If the benefit unit is based on the *final average contribution rate*, the average may be determined as the average rate applicable to the bargaining units in which covered employees worked during their last five or ten years of service. Under both of these formulas, every time a contribution rate increases, all prior contributory service benefits (and sometimes past service benefits) are automatically increased, creating substantial increases in unfunded liabilities.

This type of benefit formula can be funded on a sound basis if the actuary establishes the formula by taking into account the probable increases in contribution rates in the future. Consequently, if the benefit unit is expressed as a percentage of contributions, adjusted to reflect the final contribution rate (or final average contribution rate), the percentage will generally be substantially lower than the percentage which would apply in a plan where the benefit unit is related to actual career employer contributions made on behalf of a participant. For example, if the percentage applied under a plan to a participant's career employer contributions were 2.5 percent, then the percentage applicable under a final rate formula might be 1.8 percent since the final contribution rate would be used to establish the benefit unit payable on account of the participant's career hours worked.

Accrual of Benefits

Various benefits may be made available if the employee's service under the plan is terminated before normal retirement. These benefits may include a vested pension if the employee terminates; a spouse pension if the employee dies; a disability pension if the employee becomes disabled; or a reduced pension if the employee retires early. The amount of these benefits is seldom based on the full pension benefit at normal retirement, but on the pension "accrued" for the employee's service to date. In a joint trust pension plan, a unit of benefit is usually granted for each full year of future service. Therefore, if only future service is considered and if an individual has been fully employed for each of 20 years by the time normal retirement age is reached, the individual typically accrues $1/20$ of the full pension benefit each year. Likewise, if an individual has 30 years of future service at normal retirement age, a benefit credit is received of $1/30$ of the full pension at age 65 for each year of service.

Under ERISA, a plan must be designed so that the benefits accrued for contributory service by any single employee will at least satisfy one of three alternative benefit accrual rules. These alternative accrual rules may be referred to as the 3 percent rule, the fractional rule, and the $133\frac{1}{3}$ percent rule.

Under the 3 percent rule, the normal retirement pension must accrue at a rate of at least 3 percent of the maximum normal pension benefit for each year of service so that after $33\frac{1}{3}$ years of service a full pension can be earned. This 3 percent benefit accrual alternative may be useful when a flat dollar benefit is provided at a specified retirement age. For example, if the normal retirement pension were $300 per month, then this accrual rule would require that an employee earn at least a $9 per month future service credit for each full year of future service.

Under the fractional rule, the benefit earned each year must not be less than the prorata share of the full benefit payable at the normal retirement age. In other words, a terminating participant's benefit accruals are computed by multiplying the participant's projected benefit by a fraction, the ratio of actual years of plan participation divided by the total number of service years that would be accumulated if the participant remained covered by the plan until normal retirement age. To illustrate, if a participant were employed at age 25 and a $300 monthly pension would be payable at normal retirement age 65, then after, say, ten years of service, the participant must accrue at least $10/40$ths of the $300 monthly pension.

Under the $133\frac{1}{3}$ percent rule, a limit is imposed on the extent of difference between the level of benefit units which a participant can earn. Under this alternative, a plan cannot be designed so that the benefit unit accrued by a participant in a single year can exceed $133\frac{1}{3}$ percent of the benefit unit accrued in any preceding year. For example, a participant would not satisfy this rule if a benefit unit could be accrued of, say, $10 per year of service for the first ten years of service and $20 per year of service thereafter. If there is to be a step-rate benefit accrual, under this rule the increase cannot exceed 33⅓ percent. Thus, in this latter instance, the benefit unit could not exceed $13.33 for service after the first ten years.

ERISA's accrual rules do not apply to past service benefit credits since during that period of time an employer did not maintain the pension plan, and ERISA recognizes for a joint trust pension plan that the employer maintains the plan only during the periods when the employer contributes to the plan pursuant to a pension contribution agreement.

As will be discussed later in this chapter, ERISA requires that an employee be granted a year of vesting service if 1,000 or more hours of service are accrued during a plan year. Under ERISA's accrual rules, a prorata portion of the future service benefit credit must be granted to each individual who accrues a vesting service year during a plan year. For example, if a plan requires 1,800 hours of future (contributory) service to earn a full benefit credit, then an employee who earns a vesting service year and works 1,000 covered hours must accrue at least 1,000/1,800ths of a benefit credit, that is, 55.6 percent of a full future service benefit credit must be accrued for 1,000 covered hours. In most plans a full year of future service credit is earned if an employee works 1,500 to 1,800 hours in a year, and fractional credit is granted for less work. Often, no benefit credit is granted if less than 300 to 500 hours are worked in a single year. However, the number of hours required for a full year of future service credit should reflect the average work year of the covered group. In some construction trades 1,200 hours may be appropriate and a smaller number of hours would be used for seasonally employed groups.

Most plans provide that no more than one benefit unit may be earned in any one plan year. For example, if an individual worked 2,000 hours in a year and the plan required only 1,500 hours for a full benefit unit, such an individual would be limited to a single benefit credit. This situation has bothered a great many of the union employees covered by joint trust pension plans who believe a plan should be designed so that the benefit credit would reflect every hour worked. The plan previously mentioned could be modified to grant every covered employee a benefit credit of 1/1,500th of a full year's benefit credit for each covered hour, a covered hour being an hour for which a contribution is required or made on behalf of a covered employee. With this revised formula an individual who worked 1,800 hours would receive 1,800/1,500ths of a year's full benefit credit, that is, the individual would earn $1^1/_5$ benefits units for the 1,800 hours worked.

Some bargaining agreements require contributions to be made on every hour worked while other agreements restrict contributions to straight time hours only. The actual hours used for benefit accrual purposes should reflect the conditions stipulated by bargaining agreements, even though a different basis may be used for purposes of measuring vesting service. Future service also may be related to contributory weeks, and a full week of service may be granted when at least one hour of employment in a week has been rendered. The benefit accrual rules should reflect the actual basis on which contributions are made to the plan under the bargaining agreements.

As regards the accrual of past service credits, there probably are as many bases for determining the amount of benefit earned as there are joint trust pension plans. For example, one quarter of a past service credit may be granted for each consecutive calendar quarter immediately preceding an employee's first covered hour during which time an employer in the industry made contributions on the employee's behalf to the social security system. On the other hand, another plan might grant a full year of service for each year of an unbroken series of calendar years during which the employee was at work "or available for work" in the industry immediately preceding his or her first covered hour. Then again, still another plan might require a minimum number of hours or weeks of employment in each past service year in order to be granted past service benefit credit. There are, of course, numerous other methods employed to determine a covered employee's past service benefit accruals. In virtually all situations the trustees will generally require that a minimum number of contributory future service years be earned within a short period following an employee's first covered hour, in order for an employee to be eligible for past service benefit credits.

The definition of an hour of service for purposes of benefit accrual need not be the same as the definition used for vesting service purposes. For vesting purposes, service for which compensation is paid directly or indirectly must be counted, but for benefit accrual purposes, only *contributions which are made or required to be made* under a bargaining agreement need be recognized. The phrase "required to be made" as it applies to benefit accrual is very important because it implies that contributions may not actually be made for such hours of service. In other words, any period of time when hours of service are rendered by an employee and for which employer contributions are required under an acceptable written agreement must be counted for benefit accrual purposes even though the employer contributions may be delinquent or the employer may have become bankrupt and the plan may never receive such contributions. With this fact in mind, it is important for a plan to establish rules which determine the period of time that a written agreement is acceptable while an employer is delinquent so that a limit is placed on the extent of the benefit accrual. In other words, when an employer is delinquent in contributions for a period of three to six months, the plan may deem that the written agreement is no longer acceptable and contributions are no longer required so benefits will not continue to accrue. This safeguard is necessary in order to maintain the sound funding of a joint trust pension plan—primarily because of the danger that the required contributions will not be recovered from a bankrupt employer.

Another matter of great importance to a joint trust pension plan relates to the conditions under which past service benefits are increased from time to time as contribution rates change. If past service benefits are periodically increased as contribution rates rise, a plan could sustain a substantially increased financial burden if those benefits could not be cancelled if the employer withdraws. The IRS has issued a letter ruling in one instance concerning the cancellation of past service benefits granted under a plan when an employer withdrew from the plan. Under that ruling, past service benefits granted on account of service with an employer before that employer first contributed to the plan were allowed to be cancelled. Although ERISA clearly indicates that original past service benefits may be cancelled under such circumstances, cancellation in all instances may not be possible. Therefore, it is important for the trustees to carefully evaluate the granting of additional past service credits as contribution rates increase. Perhaps, in lieu of past service benefit improvements, trustees might decide to grant for past service only "supplemental benefits" for active employees who retire directly from service and who have originally earned past service credits. Under ERISA's "3 percent rule", as long as each contributory year's benefit credit earned is at least 3 percent of the maximum benefit payable for a specified level of employer contributions, the supplemental benefits would not have to be accrued by any individual. The supplemental benefits (for past service) would be payable only to employees who retire from active participation. Employees who become vested either before or after the employer(s) ceases to contribute to the joint trust pension plan might not be entitled to such supplemental benefits.

Age at Which Benefits Commence

Most plans establish their normal retirement age as age 65 because that is the age when unreduced benefits are payable under the social security system. Sometimes the normal retirement age is lower if the particular industry mandates a lower retirement age. For example, plans for airline pilots will typically have a normal retirement age of 60 because that is the age at which most pilots must retire from service. If the covered employment involves police or firefighters, the hazards of those occupations may call for an earlier retirement age because these employees need youthful vitality to perform their jobs effectively. Usually, a normal retirement age will include, in addition to a minimum age, a requirement that a specified number of years of total credited service (i.e., the sum of past and future credited service) be earned and perhaps a minimum number of future (contributory) service years be accumulated. Typically, 25 or 30 years of service would be required for a covered employee to receive full pension benefits when normal retirement is earlier than age 65.

There has been a great amount of confusion between the normal retirement age of a plan and a mandatory retirement age. Under a joint trust pension plan, the normal retirement age generally has not been a mandatory retirement age *unless* the underlying collective bargaining agreements stipulated an age when covered employees had to retire and receive their pensions. Even when a mandatory retirement age has been imposed under a collective bargaining agreement, some relief has usually been provided under the agreement to cover those instances when employees would not otherwise have sufficient service by the mandatory retirement age to receive a benefit under the plan.[1] Under ERISA, the normal retirement age cannot exceed the later of age 65 or the completion of a ten-year period after an employee first began to participate in the plan. If the normal retirement age is set at, say, age 60 or age 65, most plans do not require more than two to five years of contributory future service before an individual is allowed to retire and receive a pension. To fix a longer period of contributory service may impose too great a hardship on employees who are older at the establishment of the plan or who are in bargaining units wishing to adopt the plan. As previously mentioned, the normal retirement age should be set so that the plan can continually attract new employer groups and remain viable with favorable age and service characteristics. Most plans have allowed early retirement directly from service at age 55, provided that the employee has at least 15 or 20 years of total service. Generally, such service would include both past and future service and at least ten years of future service credits. However, a number of plans had more restrictive early retirement provisions for vested terminated participants and would not allow early retirement before age 60 or, sometimes, under any circumstances. With the advent of ERISA many plans now require merely ten years of vesting service and attainment of age 55 for early retirement because a vested terminated employee must have the right to retire early at the age when active employees have the right to retire early. There can be no discrimination between the two groups with regard to the age at which early retirement pensions are payable. However, if a plan requires, say, 20 years of total credited service and age 55 for early retirement, a terminated vested par-

---

[1] The California Labor Code requires, effective January 1, 1978, every employer, except a public agency, to permit any employee who indicates in writing a desire within a reasonable time and can demonstrate ability to do so, to continue employment beyond the normal retirement date contained in any private pension or retirement plan. However, the law does not require changes in any bona fide pension programs or collective bargaining agreements during the life of the contract, or for two years after the effective date of the law, whichever occurs first.

At the federal level, on April 6, 1978, the President signed H.R. 5383 which amends the Age Discrimination in Employment Act to increase the current mandatory retirement age from 65 to 70 years.

ticipant without 20 years of total credited service need not be allowed early retirement rights.

From a practical point of view, unless the benefit level is quite substantial, experience has shown that few employees will retire until they qualify for social security benefits. Since social security benefits are now payable in a reduced amount at age 62, there has been an increase in the number of early retirements at ages 62 and above. Some plans have attempted to encourage employees to retire even earlier than age 62 by introducing an early retirement benefit option that allows a temporarily increased pension until age 62 or age 65 when social security benefits are scheduled to commence and thereafter a reduced pension. This option is designed so that the reduced pension, payable when social security benefits commence, will, in combination with social security benefits, provide total monthly payments that are approximately equal to the increased pension payable before social security payments begin. (This subject is covered further in this chapter under Early Retirement.)

Normal Retirement. As previously discussed the standard or normal retirement age of most pension plans has been established at age 65, reflecting the age when full benefits are first payable under the social security system. As the years have gone by and as various industries have had difficulties maintaining work opportunities, trustees have given a great deal of attention to changing the normal retirement age of joint trust pension plans. In many industries, the normal retirement age has been reduced in recent years to age 62, when social security benefits are first available on an actuarially reduced basis. In some instances, plans have reduced the normal retirement age to as low as age 60 or even age 55. Of course, when airline pilots are involved, the normal retirement age has long been set at age 60 because that is the latest age at which a pilot is considered to be physically able to endure the stress of that occupation. Likewise, in the fields where other risks exist, retirement ages have been set at age 50 or 55; for example, the public safety employees of state and municipal retirement systems (police, firefighters, and guards at correctional institutions) often have a normal retirement age of age 55 or 60. The underlying concept that justifies these lower retirement ages is the risk of the occupation. When a person gets beyond age 55 or 60, the person may not be physically capable of handling the duties of his or her job.

When it comes to the concept of retirement age in most Taft-Hartley plans, however, the retirement age has been changed or reduced from time to time primarily because of troubles in the industry. For example, when there is a decline in the number of employees in the auto industry, great pressures are brought against the auto makers to reduce the retirement age. The auto workers plan is not a Taft-Hartley plan but it is the result of union negotiations. (In the UAW–Auto Industry plans, the union negotiates the benefit level but the employer determines how to provide the benefits.) That same pressure to reduce the retirement age has been brought to bear in many industries. In the construction trades today, the retirement age has been changed primarily because of the difficulties in maintaining work opportunities for younger workers. Many times the trustees have agreed to reduce the normal retirement age not only to age 60 or age 55 but also to allow unreduced pensions to be payable when a covered employee has rendered 25 to 30 years of service.

One difficulty that has arisen as a by-product of ERISA relates to the fact that the benefits that become vested under a plan must be the benefits payable at the normal retirement age. Therefore, if the normal retirement age is set at age 55, or age 60, or age 62, a participant's vested rights have to relate to that normal retirement age. Consequently, as a direct result of ERISA, many plans have changed their normal retirement age back to the original age 65 (in combination with a contributory service requirement) so that participants who terminate with short years of service, say, 10 or more years of service but less than 20 or 30 years of service, have a vested right to receive earned benefits in an unreduced amount only at the normal retirement age. Therefore these plans provide that unreduced pension benefits are payable at a specified early retirement age, say, 55 or 60, only to participants who retire directly from service after, say, 20, 25, or 30 years of service. The same benefit unit is earned each year by all participants, but unreduced pension benefits are not payable to vested terminated employees before the normal retirement age.

ERISA allows the normal retirement age for a joint trust pension plan to be set at the later of age 65 or the tenth anniversary of a participant's commencement of participation. Many plans may adopt this age and service arrangement in setting the normal retirement age, but there are many implications of such an approach. For example, as mentioned in previous chapters, if the older employees of new employer groups cannot retire and receive an unreduced pension before the tenth anniversary of initial participation, the plan may be very unattractive. Therefore, if the normal retirement age is the later of age 65 and the tenth anniversary of initial participation and the plan proves to be unattractive to new employer groups, the plan may eventually have financial difficulties. A plan must have new groups of employees constantly entering plan coverage—either from newly organized employer groups or from new employees of existing employer units—if it is to (1) maintain a stable population of covered employees and (2) retain a reasonable expectation that the actuary's estimated flow of contributions will be realized. Therefore, even though ERISA allows the normal retirement age to be deferred until a participant's tenth anniversary of plan participation, most plans will probably establish the normal retirement age as the later of age 65 or completion of two to five years of contributory service, but no later than the tenth anniversary of an employee's participation date. To control the cost of past service benefits for older employees who retire with only a few years of contributory service, plans may only allow one or two past service credits to be earned for each year of contributory service.

Early Retirement   Early retirement in most plans is set at about ten years prior to the normal retirement age. In other words, most plans have age 55 as the age when early retirement may first occur. However, few plans under ERISA will allow any early retirement benefits to be payable unless ten years of vesting service have been earned by an employee, and for many plans ten years of vesting service is essentially ten years of contributory service.

Under ERISA-modified plans of the construction trades, the early retirement benefits may be payable at age 55 with, say, 10 years of vesting service or at any age after 25 years or 30 years of total credited service. The benefit amount payable is often more favorable than an actuarially reduced benefit and, sometimes, is not reduced at all. However, in order to control costs and to provide more important benefits to the employees who remain in the construction trades or in the industry, many plans allow an unreduced pension to be payable only for those who retire directly from service. As previously described, under this arrangement an employee who leaves plan coverage with a vested pension at age 35 after, say, 12 years of service, may be able to retire at age 55 because ERISA requires it, but the employee may receive an actuarially reduced pension, whereas a full unreduced pension would be payable to the participant who remains in service until age 55 and then retires. This plan design is geared to give the greatest benefits to the employees who remain in service in the industry rather than to give them to employees who work a substantial period of time but not for an entire career.

Retirement concepts are not established in a vacuum. Many trustees are now becoming concerned with the possibility that the number of participants who take advantage of unreduced pensions at early retirement ages may exceed the actuary's estimates and cause the plan financial difficulties. For example, if the number of people who retire early significantly exceeds the number that the actuary projects in cost calculations, the plan may have actuarial losses. This could prove to be a significant problem if employees can retire at an early age with a full pension and then return to substantial employment at their trade or craft (but outside of the employment covered by the plan) and continue to earn a good income. Therefore, trustees have always been concerned with establishing some type of control over this situation. The typical provision contained in a plan to control costs in the past has been the suspension of benefits of retired participants for the period of postretirement employment in the industry.

Before ERISA the "industry" could include the entire geographical area of the United States. Under ERISA, this type of suspension becomes a problem. At the time of this writing, the DOL has not issued rules governing the suspension of benefits after an individual's retirement under multiemployer plans, but it is the consensus of a number of attorneys that benefits can be suspended during early retirement years for any period of employment in the industry before the normal retirement age if a participant works at the same trade or craft and in the same geographical area under the jurisdiction of the local unions participating in the plan, *and* perhaps even in those geographical areas for which service is recognized under the plan through reciprocity agreements.[2] This matter can be very important because a major purpose of liberal early retirement provisions is to give plan participants a financial opportunity to leave the industry and make jobs available for younger employees. If, in fact, liberal early retirement benefits encourage employees only to leave the industry in the geographical area covered by the plan, but to reenter the industry in an adjacent geographical area, then the general purpose of liberal early retirement provisions is undermined. In addition, the adjacent geographical area may also have a pension plan but not a reciprocity agreement with plans in contiguous regions. With these considerations in mind, trustees should be concerned with the degree to which ERISA's rules on suspension of benefits may influence the actuarial funding of a plan's liberal early retirement benefits.

Sometimes a board of trustees finds that it wants to encourage early retirement to make jobs available for younger employees but for financial reasons cannot allow unreduced pensions at ages as low as age 55 or 60. One way of accomplishing its objective is to include in the plan a "Social Security Adjustment Option" whereby the early retirement pension is increased until the social security benefits commence, usually at age 62 or age 65, as selected by the retiring employee. Allowing a retiring employee to select the age when social security benefits commence permits the employee flexibility in retirement planning. If the employee selects age 65, the plan's benefits both before and after age 65 will be lower than if age 62 is selected. Under this arrangement, a lower pension is payable after social security payments begin so that the total monthly benefits payable both before and after commencement of social security benefits are approximately level. This is one way in which employees who could not afford to retire on the standard early retirement pension might be able to retire early. It not only can give the trustees the opportunity to encour-

---

[2] Although there are no published regulations governing the suspension of benefits, the suspension of benefits for periods of employment by a pensioner after the plan's normal retirement age is allowed specifically by ERISA, provided that the employment is "in the industry, in the same trade or craft, and the same geographic area covered by the plan, as when such benefits commenced."

age early retirement but adds a degree of flexibility in the design of the plan so that employees can often make their own choice.

Assume that an employee is retiring at age 57 and is entitled to receive a level pension for life of $350 per month. The employee's social security benefit beginning at age 62 is estimated at $400 monthly. Thus, the employee's total monthly income from both sources combined would be $350 before age 62 and $750 thereafter. The employee would prefer to have a level income and would be willing to give up a part of his or her post-age 62 income to receive more before age 62.

The plan's actuary will determine the amount of additional early pension, payable until age 62, which can be provided by the value of the reduction in pension after age 62 so that the pensioner's monthly income is approximately level both before and after social security benefits commence. Instead of receiving a level $350 monthly pension from the plan, the actuary may determine that the plan benefit could be $611 monthly before age 62 and $211 thereafter. When combined with the $400 monthly income from social security after age 62, the employee's monthly income will be $611 both before and after age 62. The calculations are made so that the actuarial value of the supplemental pension before social security benefits commence is equal to the actuarial value of the reduction in pension after social security benefits commence.

In theory, the value of the employee's pension should be the same whether the employee retired early with a regular early pension or retired early and received temporarily an increased pension and after social security benefits commence, a reduced pension. The only fundamental difference between the actuarial values may be the actuary's assumption that people who retire early will be in poor health and, consequently, will have a shorter life expectancy. In the absence of a Social Security Adjustment Option, the actuary may anticipate that the value of payments to ill-health pensioners will be reduced because of their shorter life expectancies. The introduction of the Social Security Adjustment Option can invalidate this actuarial assumption because ill-health pensioners can increase the level of pension payments they receive during their shorter lifespan.

Complications sometimes arise if the employees who retire

early and make this selection reenter covered employment before social security benefits commence and have their benefits suspended. Instead of having the regular reduced early benefits suspended, they have a substantially increased early retirement benefit suspended—suffering a greater loss than similar early retirees who did not make the election but who reentered covered employment. To avoid this inequity, the option may be designed so that the special temporary supplemental early retirement benefit which is suspended during reemployment is not forever forfeited. An equitable solution of the problem adds complexity to the plan design, but it is worthy of trustees' consideration, especially when they wish to encourage early retirement and are willing to allow high temporary early retirement benefits.

As in the design of any benefit program, a plan's benefit design should, wherever practical, reflect the total benefit package provided to covered employees. For example, if the health and welfare plan has no provisions for health insurance coverage after retirement, liberal early retirement provisions of the pension plan may not achieve the trustees' goal. The health and welfare plan could encourage early retirement under the pension plan if it had some arrangements by which retirement coverage for health care purposes could be maintained at least until Medicare is available to the retired employees. Sometimes, the health and welfare plan can be designed to allow continuation of coverage to pensioners who make self-pay contributions to maintain full or partial coverage until Medicare commences. The self-pay contributions for full coverage may be $50, $60, or more per month. In other words, if the health and welfare plan were designed in such a manner, the pension plan might then effectively have to allow for the fact that the retiring employee requires a temporary pension increase of $50, $60, or more just to maintain health and welfare coverage. These are facts which should not be overlooked in the design of the early retirement provisions of a pension plan.

Delayed Retirement.   In many instances, employees have the right to retire at the normal retirement age but continue in service because the income they earn while employed is so much greater than their expected pension and they are sufficiently healthy to perform their jobs well. To place a limit on this practice, some plans incorporate a deferred retirement age; that is, an age to which the commencement of retirement benefits can be deferred but at which time the pension must begin. Generally, this is age 70. Some plans allow participants to earn additional pension credits while continuing in service after normal retirement age. For example, if an employee reaches his normal retirement age and only has ten benefit credits, the plan may allow accrual of benefit credits beyond that age until, say, age 70, when all benefit accruals would stop. In rare instances, pension benefits earned at normal retirement age are actuarially increased to reflect both the additional investment income earned on the actuarial reserve for the earned benefits and the shorter lifetime over which the payments will be made once the deferred retirement age has been reached. Presently, many plans allow either no benefit accrual during this deferred retirement period or a very limited benefit accrual since the plans have been established to encourage the older employees to retire and make jobs more readily available to the younger workers. If an employee defers retirement, death benefits normally paid upon death before the normal retirement age are often reduced or eliminated if not required to be paid under ERISA.

If a retired employee reenters employment, pension benefits usually are suspended and the employee often will receive no additional pension credits after retirement even though contributions are made on his or her behalf. Before ERISA, the suspension of benefits might have been for as long as six months even if an employee reentered employment for only a single month. However, ERISA apparently does not allow such suspension. ERISA only allows the suspension of one benefit payment for each month that an employee reenters employment after the normal retirement age. Again, ERISA allows the suspension of benefits of an employee only if employment after the normal retirement age is in the same industry and the employee is employed at the same trade or craft and in the same geographical area covered by the plan. For example, if the Sheet Metal Industry of Southern California were involved, an employee could reach normal retirement age, start receiving pension benefits, and go to work in Northern California without having benefits suspended. The suspension could be imposed only if work were recommenced in the Southern California area, unless perhaps, the Southern and

Northern California Plans had reciprocity agreements. Thus, ERISA has effected a very fundamental change in the rules of joint trust plans as they relate to the suspension of benefits. Before ERISA, most plans suspended benefits if any work were involved after retirement in the *industry*—regardless of the geographical area of work in the country.

Vesting

ERISA establishes three alternative minimum standards for vesting:

1. One hundred percent vesting after 10 years of vesting service; or,
2. A 25 percent vested interest in accrued pension benefits after 5 years of vesting service, with the percentage grading to 50 percent after 10 years of vesting service, and then to 100 percent after 15 years of vesting service; or
3. The rule of 45. Under this latter arrangement, when a participant's combined age and service equals 45, the participant must have a 50 percent vested right to his or her earned pension benefits, and the 50 percent vesting right must increase by 10 percent each year to a 100 percent vested right to benefits after 5 additional years. Also, under this rule, regardless of age, an individual must have a 50 percent right after 10 years of vesting service which then must graduate to a 100 percent right after 5 additional vesting service years. In addition, under this same rule, if an individual is age 40 or over when plan participation begins, no vesting is required until 5 years of vesting service have been accumulated, at which time the individual must have a 50 percent vested right—gradually increasing to a 100 percent vesting right after 10 years of vesting service.

A brief consideration of these three alternative vesting standards generally indicates to a board of trustees that the most practical vesting standard is the rule that provides for 100 percent vesting after 10 years of vesting service. This rule is often referred to as "cliff" vesting, that is, no vested rights are granted for the first ten years, and, thereafter, all benefit credits are vested.

The two other alternatives are complicated to administer and difficult to communicate to the covered employees. Vesting schedules more liberal than the minimum standards may be adopted, but more liberal schedules generate higher costs and may conflict with the trustees' desire to reward long-service employees rather than short-service employees.

Definition of Vesting Service. Service for the purpose of determining an employee's progress along a vesting schedule is measured according to the same rules that apply to eligibility for participation in the plan. Essentially, a year of vesting service is earned by a participant according to the particular rules of a joint trust pension plan and will be based on the 1,000-hour, 870-hour, 750-hour, or other alternative rules adopted by the plan under regulations published by the Department of Labor.

Impact of ERISA on Vested Employee Early Retirement Pensions. As mentioned previously, ERISA requires that any vested terminated participant who meets the age and service requirements must be able to retire as early as an active employee who is eligible to retire early. Therefore, many plans have to be amended to provide more liberal early retirement rights than had previously been required or allowed before ERISA. Although this factor does add cost to a pension plan, the cost is not necessarily significant if actuarially reduced benefits are payable before the normal retirement age. However, if a plan provides vesting rights to benefits geared to a final contribution rate or final average contribution rate, then vested terminated employees must receive retirement benefits based on a final or final average contribution rate, and this ERISA-required retirement right for vested employees can add significantly to the cost of a plan.

Prior to ERISA, a plan that geared benefits to a final contribution rate might have allowed vested terminated employees to retire early and receive pension benefits based on a career average contribution rate or some basic pension amount less favorable than the rate of pension payable to a participant who retired early directly from service. ERISA now precludes this different treatment for vested terminated employees since the benefit to be payable at normal retirement age must be computed on the same basis for all participants, those entering retirement from active service and those entering from a terminated vested status. Simply stated, if a participant's benefit rights while employed are based on a final contribution rate, that same rate must be employed in determining early retirement benefits. (In no event may a reduction in the final contribution rate reduce a participant's accrued benefits once the participant is eligible to retire.) However, ERISA does not require that any special unreduced pension benefits payable to participants who retire early *directly from service* have to be paid to vested terminated employees who retire early. This distinction can be very important if a board of trustees wishes to allow participants who retire early directly from service to receive a pension benefit that is not actuarially reduced. For example, many plans may allow an unreduced pension to be payable when social security benefits are first available, that is, at age 62. In some instances, plans may allow early pension benefits to be payable in unreduced amounts to those who retire directly from service at age 55 or 60. ERISA does require that the basis of determining the benefit *at the normal retirement age* be the same for all retiring participants whether retirement is directly from service or from a terminated vested status, but ERISA does not require that any special unreduced pensions payable upon early retirement be awarded to all participants, regardless of when service was terminated.

Forfeiture Due to Breaks in Service. Under ERISA a one-year break in service is a plan year during which a participant has accrued less than 501 hours of service. Obviously, if one of the alternative methods for determining a year of vesting service is used (e.g., 870 or 750 hours of service), then something other than 501 hours of service must also be used for purposes of measuring a one-year break in service. For example, the typical plan that would employ 1,000 hours of service for determining one year of vesting service might use 500 hours in determining a one-year break in service. Likewise, if a plan adopted the 870-hour rule, it would normally use 435 hours of service as the basis for a one-year break in service. Similarly, if a plan adopted the 750-hour service rule, then 375 hours of service would be used for purposes of measuring a one-year break in service.

ERISA does not require a plan to grant any benefit credit to an employee who does not work at least the number of hours required to earn a vesting service year. However, ERISA will allow a plan to cause an employee to lose vesting service years and forfeit all benefit credits when the number of consecutive one year breaks in service first equals the accumulated number of vesting service years, provided the employee has not already obtained a vested right (or partial vested right) to earned benefit credits. This ERISA provision governing the forfeiture of earned benefit credits is often referred to as the "rule of parity." If a board of trustees literally follows ERISA's rule of parity in establishing plan provisions, an employee who just became a participant, by accruing one vesting service year, could immediately thereafter forfeit earned benefit credits if a one year break in service is accumulated in the following plan year. To avoid this situation, many boards of trustees will include in the plan a special provision, sometimes called a "grace period." The grace period is a period of two or three plan years during each of which an employee must have accumulated a one year service break before earned benefit credits will be forfeited. This technique gives employees who are temporarily out of work some relief if they become reemployed and also assists in plan administration; that is, the administrator only has to purge the records for those whose employment status has permanently changed.

In determining the hours of employment for purposes of measuring vesting service years and one year breaks in service, the plan administrator must also count hours of service while in uncovered employment with the same employer. In addition, if an employee performs military service, the plan may have to allow credit for hours of service while the employee is in the military service for purposes of avoiding a permanent break in service under the plan and may now be required to grant benefit credit.[3]

Some plans are structured in a manner that simplifies the calculation of hours of service while employees are in military service, on disability leave, or on a leave of absence. Under such situations, plans may allow, say, eight hours of service for each day of military service, disability, or approved leave of absence. The trustees may adopt a more restrictive method of determining hours of service under DOL rules, but to do so would add administrative

---

[3] *Alabama Power Co.* v. *Davis,* — U.S. —, 95 L.R.R.M. 2569, ———— L.C. ———— (U.S. Sup. Ct. 1977). This court decision mandates a reappraisal of long-standing practice. It appears that military time must now be counted and, in turn, trustees, administrators and their advisors must determine the method of resolving this problem and, possibly, of financing the additional benefits.

complexity. Use of the simple practice of allowing eight hours of service in the indicated situations simplifies the basic administration of the pension plan.

If an employee has a one-year break in service, the employee no longer has to be counted as a participant under the plan if he or she is not already vested. However, if an employee then accumulates a number of consecutive one-year breaks in service equal to accumulated vesting service years, the employee forfeits all benefit and service credits under the plan. On the other hand, for example, if an employee has three years of vesting service, then accumulates two consecutive one-year breaks in service but earns only one hour of service more than the number of hours required for a one-year break in service, the employee "breaks the chain" of consecutive one-year breaks in service and again has three vesting service years to his or her credit. If additional vesting service years are not earned, the employee would have to accumulate, once again, three consecutive one-year breaks in service before benefit and service credits earned under the plan would be permanently forfeited. This fact can be extremely important to employees who have some degree of measurable service under a plan but, because of economic circumstances, are temporarily out of the industry and unable to work in covered employment. If such employees make themselves available for employment and remain on a union seniority list, they may be able to return to covered employment and retain their rights to earn benefit credits and vesting service, avoiding permanent forfeiture of earned benefits.

The operation of this rule of parity probably will have a very significant impact on those industries in which employees work sporadically, that is, a great number of hours of service in one, two, or three years and very few hours of service in one or two following years. It is possible for employees to have worked continually for the same employer and, because of relatively stringent pre-ERISA break-in-service rules, to have forfeited virtually all service and benefit credits because of a history of fluctuating employment. Yet, many of these employees will be protected from benefit forfeitures under the rule of parity established by ERISA. This fact can be very important in industries where the product tends to be somewhat cyclical in nature. For example, in the fish canning industry, there are years when an abundance of fish is harvested and, consequently, a great amount of work is available. However, periodically very little work is available and employees far down on the union seniority list are temporarily out of employment. For those employees in cyclical industries who remain in the industry, this rule of parity may significantly improve their prospects for retaining earned benefits and rights and, ultimately, to receive a pension.

Problems of Seasonal Industry Workers

As of this date the Department of Labor has not yet defined a seasonal industry and, consequently, has not issued rules governing the participation, vesting, and benefit accrual rules which must apply to seasonal industry employees. Some pension funds that cover seasonal workers have established both the number of hours of service required for a vesting service year and the related rules governing a one-year break in service at lower levels than required for regular employees. For example, if a seasonal employee works an average of, say, 600 hours in a calendar year and a regular employee works an average of, say, 1,200 hours, then the hours of service of a seasonal employee required for one vesting service year might be set at 500 hours. A lower number of hours of service, depending upon the relationship of the average number of hours worked by the seasonal employee to the average number hours worked by the typical full-time employee may, of course, be selected.

The seasonal type of employment reflects the industries in which there is a great amount of work for a short period of time in a year and little or no work for the remainder of the year. This kind of employment is common in certain portions of the food processing industry where vegetables or fruit are processed through canning or freezing, and the canning or freezing takes place where the product is harvested. Similar circumstances could occur in areas where the industry depends on seasons, for example, the skiing industry in winter and other recreational industries in summertime. Whether or not seasonal employees in those industries are covered depends on the type of employee that the industry attracts. For example, recreational industries normally attract many young people from colleges and schools who are not interested in pension plans. Often, they are not represented by unions and, consequently, there are no pension plans. However, in the areas where vast quantities of food are grown, picked, and processed, employees are frequently represented by unions and sometimes contributions are negotiated for pension plans. Oftentimes, the employees in the seasonal occupations are primarily females and other minority employees. Many female employees have families and cannot work full time but are available periodically to earn a supplemental income. In many situations the minorities are not trained or well educated but they can perform well at manual tasks in seasonal industries. If the season is long and/or the harvest is substantial, a seasonal employee may accumulate over 1,000 hours of service in a single year. Typically, the number of hours of service will average considerably less than 1,000 in any given season. Often, from year to year there can be cyclical swings in the amount of food that is picked, harvested, and processed and so the number of hours of service from year to year will vary significantly. For these reasons the rules which govern the rights under a pension plan should be less stringent than the rules which apply to full-time employees.

In recent years another factor has affected pension plans governing seasonal employees, namely, the actions of the Equal Employment Opportunities Commission. This Commission has brought court action against both the union and the employers in the food processing industry in California to require that one half of the available full-time (regular) jobs must be offered to all female or minority group seasonal employees who meet the job's requirements. This suit was settled by the parties involved and reflects the federal government's affirmative action program to assist females and minorities in improving their work opportunities. The settlement included, among other things, an agreement to give special pension benefits to seasonal employees who become regular employees.

Under such circumstances a new factor is introduced into a joint trust pension plan. In this instance, for example, those short-service years of seasonal employment which may have allowed an employee to become vested more rapidly now also may count in determining the vesting service years and benefit accrual rights of an employee who is newly classified as a full-time employee.

In addition, the benefit accrual rules of ERISA establish a framework within which the benefit unit earned by an employee for an hour of service must be determined. Since the contribution rates and benefit units for seasonal and regular employees covered by the same plan may have been substantially different, the benefit accrual rules may require seasonal employee benefit units to be increased or regular employee benefit units to be decreased to satisfy the accrual rules. These ERISA rules can have a very significant impact on the bargaining parties related to a pension plan that covers both seasonal and regular employees because:

1. Seasonal employees may not really be interested in increased pension benefits since the extra cost may reduce the cash wages that can be negotiated; and
2. Regular employees are usually older, longer service employees who are very much interested in pension benefits. Reduction of benefit units may be impractical, and, in addition, any negotiated increase in benefits automatically may require an increase in seasonal pension benefits.

The same kind of concept may also apply to a pension plan that covers different kinds of groups and perhaps even different bargaining units (or different worker classifications within a single bargaining unit), but where employees in one bargaining unit (or classification) often move into the orbit of another bargaining unit (or classification) for the same employer who is contributing to a single joint trust pension plan. The benefit accrual rules may apply in such instances so that there would have to be a consistent relationship between the benefit units applicable under a single pension plan for employees of the same employer who might move from one bargaining unit (or classification) to another. The only occasion when a significant difference in benefit units could apparently exist occurs when the bargaining units (or classifications) and the work performed are mutually exclusive, and there is no significant movement from one unit to another while the individual is employed with the same employer.

The status of seasonal employees is also affected by the fact that different employers within the same industry may process different types of products at different times throughout the calendar year. Consequently, seasonal employees may work for many employers during a single season. Sometimes, the employees can work for several employers during the same month of a given season. All of these facts make the application of all ERISA rules governing hours of service, breaks in service, and the recording of benefit credits more complicated.

Meeting the Problem of Inflation

There are several ways in which the plan can provide for the effects of inflation. One method is for the bargaining parties to continually negotiate increased contributions to the pension plan and, as contributions are increased, to update all pensioner benefits. At the outset of a plan, the granting of past service benefits is usually not a great problem because there are very few pensioners receiving benefits, and the levels of pensions tend to be low. However, after a plan has been in effect for many years and there are a large number of pensioners with substantial pension benefits, the cost of updating pension benefits increases significantly. If plan benefits for pensioners are frequently updated because of increases in the cost of living, there is a danger that too high a proportion of the total contribution will be required to pay for such increases and, ultimately, the younger employees who are to replace those who retire, die, or become disabled will become dissatisfied with an unduly low level of benefits. A general rule of thumb from an actuary's viewpoint is that not more than 50 percent of all contributions should be applied to amortize a plan's total unfunded prior service benefits. If this rule is applied, there is a practical control over the level of benefits that can be afforded when a plan is updated and reasonable assurance that younger employees will earn an acceptable level of benefits during their continued employment.

Preretirement Solution. The type of benefit formula that solves this updating problem automatically for active participants in a joint trust pension plan is a final, or final average, contribution rate benefit formula. Under this type of formula, benefits earned for all service are often automatically increased to reflect higher contribution rates. Clearly, this approach will increase unfunded liabilities from time to time as the contribution rates rise, but it also has a built-in feature that benefit units are constantly updated as increased contribution rates are negotiated, especially if all service is recognized in the update. However, few joint trust plans are designed to *automatically reflect* changes in the rates of negotiated employer contributions because, as previously mentioned, (1) significant contribution rate changes can dramatically increase a plan's unfunded liabilities and (2) there may be no relationship between changes in contribution rates and desirable changes in the plan's level of retirement benefits.

Few defined benefit joint trust plans directly relate employer contributions to the wage levels of the covered employees. Consequently, the benefit unit earned for each year of service does not necessarily reflect either changes in the cost-of-living or productivity gains. Benefit adjustments are usually made on an ad hoc basis by the plan trustees in response to negotiated changes in contribution rates or changes in actuarial assumptions resulting from higher than anticipated units of production, employee turnover, investment income, or other factors. Adjustments to earned benefits are intentionally made on an ad hoc basis so that the trustees can exert strict control over the plan's unfunded prior service liabilities. Even when earned benefits are periodically adjusted, past service benefits often are not adjusted and, when they are, the increase in past service benefits may be strictly limited.

Postretirement Solution. The most effective method of assisting pensioners to meet the effects of inflation is, obviously, to grant automatic cost-of-living benefit adjustments. If a plan were to grant a lifetime cost-of-living increase of as little as 3 percent per year to both current and future pensioners, the annual costs of the plan could increase by as much as 25 percent to 35 percent, or even more, depending upon the age distribution of employees when they retire. If a typical employee retires at age 60, a plan's annual cost could increase by as much as 35 percent or more. In other words, 35 percent or more of all future employer contributions might be needed to fund this modest cost-of-living benefit improvement if it were automatically (or, in fact, on an ad hoc basis) provided for each pensioner's lifetime under a plan. The annual cost of this kind of cost-of-living pension could be reduced if the cost-of-living adjustment were made only every five years for those pensioners who survive in retirement. For example, a person could retire at age 65, and the cost-of-living adjustment would only be made if the person survived to age 70; and, then to age 75, and so forth. Although this cost-of-living provision would cost less than one that grants annual adjustments, the minimum additional cost would generally be at least 20 percent of the plan's cost without this benefit feature.

In view of the substantial cost impact of cost-of-living adjustments, for a specified level of employer contributions, the initial pension at retirement under a cost-of-living formula would have to be reduced so that it could rise automatically over a pensioner's remaining lifetime. A pensioner generally would have to live at least 10 to 12 years following retirement before his or her pension would reach the level it could have been under the plan if a cost-of-living pension were not provided. Consequently, this type of benefit is rarely, if ever, provided under a joint trust pension plan.[4]

DEATH BENEFITS

There are few joint trust pension plans that do not provide some form of death benefit if death occurs before retirement. Before the enactment of ERISA, little or no death benefits were provided after retirement unless the pensioner elected some optional form of pension. However, ERISA requires that all pension plans that allow early retirement give active participants who have been married at least one year an opportunity to elect a joint and survivor form of protection in case death occurs after eligibility for early retirement but no earlier than ten years before the normal retirement age. Also, ERISA requires that a married participant who has been married for at least one year at retirement be provided a joint and survivor pension unless the participant elects to receive either the normal pension form or some other available optional pension form. The introduction of these forms of death benefits has resulted in joint trust pension plans making major

---

[4] The book *Preservation of Pension Benefit Rights* by Dan M. McGill published by the Pension Research Council (Homewood, Ill.: Richard D. Irwin, Inc., 1972) contains a comprehensive discussion of techniques which may be employed to adjust pension benefits for inflation and productivity gains.

revisions in their plan provisions so that there will be a coordination of the death benefits which were provided under the plan before ERISA and these ERISA mandated forms of death benefit protection.

Preretirement Death Benefits

Under most joint trust pension plans providing a preretirement death benefit, the benefit was not payable until a participant had met the vesting requirements of the plan. Before ERISA, these requirements were often integrated with early retirement provisions. For example, vesting may not have been granted until a participant reached age 55 and had accumulated 10 years of total credited service or, alternatively, had completed 20 years of total credited service, at least 10 years of which was credited future service. Sometimes, a plan would allow a participant to become vested after 15 or 20 years of future service, and death benefits would be available upon meeting that condition. Very few plans allowed a participant to become vested after ten years of service, yet this is the common requirement for vesting under ERISA-revised plans. Occasionally, if a high level of contributions was negotiated for a joint trust pension plan, the death benefits might be provided after less than ten years of service; for example, sometimes five years of future service credits would be the basis for allowing some form of death benefit.

Before ERISA, it was quite common for a lump-sum death benefit to be a percentage of the employer contributions made on behalf of a participant. For example, the payment might have been 30 percent, 50 percent, or even 80 percent of employer contributions. When this type of benefit was allowed, a limit on the amount of benefit often was imposed. The limit might have been, for example, $100 for each year of future service, but in no event more than $2,000. On the other hand, the maximum benefit might have been simply a flat $3,000 or $5,000. In recent years when such benefits have been provided under joint trust pension plans, considerable effort has been made to raise or eliminate the maximum amounts of single sum death benefits because of the relatively high contribution rates negotiated under some plans, such as the construction trades joint trust plans where the average hourly contribution rate today might be $1.00 or $1.50.

Another relatively common form of death benefit provided in joint trust pension plans has been a temporary monthly income payable to a designated beneficiary for a period of, say, three or five years. The amount of the monthly income has usually been equal to the earned pension benefit of the participant at the time of death. Sometimes the benefit has been limited to the earned pension benefits related to future service only.

In a number of plans, the income payments have been made in the form of dependent benefits and the income has been payable to a participant's spouse as long as there were dependent children under age 18 or 21, or to the guardian of the children if there were no spouse. Occasionally, if there were neither a spouse nor children, the income payments might be made to the dependent parents of the participant for a period of up to, say, ten years. Rarely, benefits have been payable to the participant's spouse for life or until remarriage. In a number of plans the monthly income payable to a spouse would cease upon commencement of social security benefits to the spouse when the spouse reached age 62. When dependent benefits or spouse pension benefits have been payable, the monthly income has often been limited to 50 percent of the participant's earned pension credits. Sometimes the monthly income has been fixed at, say, $20 per month per dependent child with a limit of $50 per month, adjusted upwards if the contribution rate exceeded, say, 20 cents per hour. For example, in this situation, if the contribution rate were 50 cents per hour, the monthly benefit per dependent child might be $50, and the maximum monthly benefit might be $125.

As previously mentioned, ERISA requires certain forms of spouse pension protection if a participant dies before retirement. The law requires that a participant who has been married at least one year have an opportunity to elect to provide a spouse with a survivor annuity, if the participant is within ten years of normal retirement age and eligible to retire early. The survivor annuity must be at least as great as the life pension the spouse would have received if the participant had retired the day before his or her death under a joint and 50 percent survivor form of pension. For example, if a participant had accrued a monthly pension of $100 on the day before his or her death and could have retired under a joint and 50 percent survivor pension of $80, payable while both were alive, the participant's spouse would receive a lifetime pension of $40.

A plan can require that the participant pay for the cost of this protection, with the cost being assessed by a reduction in the amount of pension. Actuaries have generally established the cost of this protection at approximately one half of 1 percent of the amount of earned pension for each full year of coverage. Under IRS rules and regulations, each participant must be given adequate notice of his or her right to elect this benefit and the participant must have the right to revoke the benefit protection from time to time. In order to protect the plan against adverse selection, the plan may provide that an election or revocation will not become effective if the participant dies within a two-year period after the election or revocation except if the participant dies from accidental causes.[5]

Under joint trust pension plans, the administrative complexity of the notice requirements and tracking each participant's election and revocation can be onerous. Consequently, the trustees of many plans have decided to provide this form of protection as an additional benefit under the plan. Depending upon the age/service/benefit cost characteristics of the participants, this additional benefit can increase a plan's cost by as much as 5 percent to 10 percent. For those plans that have provided a significant preretirement single sum death benefit (e.g., 80 percent or 100 percent of employer contributions), the cost of this survivor annuity can be offset against the death benefit otherwise payable so that there is little added cost to the plan. Likewise, if a plan already has provided a form of spouse pension protection, the cost of providing this ERISA-required benefit may be inconsequential if the plan's pre-ERISA spouse pension were payable for a lifetime and only cancelable upon remarriage. Sometimes, plans that provide a limited form of spouse pension protection before a participant is eligible for early retirement wish to maintain that benefit and can do so at little cost. The principal cost results from eliminating the remarriage clause after a participant is eligible for early retirement.

---

[5] See Qualified Joint and Survivor Annuity Benefits in Chapter 7 for details on administrative requirements.

Postretirement Death Benefits

Before ERISA the most common postretirement death benefit was a guaranty that the plan would pay the remaining balance of 36 or 60 monthly benefit payments if the participant died before that number of payments had been made. Many plans provided only a straight life pension with no form of death benefit protection. Under ERISA, if a participant has been married at least one year at the time of retirement, the participant must receive the earned normal pension benefit in a reduced amount in the form of a qualified joint and survivor annuity *unless* he or she elects to receive either the normal form of pension or some optional form of pension available under the plan. The qualified joint and survivor annuity is the actuarially reduced equivalent of the participant's earned normal pension. Upon the retired participant's death, his or her surviving spouse must be provided with a lifetime pension of at least 50 percent of the participant's reduced pension. The participant must have the right to make such an election within a reasonable period of time prior to actual retirement. In general, if this automatic joint and survivor form of pension becomes effective, there may be a 12 percent to 15 percent reduction in the participant's normal pension benefit to pay for the cost of the death benefit provided to the spouse if the normal form does not provide for a guaranteed number of payments. The reduction will be smaller if 36 or 60 pension payments are guaranteed under the normal form. Most plans do not subsidize this actuarial reduction, and probably few participants will allow this reduced joint and survivor pension form to become effective unless the amount of their monthly pension is substantial or they have a health impairment. In other words, unless a participant determines that the reduced joint and survivor pension and the participant's social security benefits will allow him or her to receive a reasonable retirement income, most participants would probably elect *not* to receive this joint and survivor pension.

There is a question concerning the right of participants to make this election without the joint agreement of the spouse in community property states. In such states the pension benefits earned by the participants have been deemed by the courts to have been earned equally by both the participant and the spouse to the extent that the benefits have been earned during marriage. Some joint trust pension plans, consequently, are requiring that any election *not to receive* a reduced joint and survivor pension form must be made jointly by the participant and spouse. This joint election requirement is intended to provide a measure of protection to the pension plan if the participant would otherwise die and leave a surviving spouse with no pension benefit. Even in non-community property states, trustees need to protect themselves from legal suits by widows who may claim that they were improperly deprived of pension protection upon the death of a pensioner who "opted out" of the automatic joint and 50 percent survivor pension. Careful records should be retained to prove that the pensioner, in fact, communicated the "opting out" of this joint and survivor pension to his or her spouse and that the spouse understood the effect of this action.

Occasionally, other forms of death benefits are provided after a participant's retirement. They tend to be single sum payments of relatively modest amounts, such as $2,000, $5,000, or the sum of one year's pension benefits. The death benefits do encourage reporting of the death of a pensioner.

DISABILITY BENEFITS

In recent years most plans have adopted some form of disability income protection for plan participants. In general, these benefits have been provided after 10 or 15 years of total credited service, including 2 to 5 years of future credited service. Sometimes the benefit has been available only when a participant has become vested under the plan. With the general adoption of a ten-year vesting schedule by joint trust pension plans, many plans now allow disability benefits to be payable only when an individual becomes vested under the plan.

One of the least expensive forms of disability benefit is a monthly pension actuarially equivalent to a participant's earned pension benefits. If a plan provides an actuarially reduced benefit when an individual becomes disabled, the reduction is very sharp when disability occurs more than ten years before the normal retirement age. The cost is further reduced by the fact that the disability benefit reflects only the pension benefit earned to date of disability, and this will be small for an employee at the younger ages. The more common form of disability benefit is to allow as a monthly pension, say, 50 percent of the participant's unreduced earned pension benefit or, if greater, the benefit that a participant could receive if he or she were to retire early. In a number of joint trust pension plans with relatively high contribution rates, the full accrued pension benefit without actuarial reduction is often paid upon a participant's disability. Sometimes the full accrued pension benefit will be payable if a participant is totally and permanently disabled and unable to perform work of any kind. On the other hand, a lower benefit, for example, 50 percent of the participant's accrued pension, may be payable if the participant is disabled and unable to perform work at his or her particular trade even though the participant may be capable of performing some other type of work. In most instances, the disability pension terminates when a participant dies, recovers from the disability, or reaches normal retirement age. Often, if a disabled participant reaches normal retirement age, he or she will be reclassified as an age pensioner. However, if any death benefits are payable under the plan after retirement, the amount of such benefits is generally reduced by any disability benefits that may have been paid to the participant.

Sometimes, in an effort to control disability claim costs and to reflect all sources of income to a participant when disabled, the plan's disability benefit provisions will coordinate all benefits available upon the participant's disablement. For example, a substantial temporary or permanent disability benefit may be payable under a welfare plan in which the employee participates, and if the disability is service connected, the participant will be entitled to workers' compensation benefits. Social security benefits may also be available. The pension plan's disability benefit provisions may be designed so that a participant's combined sources of income while disabled are not so generous as to encourage malingering. This means that disability benefits from other sources (except individual insurance policies) may be offset or deducted from the benefits payable under the pension plan. The integration rules of the IRS limit the offset for social security to 64 percent of the participant's own disability benefit, no recognition being given to benefits for dependents. However, these disability offsets rarely are incorporated in joint trust pension plans.

For most joint trust pension plans, it is impractical for the trustees to establish whether a participant is, in fact, eligible for a disability pension. Consequently, most joint trust pension plans often rely exclusively upon the Social Security Administration's determination of whether or not an individual is disabled. In general, the SSA requires that an employee be totally disabled and that the disablement be expected to last at least one year. (In addition, before any disability benefit award is granted, the SSA requires that the disability be considered permanent and that the employee not be capable of being rehabilitated to perform other work.)

Because of these several conditions, many employees who are disabled sufficiently so that they can no longer perform the tasks required of their trade or craft are not granted a social security disability award. They can be retrained to work at other occupations. For example, an employee who is relatively young, say, under age 45 or 50, may be retrained, but one who is in the middle to late 50s generally would be considered not retrainable. In any event, if an employee is granted a disability award, the joint trust pension plan normally will commence disability payments at the later of the date of the social security disability award or the date when the participant applies for the disability pension. If the application for benefits is late, retroactive payments are occasionally made—back to the effective date of the disability, but generally not for more than one year.

If an employee is, in effect, disabled from performing work required of his or her trade or craft but is unable to receive a social security disability award, sometimes joint trust pension plans allow a *partial disability* pension and will require objective evidence that the participant is disabled. The evidence may involve medical and/or psychological examination by one or more physicians designated by the plan administrator. Sometimes a board of trustees will retain a physician as a consultant and will require certification of disability by a physician who is designated by the local medical board of review as qualified to perform the examination and to give an informed professional opinion.

There has been a considerable increase in both the disability claim rates and claim values under the social security benefit program,[6] and, correspondingly, joint trust pension plans that allow disability benefits and rely on social security disability awards for benefit entitlement have experienced escalating claims in recent years. With this fact in mind, trustees should request the plan's actuary to assist them periodically in evaluating the standards for granting disability pensions under the plan and in making necessary adjustments to control the incidence of plan cost.

---

[6] *Social Security Actuarial Study No. 74* (Washington, D.C.: Social Security Administration, 1977).

CHAPTER 7

PLAN ADMINISTRATION

In many respects, the administration of the plan is the most visible aspect of the joint trust pension plan because it concerns the day-to-day operation of the plan, including:

The billing and receiving of employer contributions.

Transferring of funds to and from the investment manager.

Determining and paying benefits.

Preparing data for the plan actuary to evaluate the cost of the plan.

Submitting data as required for various governmental filings.

The liaison function of the administrative office is also very important since the office is usually the intermediary between the trustees, the plan participants, and the professional advisors of the fund. In addition, the record-keeping operation is critical to the sound management of the plan. It is imperative that accurate and up-to-date records be kept on the participating employees since the pension benefits often do not become payable for 20 or 30 or more years after the benefit credits were recorded.

These basic administrative functions have been quietly revolutionized by the requirements of ERISA. Since the passage of ERISA, the plan administrator must also be concerned with "reportable events" (notices required to be given to the PBGC), statements of accrued and vested benefits upon individual request, statements of vested rights upon termination of service, determinations of hours of service under complicated rules, the impact of ERISA's rule of parity on benefit forfeitures, and the requirements of ERISA's joint and survivor annuity protection afforded to plan participants.

This chapter briefly describes:

The types of organizations that are available to plan trustees in carrying out administrative functions,

The traditional functions of the plan administrator, and

The unique duties imposed on the plan administrator by ERISA.

At the outset, it is important to distinguish between the legal "administrator," that is, the persons who are responsible for the administration of the plan, and the administrative personnel to whom all or certain duties are delegated. ERISA Section 402(a)(1) provides that "Every employee benefit plan shall be established and maintained pursuant to a written instrument. Such instrument shall provide for one or more named fiduciaries who jointly or severally shall have authority to control and manage the operation and administration of the plan." Therefore, the plan or trust agreement must either specify who the named fiduciaries are or the procedure by which the individuals are selected. Usually, for joint trust pension plans, the labor and management parties who negotiated the collective bargaining agreement(s) that resulted in the establishment of the plan are the entities who select the trustees. Normally, the plan trustees are the named fiduciaries and are granted the duty under the trust agreement to administer the plan.

ERISA Section 402(b)(2) requires the plan documents to "describe any procedure under the plan for the allocation of responsibilities for the operation and administration of the plan. . . ." Further, the act, in Section 405(c)(1), allows the plan documents to provide for procedures to allocate fiduciary responsibilities among named fiduciaries or for named fiduciaries to designate other persons to carry out their responsibilities. Plan documents commonly provide for such procedures and allow the trustees to hire professional assistance including administrative personnel. It is important for the protection of the trustees that such allocations of responsibility or delegations of duties be in conformity with the plan instruments.

Normally, the board of trustees of a joint trust pension plan which is the legal "Administrator" will contract with or hire a professional "administrator," more properly called an "administrative manager," "fund manager," or "contract administrator" to perform all or most duties of administration. Therefore, for purposes of this chapter, the term "administrator" will refer to the administrative manager, the organization actually carrying out the duties of administration on behalf of the legal plan administrator, the board of trustees.

ADMINISTRATIVE ORGANIZATIONS

There are essentially two types of organizations that perform administrative services for a board of trustees, that is, a salaried administrator and a contract administrator.[1] Although insurance companies occasionally have performed administrative services for joint trust pension plans, this discussion will not consider them because their involvement has been rare. The following comments briefly describe the two principal types of administrative organizations that trustees retain.

Salaried administrators are employees of the board of trustees and devote full time to the plan's operation. They implement the policies and decisions of the board of trustees as regards the continuous operation of the fund. Since they are fully occupied in managing the plan's operations, they tend to become quite familiar with the changing needs of the trade, craft, or industry related to the plan. They are immediately and constantly available to service the many detailed problems relating to the collection of contributions, record keeping and accounting, the processing of benefit applications, governmental filings, relationships with the participating local unions, and so forth.

In addition to the specific functions previously outlined, salaried administrators hire, train, and personally supervise the personnel of the trust fund office; design and implement record-keeping systems (often including the administration of data processing systems and equipment); design employer reporting forms; maintain employer contribution records, and process claim

---

[1] The selection of an administrator is discussed on pages 33–35.

forms and employee/participant enrollment cards. They also supervise the processing of benefit claims and analyze pension applications for submission to the board of trustees for approval.

Contract administrators are most often organizations that specialize in plan administration for a number of joint trust pension plans (and often provides similar services for the other types of joint trust benefit plans). They generally perform the same operational functions as salaried administrators, but as independent contractors, they utilize their own employees as administrative personnel in the performance of these duties. Office space and furnishings, including data processing equipment, are usually the property of the contract administrator. Sometimes the contract administrator subcontracts the data processing functions to a service bureau or other organization specializing in computer software or processing services. Administrative service fees, often expressed in terms of a specified number of dollars per month per employee and expense allowances for personnel and equipment, are set at the time the contract administrator is retained by the board of trustees.

TRADITIONAL FUNCTIONS OF THE PLAN ADMINISTRATOR

The traditional functions of plan administration can be broadly categorized as:

Accounting.
Data management—long-term responsibilities.
               —day-to-day duties.
Benefits administration.
Office administration.
Trustee services.
Governmental reporting.

The specific functions outlined below will indicate the broad scope of the plan administrator's duties and, it is hoped, will provide an insight into the day-to-day requirements of an administrator. The responsibility for the performance of these functions may vary among different plans and administrative organizations.

For example, a corporate bank trustee, not the administrator, may mail pension checks and pay bills by voucher; the auditor may perform some of the accounting functions described, and the benefit calculations may be made by a consulting actuarial firm. In spite of these possible variations, the enumeration that follows is a general guide to the broad functions and responsibilities of administrators.

Accounting Functions

Administrators must:

1. Maintain a double-entry bookkeeping system and general ledger, reflecting all contribution receipts, benefit and expense disbursements, plan assets and liabilities.
2. Reconcile each month the trust's bank statement to the general ledger accounts.
3. Prepare and submit to trustees and professionals detailed financial statements each calendar month or quarter, reflecting the plan's financial activity. (These statements may be on a cash or accrual accounting basis.)
4. Assist plan auditors and other interested parties in their audits or reviews of plan records, procedures, and practices.

Data Management—Long-Term Responsibilities

Administrators are required to:

1. Maintain current and historical records for each participant of hours or weeks worked, contributions paid, applicable bargaining agreement, and other relevant data under the plan. Depending on the plan's definition of an "hour of service," administrators must record monthly all information received regarding disability or other leaves of absence, jury duty, military absences, and other information, as may be needed to determine years of service and one-year breaks in service. They must also record for each participant an identification number (usually social security number), date of birth, and sex for claim processing and actuarial valuations. The record should also contain the date of entry into the plan,

data on any break in service, and the date from which any past service is measured. (Recording accurate past service data is a serious problem for many plans since it relates to service *before* the date administrative records were established. The problem is discussed more fully below in connection with the required notice of vested participant rights.) Administrators must establish a practical system for obtaining information relating to covered employees who have been granted back-pay awards and to covered employees who have transferred to nonbargaining unit employment with the same employer. This data is required under DOL rules so that records can reflect hours of service for which no pension plan contributions are made.

2. Develop and maintain procedures for updating data (by computers to the extent practicable) to record:

   a. New entrants and initial contribution date, rates, bargaining units, where applicable;

   b. Deaths, nonvested and vested terminations, dates and related benefit information;

   c. Disabilities and their effective date, together with the effective dates, where applicable, of social security awards;

   d. Pensioners, together with the form of pension, the retirement date, designated beneficiary, amount of pension, termination date for expiry of any pension guarantee period, and spouse or beneficiary information, where applicable.

3. Provide the plan actuary with participant census information, often on an annual basis, for the actuarial valuation of the plan. Such information may include past service data, yearly hours of service and employer contribution information for each active participant, amount of deferred pension for each vested terminated participant, data on participants who have accrued one or more one-year breaks in service, data on pensioners, disability retirements, and other items required by the actuary.

4. Maintain updated records regarding contributing employers and applicable bargaining agreements, including expiry or renewal dates. If applicable, administrators must send notices to contributing employers of increased contribution rates re-

quired to maintain benefits or of penalties assessed because of an ERISA funding deficiency.

Data Management—Day-to-Day Duties

Administrators also have to:

1. Prepare and mail each month checks to all pensioners, ensure that endorsements on canceled pensioner checks are periodically compared with signature cards on file, and follow-up on all doubtful signature cases.
2. Once each year, if practicable, prepare individual statements for all participants in the plan showing hours of service, reported by month, during the last year. (This procedure will enhance the administrator's assurance of the adequacy of the records in calculating vesting and benefit credits.)
3. Each month address employer remittance forms and mail to all active contributing employers.
4. Process employer remittance forms received from the custodial bank (employers often will remit directly to the bank under a lockbox arrangement); check contribution rate against the rate required by the bargaining agreement, and balance reported contributions tabulated on remittance forms to bank deposit slips; check forms for errors in employer remittances; contact and follow-up with employers who have erred in reporting and correct discrepancies; and "batch" forms for data processing.
5. Prepare a monthly list of delinquent employers, together with specific information concerning due dates, estimated amounts of delinquent contributions, and any other pertinent information; and report information to applicable local union and to collection attorney, according to the practices of the plan.

Perhaps the most onerous daily task of administrators involves their responsibility to collect all of the pension contributions payable under a collective bargaining agreement—especially if employees may be employed continually in an industry but are employed by a number of contributing employers and often for very brief periods of time. In the latter instance, a given employee may not be on an employer's payroll for more than a few days in a single month, and the employer may fail to report the employee's hours of service and pay the required contributions. Sometimes, an employer may control more than a single firm operating in the same industry and in the same geographical area. If a collective bargaining agreement does not apply to all of the employees of all firms, it is possible that an employer may avoid making the required pension contributions by placing employees on the payroll of the firm whose employees are not subject to a collective bargaining agreement. These considerations and the concern of trustees to ensure that all employers share equitably the responsibility of contributing to the plan mandate that random periodic audits be made of the contributing employers' payroll records. Only through such field audits can administrators effectively carry out the responsibilities delegated to them by the trustees to collect the employer contributions payable under pension agreements and to maintain proper records of hours of service necessary to establish employee participation, vesting, and benefit rights.

Benefits Administration

To serve the plan participants properly, administrators must:

1. Process all retirement and death benefit information requests and applications; accumulate all necessary documents to support applications (e.g., proofs of dates of birth, past employment); calculate pension benefits, including optional forms of benefits; and process benefit applications made pursuant to the plan's reciprocal agreements.
2. If the plan provides for elective preretirement qualified joint and survivor annuity protection during eligibility for early retirement, notify all participants at least 90 days immediately before the earliest date by which an election can be made of benefit rights and costs, and record all elections and revocations and related periods of coverage.
3. Answer all questions, upon request, from pension applicants and other beneficiaries of the plan concerning death, disability, or pension benefits; and if practicable, issue statements of benefits earned and vesting service accrued to date for participants not yet eligible for retirement. ERISA Section 105 re-

quires administrators to furnish this information upon written request no more often than once a year, although the extent to which this applies to multiemployer plans is to be determined by regulations not yet issued by the Secretary of Labor. If practical, trustees may wish to direct the automatic preparation and distribution of statements of benefit accrual for all participants on an annual basis to eliminate the continuing administrative burden of responding to individual requests. This practice would fulfill the legal and moral responsibilities to communicate benefit status and data to plan participants.

4. Arrange for appropriate notice and review of all denied claims, within applicable time restraints, under DOL rules and regulations.
5. Assist legal counsel and actuary, as required, in meeting court requirements relative to divorce settlements of benefit rights.
6. Maintain a supply of and distribute the pension booklets (summary plan descriptions), as required under DOL rules and regulations, to the participants and beneficiaries.

Office Administration

To achieve efficient and effective benefit administration, administrators generally should:

1. Maintain office space in the immediate geographical area of the plan.
2. Provide complete office facilities for performing plan administration. (If a salaried administrator, he or she will arrange and maintain adequate insurance coverage of plan administrative facilities pursuant to trustee policy.)
3. Pay all postage and other normal business expenses for supplies and forms.
4. Provide directly or arrange for all data processing facilities necessary, including systems, procedures, and programs, to process the plan's reports, benefit payments, and record keeping.
5. Perform all filing, typing, correspondence, reproduction work, and miscellaneous services necessary to perform the administration of the plan.

Trustee Services

As the liaison between the plan participants, professional advisors, and the board of trustees, administrators are required to:

1. Pay all trust expenses and arrange for checks to be signed by one employer trustee and one union trustee, where authority is not granted to the administrator.
2. Arrange for the regular and special meetings of the trustees and prepare and issue a meeting agenda in advance. The agenda, together with a file of all pertinent documents to be discussed, should be distributed to the trustees, accountant, actuary, legal counsel, and investment advisor.
3. Provide a qualified administrative representative to attend all trustee meetings, take minutes, and prepare the official record of trustee meetings. (Sometimes, these latter functions may be performed by a plan consultant or other advisor.)
4. Assist plan's consulting actuary and legal counsel in implementing necessary revisions of the trust document, pension plan, subscription agreements, policy governing acceptable bargaining and subscription agreements, bank agency agreements, and employee booklets.
5. Prepare or assist in the preparation or revision of administrative forms used by the plan.
6. Assist legal counsel in obtaining and maintaining adequate fiduciary liability insurance coverage for protection of the trustees and, if a salaried administrator, the administrator.
7. Obtain evidence that the investment advisor, if other than a life insurance company, maintains adequate fiduciary liability insurance to inure to the benefit of the pension plan.

Governmental Reporting

In effecting ERISA compliance, administrators must:

1. Prepare annual tax statements for each pensioner.
2. Prepare the annual report (Form 5500) for the IRS with the assistance of legal counsel, the actuary, and the accountant. (Form 5500 includes, among other things, information concerning changes in designated trustees, administrative man-

ager, accountant, actuary, and investment advisor, and amendments to the plan and trust.)

3. Submit to PBGC the premium payment for plan termination insurance.

The trust attorney generally files requests with the IRS for approval of the continuing tax qualification of the amended plan after all materials have been reviewed by the plan's actuary.

Appendix E includes a more detailed outline of the numerous reporting and disclosure requirements of ERISA, some illustrative administrative forms which the administrator might use, and an outline of the census data required by the plan actuary in performance of periodic actuarial valuations.

NEW ADMINISTRATIVE DUTIES IMPOSED BY ERISA

It is apparent that the administration of a joint trust pension plan encompasses a vast array of duties and functions. The function is complex because, unlike a corporation, administrators must rely on the cooperation of many contributing employers and local unions, over which the administrators have little or no control.

Although the traditional functions of the plan administrator are significant, ERISA imposes onerous new responsibilities which alter the administrative operations of joint trust pension plans. As mentioned, vastly increased reporting and disclosure requirements have been imposed on plan administrators; they have to be concerned with "reportable events," notices to participants of their vested rights, determination of years of service and breaks in service under difficult new definitions, the operation of a unique rule of parity which governs benefit forfeitures, and joint and survivor annuity protection. In addition, administrators now must follow a very detailed procedure in processing claims, handling denials of claims, and in reviewing appeals relating to denied claims. The following sections briefly discuss these new problem areas and some related administrative requirements.

Reportable Events

There are numerous reportable events under Title IV, Section 4043 of ERISA, that affect the responsibilities of plan administrators. When plan administrators know or have reason to know that a reportable event has occurred within specified time limits, they must notify The Pension Benefit Guaranty Corporation of such event. Some of the principal reportable events which concern joint trust pension plans arise when—

An ERISA funding deficiency occurs;

There has been a substantial decline in the number of plan participants;

Plans act to merge, consolidate, or transfer assets;

A plan amendment may decrease accrued benefits payable to any participant;

A partial or complete plan termination has occurred; and

A plan is unable to pay benefits when due.

In addition to reportable events, if a "substantial employer" withdraws from plan participation, the administrator must report the event to the PBGC. Therefore, each year the administrator must determine which contributing employers are substantial employers[2] and notify those employers of their status because of the importance of the contingent employer liability scheduled to be imposed on substantial employers as of July 1, 1979, under Title IV of ERISA as amended.[3]

Finally, plan administrators must report other events to the IRS. (The IRS communicates information to the DOL, as necessary.) If the accountant, actuary, or contract or salaried administrator is terminated, the occurrence is reportable on Form 5500. Notice of such terminations may prompt inquiries concerning the reasons for the trustees' actions.

Notices of Vested Participant Rights

The plan administrator is required to file annually with the IRS a notice (Schedule SSA) that lists the social security number and

---

[2] In general, a substantial employer in a given plan year is a contributing employer who contributed at least 10 percent or more of the aggregate employer contributions to a pension plan covering employees of more than one employer during each of the immediately preceding two plan years or during each of the second and third immediately preceding plan years.

[3] See pages 181–84 for more specific details of the process involved with the withdrawal of a substantial employer.

name of each vested terminated participant, the nature, amount, and form of the deferred vested benefit. The IRS has published regulations governing the reporting of this information for each plan participant who has "separated from service." The regulations specifically recognize some of the difficulties that joint trust plans have both in establishing if a participant has a nonforfeitable right to a deferred pension benefit and if a participant has, in fact, separated from service. The following discussion outlines some of the unique problems that joint trust plans face in preparing Schedule SSA for vested terminated participants.

The structure of the typical joint trust pension plan does not determine a date of termination of employment. Rather, a date when a break in service occurs may be determined as of the end of a one, two, or three plan-year period during which the participant failed to earn, say, at least 500 hours of service in each plan year. Therefore, a participant may, in fact, have actually left covered employment more than one, two, or three years (depending upon each plan's specific break-in-service provisions) before the plan administrator will consider a participant to have terminated covered employment. This break-in-service treatment is an inherent characteristic of many joint trust pension plans because these plans are designed to allow a degree of benefit portability more liberal than strictly required by law, in order for a covered employee to maintain continuity of employment if he or she moves from one employer to another within the same trade, craft, or industry.

Plan administrators face several other areas of great potential difficulty in meeting ERISA's administrative requirements. For example, the plan will often count combined past service and future service years to determine benefit amounts, and the plan's vesting rights may also be related to both types of service. Years of past service may be, as they often are, incomplete or incorrect in the administrator's records—implying that an employee is not vested when a break in service occurs; yet, correct and complete information may prove the participant to be vested and also change the amount of benefits accrued. Prior to ERISA, past service was often verified only at the time a claim was filed to avoid expensive and time-consuming requests for information from employers or the Social Security Administration. This requirement to report vested benefits for terminated participants, as well as the requirement, previously mentioned, to respond to requests for accrued and vested benefit information from active participants, imposes on the plan administrator the added burden of establishing a continuing program to (1) carefully examine the employment records of newly entering groups to obtain complete past service information, (2) obtain past employment information on existing participants, and (3) consider methods of plan design to eventually eliminate (or relieve) the continuing administrative expense incurred in this effort.

Yet another problem exists. A participant may not be reported on remittance forms returned by his or her employer and may be eventually considered a terminated participant without a vested interest—according to administrative records. The employee, however, may merely have been transferred, or promoted, to nonbargaining unit employment with the same employer, requiring this contiguous employment to count toward the plan's years of service required for vesting. The plan administrator can request information from the employer and, perhaps, from the employee (if the employee's address is available), but there may be no practical method by which the plan administrator can force either the employer or the employee to respond. If the administrator automatically provides a statement of benefit accrual and status to each participant, problems of this type may be minimized.

Because of the difficulties previously outlined, IRS regulations require the plan administrator to file Schedule SSA with the annual report (Form 5500) required for the plan year within which a participant completed the second of two consecutive one-year breaks in service, as defined in the particular plan. In addition, recognizing that the plan administrator's records may be incomplete, the regulations allow the administrator to complete Schedule SSA by relying only on information relating to service specifically covered by the plan. For example, service of an employee rendered with a contributing employer which is not "covered employment" under the joint trust plan, may be disregarded, and the administrator may indicate on Schedule SSA that the amount of deferred pension is not absolutely accurate. Also, if the administrator's incomplete records do not clearly indicate that a terminated participant has a vested right, Schedule SSA may be filed with a notation that the terminated participant "may be entitled to a vested deferred benefit," but the amount may be omitted. Finally, a statement including the information, if any, filed on Schedule SSA must be mailed to each terminated participant or forwarded to him at his last known address no later than the date by which Schedule SSA is required to be filed.

In spite of the relief granted by IRS regulations, as a fiduciary the plan administrator must make a substantial additional and continuing good faith effort to obtain and maintain adequate participant benefit records.

Determinations of a Year of Service and a One-Year Break in Service

Establishment of correct records of these types of service involves a modest amount of additional record keeping or a significant increase in administration, depending upon whether the plan employs one of the DOL's alternative methods of measuring a year of service or uses the standard 1,000 hours of service rule. If the standard 1,000 hours of service rule is employed, an hour of service must be granted to reflect "service," if compensated, while on jury duty, holiday or vacation, layoff, leave of absence, in military service, or while ill or disabled, service for which back pay is awarded, and for "contiguous service"—in addition to the hours for which contributions were made and reported directly. Unless a joint trust pension plan involves only a few contributing employers whose employees rarely change employment, it is difficult to understand how a plan administrator can reasonably expect to obtain complete information and to maintain complete records. Also, if the standard 1,000 hours of service rule is employed, the plan administrator must ensure that all bargaining agreements require contributions on all hours worked and establish rules which reject, as unacceptable, agreements which do not comply.

A major portion of these administrative complexities can be eliminated by use of the 870-hour or 750-hour alternative rules allowed by the DOL to establish a year of service. Both of these alternate methods allow an administrator to rely on actual hours worked as the basis for determining hours of service and to disregard such items as time involved with jury duty, leaves of absence, disability, and so forth. Use of the 750-hour rule allows overtime to also be ignored, but neither alternative allows contiguous service and back-pay awards to be disregarded. If the 870-hour rule is adopted, the plan administrator must still mandate the bargaining agreements require contributions on all hours worked including overtime.

Finally, the administrator must establish a system of obtaining information concerning all back-pay awards for plan participants and apply the DOL rules to convert the back-pay award values to hours of service for record-keeping purposes.

Rule of Parity

Assuming that the plan administrator has established a practical system for recording all hours of service to determine years of service for vesting purposes and breaks in service, he or she still has the responsibility of determining when an inactive participant has permanently forfeited all benefit and vesting service under the plan. This permanent forfeiture can only occur for a nonvested participant when and if the accumulated number of *consecutive* one-year breaks in service equals the accumulated number of vesting service years. If, before the latter condition exists, a covered employee accumulates just an hour more than one half the number of hours of service required for a year of service (under ERISA and the DOL regulations), the total accumulated record of vesting service years is restored, and the possible forfeiture of benefits and service credits is deferred. These circumstances require the plan administrator to maintain benefit and hours of service records virtually in perpetuity. The discovery by the plan administrator at some future date of previously unreported hours of service, of whatever type, may generate many records of participants who are, in fact, vested but who previously appeared to have terminated without vested rights.

Qualified Joint and Survivor Annuity Benefits

As described previously, ERISA mandates that a plan allow a married participant to elect spouse pension protection if he or she will be eligible to retire early during the ten years immediately before normal retirement age. Also, ERISA requires automatic spouse pension protection for a married participant who retires from active service, remains in service on or after normal retirement age, or terminates service after eligibility for commencement of benefits—unless the participant elects otherwise.[4] The following sections discuss the administrative problems and concerns regarding each of these important ERISA requirements.

Preretirement Spouse Protection.   Under a plan that grants early retirement benefits, a married participant who is eligible for early retirement and is within ten years of normal retirement age has reached the qualified early retirement age; that is, the age when spouse pension protection must be available. If the married participant has elected the preretirement spouse protection, a spouse pension will become payable if the participant dies while in active employment after the coverage becomes effective and before normal retirement age.

Assuming that the joint trust pension plan does not provide this protection automatically as an additional benefit, there must be an election period which can begin no later than the 90th day *before* the attainment of the qualified early retirement age. The plan administrator must notify plan participants of their eligibility for this benefit on or about 90 days before the election period begins. This notice must include information concerning the option, the election procedure and the financial effects of an election. The notification may be by mail, by personal delivery, or otherwise, by permanent posting or repeated publication, if reasonably expected to be timely and to continue to reach the attention of participants during the election period.

Except in the event of accidental death, ERISA allows plans to require a waiting period of up to two years after the election is made before the coverage is to be effective. If, for example, early retirement is available at age 55 and a two-year waiting period is provided, the election period must begin 90 days before the participant reaches age 53 and the notice must be provided 90 days before the beginning of the election period so the participant will have time to make the election and obtain coverage at age 55. If

---

[4] See pages 103–4 for details of the preretirement coverage and pages 105–6 for details of the postretirement coverage.

the election is made by the participant, then the plan administrator must record the fact and arrange to charge the participant for the cost of the death benefit coverage. The charge may be assessed as a reduction of the participant's pension, determined, for example, as $1/24$th of 1 percent of the accrued pension benefit for each month of coverage. Again, under this elective form of qualified joint and survivor annuity coverage, the participant who has made the election also has the right to revoke it. If a revocation is made, the plan administrator must record its effective date. The elimination of this death benefit coverage may be deferred so that coverage ceases at the end of a time period equal to the waiting period following the election of this coverage. In other words, if the waiting period following election of the coverage were two years, then a revocation need not become effective for a two-year period.

Clearly, this elective form of joint and survivor protection adds significantly to the plan administrator's record-keeping problems and the administrative responsibility to communicate adequately the nature of the available protection and the meaning of a revocation.

The complexity of administration of this benefit on an elective basis has encouraged many boards of trustees to consider the financial feasibility of providing the required protection to spouses on an automatic basis at no cost to the participants. In this case, the administrative burden is reduced to the processing of claims for deaths that actually occur while the participant was within ten years of normal retirement date and eligible to retire early. Presumably, if a participant's spouse is aware that the plan provides such survivor pension protection, the spouse will generally make a timely claim for the benefit upon the participant's death. Administrators' responsibilities are limited to the proper communication of plan benefits and claim payments; they do not have the onerous and difficult tasks involved with elective qualified joint and survivor annuity protection.

Postretirement Spouse Protection. ERISA requires that the pension be paid on the joint and survivor form *automatically* for a participant who retires on or after the normal retirement age. Also, if early retirement benefits are available, this protection must be provided automatically when a participant retires after the qualified early retirement age—*unless* the participant elects otherwise. This protection must be provided on the same basis to (1) participants who separate from service on or after satisfying the stated age requirements while eligible to receive benefits, and (2) participants who die in active service on or after the normal retirement age.

If a joint trust plan has no early retirement provisions, information concerning this automatic joint and survivor annuity form of pension and any elections available must be communicated to a participant nine months before normal retirement age. The information provided must indicate the financial effect of any election. In lieu of delivery by mail or in person, this information can be published in an employee newsletter or can be disseminated by arranging with employers and the union to permanently post a notice if (1) all participants have reasonable assurance of seeing it, and (2) the information is distributed regularly and continually.

If early retirement is allowed and the preretirement spouse pension protection is granted *automatically* to active participants, then the information concerning the automatic joint and survivor annuity form of pension must also be communicated to an active participant nine months before the qualified early retirement age—in the same manner as stated previously.

Since many plans offered optional forms of pension before enactment of ERISA, this requirement to provide information to prospective pensioners on postretirement spouse protection' should not add substantially to the administrative burden of processing retirements. However, the protection of eligible terminated employees or participants working after normal retirement age adds administrative difficulties, unless the protection is provided without charge.

Claims Procedure

To ensure that all plan participants' claims for benefits are properly and carefully evaluated and processed, the DOL has established rules and regulations governing the claims procedures to be followed by all employee benefit plans. Consequently, each plan administrator must have such rules incorporated into the plan document and effect procedures which will implement these DOL rules and regulations.

Briefly, the DOL required claims procedure establishes a framework of practices relating to claims for benefits, the notice of any claim denial, the review procedure required when a participant appeals a denied claim, and the final notice of a decision on a "denied claim" review by the plan administrator. It is imperative that the organization performing administrative services on behalf of a board of trustees carefully follow an approved claims procedure that encompasses these DOL rules—since the administrator must simultaneously act on behalf of all plan participants and protect the board of trustees from possible legal suits that could result from failure to follow the mandatory DOL practices.

Processing Claims. Each claim that has been filed on the plan's forms must be considered filed as soon as it is received by the administration office, provided the form has been properly completed. If necessary information is missing, the administrator must immediately notify the claimant of the additional data required. If a claim is denied (wholly or in part), the administrator must give the participant a written notice of denial, written in a manner expected to be understood by the participant, and which—

Cites the specific reason or reasons for the denial.

Provides definitive reference to plan provisions on which the denial is based.

Gives a description of any additional material or information necessary for the claimant to perfect the claim for benefits and the reasons why the material or information is required.

Describes the steps to be taken if the claimant wishes to submit the claim for review.

The administrator is required to give a participant the notice of denial within 90 days after receipt of a claim unless special circumstances require the administrator to extend the time for processing the claim. If an extension is required, the administrator must furnish the participant a written notice within the original 90-day time limit for processing the claim. This notice must indicate the special circumstances that have caused the processing time to be extended and state the date by which the decision can be expected—but not more than 180 days after the date the claim was received. If the administrator does not give a timely notice of denial as indicated, the participant has the right to demand an immediate review of his or her presumed denied claim.

Reviewing a Denied Claim. The participant, or a duly authorized representative, may request a review of a denied claim for benefits by filing a written application within 60 days after receiving the written notification of a denial (or, if no written notice is received, after expiration of the administrator's time limit for giving the participant a written notice of denial). The 60-day time limit for submission of an appeal may be extended by the plan administrator if it is believed there was reasonable cause for a delayed submission.

In reviewing a denied claim, the plan administrator (board of trustees), or a designated subcommittee of trustees, must give a full and fair review of the claim. As part of the review procedure, the claimant (or representative) may examine pertinent documents and may submit issues and comments in writing. However, the claimant does not have a right to appear personally before the board of trustees or, if applicable, the designated trustee subcommittee, *unless* the reviewing entity determines that a personal appearance would be of valuable assistance in reaching a decision.

Notifying Participants of a Claim Review Decision. The administrator must provide the claimant with a written notice of the decision concerning a claim denial that has been appealed. The notice must include specific reasons for the decision, written in a manner calculated to be understood by the claimant, and citing specific references to plan provisions on which the decision was based.

It is important that the administrator furnish the notice to the claimant as quickly as possible after the reviewing entity has met—the date generally being the first regularly scheduled meeting that is at least 30 days after receipt of the claim. In this instance, the meetings must be regularly scheduled at least on a quarterly basis to comply with the DOL rules. However, if special circumstances require an extension of time for processing the appealed claim, the decision can be delayed, but not beyond the third regularly scheduled meeting. Under all other circumstances, the decision must be made not later than 60 days following receipt of an appeal, unless unusual conditions or causes require an extension—but in no event beyond 120 days after receipt of the requested review of the denied claim. Whenever an extension of time is required, a written notice must be given to the claimant before the extension period begins.

The board of trustees must ensure that these DOL-mandated rules governing claim and appeal procedures are assiduously followed to carry out its fiduciary responsibilities under ERISA. In this era of class action suits and great emphasis on participant benefit rights, a board of trustees must demand that the administrator carefully monitor the timeliness of all claims processing and the communications concerning denied claims. If a board of trustees (or the trustees' committee responsible for review of claimant appeals) has not scheduled a systematic timetable for reviews, it behooves the administrator to arrange a formal schedule of at least quarterly claim review meetings to adequately comply with DOL rules and regulations.

CHAPTER 8

RECIPROCITY

The purpose of reciprocity between pension plans is to provide benefits to covered employees who would otherwise be ineligible for a benefit because their years of employment have been divided between covered employment creditable under a given plan and employment creditable under another pension plan or many other pension plans.[1] Also, such benefits may be allowed a covered employee who, though eligible to receive benefits under a given plan or a related plan, could receive a larger pension by utilization of a related credit. When plans enter into reciprocal agreements, the plan with which reciprocity exists is referred to as a *related plan* and the creditable service under that plan is referred to as a *related credit.*

Reciprocal agreements, in combination with vesting provisions, provide a degree of portability of pensions for the populations of covered employees who are becoming progressively more mobile. However, the only totally portable pension system in this country is the social security pension system under which an employee can terminate employment with many employers and still carry all the pension credits earned during a lifetime. It is impossible for private pension systems to achieve the same degree of portability as a federally established program, unless the federal government

---

[1] The book *Reciprocity among Private Multiemployer Pension Plans* by Maurice E. McDonald, published by Richard D. Irwin, Inc., Homewood, Ill., 1975, for the Pension Research Council is a source of substantial information on this subject. Also, the chapter on Reciprocity Agreements in Dan M. McGill, *Preservation of Pension Benefit Rights* (Homewood, Ill.: Richard D. Irwin, Inc., 1972) contains helpful information on this topic.

were to impose a rigid and uniform set of rules for all pension plans. Therefore, the plans that enter into reciprocal agreements have the more limited but still important goals of—

1. Protecting older, long-service employees from loss of pension credits because of job changes, and
2. Reducing the number of breaks in service and consequent losses of pension credits of younger employees as they move from one employer to another.

COMPARISON OF VESTED PENSIONS WITH RECIPROCAL PENSIONS

Just what is the difference between a vested pension and a reciprocal pension? Simply stated, a *vested pension* is a pension benefit earned by an employee under a given pension plan that is not forfeited or canceled by termination of the employee's service prior to early or normal retirement. To this extent, a vested pension is portable. Although a vested pension is portable, it is possible that the benefit may not be paid. The loss of a vested benefit could occur if the plan is terminated when the funding of the plan's liabilities is inadequate and the PBGC does not insure the full amount of vested benefits of the terminated plan. This situation can occur when there have been significant benefit improvements in the year or years immediately preceding a plan's termination. When plan termination insurance does apply to joint trust pension plans, the PBGC will fully insure only those benefits which have been in effect for several years, subject to certain statutory maximum benefit limits. With ERISA's funding standards, a plan's original unfunded liabilities are systematically funded and a plan's benefit improvements are likewise funded. Therefore, the vested pension benefits of most plans in the future gradually should become quite secure.

A *reciprocal pension* is a pension benefit earned by an employee under a pension plan that has a reciprocal agreement with another plan established within the same industry or trade union group, but usually in a different geographical area. Under this arrangement, an employee can terminate employment covered by one plan, move into covered employment in another geographical area, and avoid a break in service so that pension credits are retained. This arrangement enhances the probability that an employee who moves from one geographical area to another will receive a benefit, but it does not necessarily mean that the combined service of two or more plans will allow the employee to become vested before all of the requirements necessary to retire have been met. The employee's combined service, if rendered under a single plan, might allow the employee to be vested before retirement eligibility; but each plan may require, say, ten years of vesting service to be earned under its provisions before an employee becomes vested in accrued benefits, unless combined service and age make the employee eligible to retire.

As can be recognized, vesting provisions and reciprocal agreements assist in providing different degrees of portability, but it is a limited form of portability. Also, many employees are not covered by pension plans that have reciprocal arrangements with other plans, and reciprocal agreements are generally limited to the same trade, craft, or industry. Finally, if two reciprocating plans require ten years of active participation for an employee to be vested, the years of active participation in one plan are not necessarily counted as active participation for vesting purposes in a reciprocating plan. Whether or not such active participation is mutually recognized for vesting purposes is determined by each separate board of trustees, and its determination will be reflected in the plan's provisions.

ACTUARIAL ESTIMATES OF RECIPROCITY COSTS

The costs of reciprocity depend primarily on—

The level of pension benefits,
Vesting schedules, and
Rates of employee turnover.

Reciprocal agreements between plans increase pension costs because they reduce the number of breaks in service of employees who move from the covered employment of one plan to the covered employment of another, reducing the forfeitures that would otherwise occur for employees who are not yet vested. Consequently, reciprocity agreements reduce the effect of employment turnover discounts that an actuary uses in determining a plan's estimated cost. ERISA has done much to reduce the cost of reciprocal agreements because most plans have improved their vesting provisions (generally, by adopting the ten-year vesting schedule). Thus, a substantial portion of forfeitures resulting from breaks in service has automatically been eliminated. Very little is currently known of the probable cost to any given plan of its entering into a reciprocal agreement. The reason is that reciprocal agreements are relatively new for many plans, and no central agency has collected experience data.

To provide some insight into the probable long-range cost implications of reciprocal agreements, calculations have been made of the annual pension costs for a group of employees that might typically be covered by an industry-wide pension plan. Assuming that the pattern of employment termination follows one of five employee turnover tables, pension costs have been calculated on two alternate assumptions:

1. That a plan provides 100 percent vesting after ten years of active participation (the most common vesting provision in ERISA conformed plans), and
2. That a plan allows 100 percent full and immediate vesting. This assumption effectively presumes that benefits that would have been forfeited upon an employee's termination are not forfeited because each individual who withdraws during the first ten years of active participation moves to a reciprocating plan and remains covered until eligible to retire.

The percentage increases in annual pension costs, determined by dividing the costs from (2) by (1), above, for each of the five turnover tables, can be considered to represent the maximum percentage cost increase to a typical plan because of entering into reciprocity agreements. The percentage increase in annual cost is tabulated below for each of five turnover tables.

Employee Turnover Table	Percentage Increase in Annual Pension Cost
1 (low turnover)	3
2	7
3 (medium turnover)	13
4	24
5 (high turnover)	34

As can be seen, the cost increases range from 3 percent to 34 percent. For example, if the annual cost of a pension plan with a standard ten-year vesting schedule were $100,000 and reciprocal agreements effectively prevented any withdrawing employee from forfeiting benefits, the annual cost could increase to as little as $103,000 or as much as $134,000 depending upon the plan's turnover experience assumptions. The higher the employment turnover in the early years of participation, the greater will be the increase in the total pension cost when reciprocal arrangements are entered into. However, there is an essential overstatement in the development of this range of costs for reciprocal agreements. The assumption is that employees who withdraw from a plan with less than ten years of service will stay in the same trade, craft, or industry and move to a reciprocating plan. In all probability, such employees will not do so. Actual experience will probably develop cost increases which would be not more than 15 percent to 25 percent of those shown in the table.

Although there is no truly typical group of employees covered by a pension plan, using reasonable actuarial judgment, reciprocal agreements could add as little as one half of 1 percent or as much as 8 percent to 10 percent to a plan's costs—depending upon the plan's general level of employee turnover.

TYPES OF RECIPROCITY AGREEMENTS

From the standpoint of implementation, reciprocity agreements may use one of two approaches, the pro rata or the money transfer.

Pro Rata Approach

The pro rata approach has been more suitable to funds whose participants change geographic locations on a permanent basis. As an example of how eligibility for benefits and benefit amounts are preserved under this method, assume the following basic data for a particular employee:

1. Age at retirement = 61.
2. Years of vesting service under Plan A = 10.

3. Years of vesting service under Plan B = 8.
4. Eligibility requirement for retirement under Plan A = Attained age 55 plus 15 years of vesting service.
5. Eligibility requirement for retirement under Plan B = Attained age 60 plus 10 years of vesting service.
6. Monthly benefits under Plan A = $20 per year of service.
7. Monthly benefits under Plan B = $30 per year of service.

The employee's total monthly pension and the payment(s) due from Plan A and Plan B, respectively, would be determined as follows:

	Plan A	Plan B	Total
Years of vesting service	10	8	18
Monthly pension	$20 per month per year of benefit service	$30 per month per year of benefit service	

The participant is eligible to retire after combining vesting service from both plans (18 is greater than 15 under Plan A and is greater than 10 under Plan B). Benefits are prorated, based on total combined service and are as follows:

Plan A: Since the employee has worked 10 of the 18 years under Plan A, a pension of $200 (= 10 × $20) is received.

Plan B: Likewise, since the employee has worked 8 of the 18 years under Plan B, a pension of $240 (= 8 × $30) is earned.

The participant's total monthly pension is therefore $440 (=$200 + 240).

Note that without the reciprocal arrangement the individual would not be eligible to retire early and receive benefits under either plan because the individual would not have had the required 15 years of vesting service under Plan A or the 10 years of vesting service under Plan B. Unless an additional two years were worked under Plan B, the employee would not be able to retire at normal retirement age under that plan without a reciprocity arrangement.

The next example will serve to illustrate how reciprocity can be utilized to avoid a break in service and forfeiture of service. It will also illustrate how reciprocity can be used to allow a covered employee to earn a vesting service year. Again, assume certain basic data:

1. *The break-in-service rule under Plan A or Plan B.* When a participant fails to work at least 435 hours in each of two consecutive plan years, a service break occurs and the covered employee is no longer an active participant. (This does not mean that the covered employee has forever forfeited vesting service credits under ERISA rules.)

2. *Forfeiture of service rule under both Plan A and Plan B.* When the number of consecutive plan years during which a participant fails to earn 435 hours of service (vesting hours) equals or exceeds accumulated vesting service years earned prior to his or her first one year break in service, all accrued benefits and vesting service credits are forfeited if an employee has not accumulated ten vesting service years.

3. *Vesting service year rule under both Plan A and Plan B.* One vesting service year is granted if a participant earns at least 870 hours of service in a plan year.

4. *Record of hours of service (vesting hours) earned year by year:*

Plan Year	Vesting Hours— Plan A	Vesting Hours— Plan B	Total Vesting Hours
0	1,200	400	1,600
1	2,000	0	2,000
2	1,800	220	2,020
3	190	200	390
4	210	280	490

Under Plan A the participant has earned three vesting service years as of the end of Year 2. Under Plan B zero vesting service years were earned without reciprocity and three such years after combining hours of service. In Year 3, no vesting service year was earned under either plan *separately* or even after combining hours. However, in Year 4, when the participant again earned no vesting service year under either plan, due to reciprocity, a break in service is avoided because more than 435 hours of service were earned. Similarly, if the aggregating of hours of service results in a total that equals or exceeds 435 hours in subsequent years, the forfeiture of vesting and benefit credits that would otherwise occur under the break-in-service rules of either plan would be prevented.

Money-Transfer Approach

The money-transfer approach is implemented through an agreement which provides that all contributions made on a participant's behalf are transferred to the participant's "home" pension fund. This method has generally been used as a means of permitting participants who temporarily work outside of the jurisdiction of their home pension fund to continue to receive all or a portion of their home pension credits solely from the home pension fund. The amount of pension credit, of course, depends upon whether or not the contribution rate while participants are in another jurisdiction is the same as the contribution rate of their home plan.

Again, an example will help to illustrate the operation of this method. Assume that a participant covered under Plan A is employed temporarily in Plan B's jurisdiction. The employer under Plan B remits his or her contribution to Plan B's office. Periodically, contributions will be remitted by Plan B to Plan A. The participant is then credited by Plan A for all or a portion of his or her regular home pension credits. To be eligible for benefits, the employee must satisfy the rules and regulations of Plan A. Obviously, under this method no pension would be payable under Plan B.

ISSUES AND PROBLEMS

The previous two examples are highly simplified. There are many difficult problems to resolve in arranging reciprocity agreements between plans. For example, how are past service credits handled under the pro rata method? What benefit credits are provided when the money transferred is based on a different contribution rate or on an hours worked base less favorable than the contribution rate or hours worked base of the home fund. For instance, one plan may have contributions on *all hours worked* while the other may have contributions on *only straight hours worked,* and so forth. Also, under the money-transfer method, how should excess contributions arising when and if the Plan B contribution rate is greater than the Plan A contribution rate be handled? Should these excess contributions be used to purchase additional benefits for the temporarily transferred participant, or should the excess contributions be retained in Plan B's fund—producing a profit for that fund? Instead of Plan B having a greater contribution rate than Plan A, Plan B may have more liberal benefit entitlement provisions or a better pension benefit structure. Under ERISA, can Plan B deny these benefits to a "temporarily" transferred participant who is covered under a money-transfer type of reciprocal agreement but who remains covered for a long period under Plan B's jurisdiction? Finally, what are the future possibilities of a full money transfer, that is, a "roll over" of the actuarial value of the accrued benefits/vesting years up to the date of transfer following the participant to Plan B, if the participant eventually were to become a long-service employee covered under Plan B?

While each of these reciprocity methods has certain advantages, the pro rata method is preferred by most joint trust pension plans, mainly because it achieves greater equity among reciprocating plans in respect of actuarial gains generated by withdrawing employees who never qualify for benefits. Under the money-transfer method, such gains generally accrue to the home pension fund only. If there is a balanced movement of employees and contributions between plans, equity would not be significantly disturbed under either approach.

Under the pro rata method, plans must maintain separate employment records of employees until the employees who might qualify for a partial pension have retired. On the other hand, under the money transfer method the periodic transfer of records and money to the home pension fund fully discharges the plan of responsibility for maintaining records of temporary employees. Since more long-term administrative complications arise under the pro rata method, it may be useful to examine a few areas where fundamental decisions need to be made by trustees so that withdrawing employees can understand their rights and the administrative office can efficiently determine when partial pensions are payable.

Under most plans both past and future service benefits are

payable. The date that a contribution is first made on behalf of a participant generally establishes the "participant contribution date" and fixes the point in time from which past service and future service are measured. Therefore, future (contributory) service under a related plan prior to a participant's contribution date may be recognized by a plan as past service, and only service after that date may be recognized as future service. The rules of either plan can be accepted in determining whether or not service has been continuous, and, sometimes the more liberal plan's rules are used to establish whether a covered employee has had a break in service. On the other hand, a reciprocal agreement might allow past service and future service to be measured from an employee's earliest contribution date regardless of the plan under which contributions were first made. The trustees' decision in this regard can have a substantial effect on the determination of an employee's vesting rights under reciprocating plans and, consequently, on the amount of benefits payable. If the trustees of a plan wish to recognize contributory service in a related plan for vesting purposes, employees who transfer into the area with sufficient years of related credit could begin to accrue benefits under a plan on a 100 percent vested basis. This situation could well be considered as discriminatory to the regular participants of the plan who may have several years of contributory service and still are not vested in their accrued pension credits. If, for unpredictable economic reasons, substantial groups of employees are transferred from a related plan to the coverage of a reciprocating plan, serious inequities could be created.

It is estimated that 80 to 90 percent of joint trust pension plans have reciprocal agreements, and those agreements are affording pension benefits to numerous pensioners who would have otherwise forfeited some or all of their pension credits. However, the author believes an analysis of experience will demonstrate that the preponderance of those benefits would have been provided if the plans involved always had a ten-year vesting schedule. With the general introduction of ten-year vesting into joint trust pension plans, the importance of reciprocal agreements will diminish in the future. In addition, once ERISA compliance has been achieved by most plans, there will undoubtedly be political pressure for further liberalization of the vesting provisions in private plans, perhaps requiring at least a 50 percent vested interest in all pension credits earned after five years of contributory service and 100 percent vesting after ten years of such service. Such a liberalization would gradually diminish the need for and value of the pro rata method under reciprocal agreements. If and when much further vesting liberalizations occur, the money-transfer method may become the only practical method of accommodating transfers between plans so that undue administrative burdens and expenses can be avoided.

Reciprocal agreements between joint trust pension plans have served and are serving a very important and useful function in providing increased security of earned pension rights. The cost of these special rights has been difficult to assess, but the vesting requirements of ERISA have diminished anticipated future costs to moderate, if not modest, levels. If further liberalizations in vesting schedules are legislated, the need for expanding the use of such agreements will be reduced except for those industries where there may be relatively continuous movement of employees from one geographical area to another. More time and experience will be needed before the future of pension reciprocity can be safely predicted.[2]

---

[2] Appendix B, the specimen joint trust pension plan, includes an example of how the trustees' policy regarding pro rata reciprocal agreements could be implemented as part of the rules and regulations of the plan document itself.

Specimen reciprocal agreements (in pre-ERISA language) of both the pro rata and money-transfer types may be found in McDonald's *Reciprocity among Private Multiemployer Pension Plans*. A specimen post-ERISA reciprocal agreement of the pro rata form may be found in Appendix G of this book.

CHAPTER 9

ACTUARIAL CONSIDERATIONS

When a plan actuary performs an actuarial valuation of a proposed or established plan, he or she must make numerous assumptions to develop a "best estimate" of the present value of expected future benefits and expense payments, the level annual cost (often referred to as the "normal cost") associated with the plan's benefits, and the values of the anticipated flow of future employer contributions to the plan. The current annual costs that the actuary develops are then compared with the current employer contributions, and the present values of expected benefits and expenses are compared with the total of expected future contributions *plus* the plan assets, if any, to determine the funding status of the plan.

In calculating these present values, a number of actuarial assumptions must be made. These assumptions include rates of investment return, expense levels, probabilities of death, employment termination, disability retirement, age retirement, and the expected number of hours worked in future years. There are two other very important assumptions that the actuary almost always makes: (a) the normal cost and current number of covered employees will not change over time and (b) the plan will continue indefinitely into the future. For a group to maintain its present size, the actuary assumes that the number of new entrants will equal the number of covered employees who depart because of termination of employment, death, disability, and retirement.

This chapter explains—

The nature of the many assumptions used and the concepts underlying their selection by the actuary;

The actuary's cost methods used in making calculations;

The ERISA-mandated funding standard account established to measure a plan's funding progress; and

Several other practical factors that influence the actuary's work.

ACTUARIAL ASSUMPTIONS

Investment Earnings Rates

The investment earnings rate is used to discount a future benefit value for interest between the valuation date and the expected date of payment. The assumed earnings rate has a direct effect on the estimated costs: the higher the earnings assumption, the higher the level of pension that an actuary can recommend for a given annual cost, and vice versa. The compounding effects of interest over time are substantial as any individual who is paying off a mortgage or an installment debt realizes. With a pension plan, however, interest has an opposite effect, that is, it reduces the present value of future obligations. As an example, the value today at 5 percent interest of a single sum of $10,000 due at age 65 for a male worker who is now age 45 (assuming the worker lives to age 65) is $3,769. In other words, the effect of compound interest discount at 5 percent per year for 20 years reduces by 62.31 percent the number of dollars needed today to provide $10,000 in 20 years. Viewed from another perspective, an investment today of $3,769 accumulated with compound interest at 5 percent per year for 20 years grows to $10,000.

In view of the long-range nature of pension obligations and the fact that investment earnings are not very predictable for a period of 25 or more years, actuaries usually use a relatively conservative investment earnings assumption in their cost calculations. The interest rate must not merely reflect the current earnings rate available on new investments but also the rates *expected to be earned* over the period when the plan liabilities will be paid. For example, if a relatively new plan has $1 million wholly invested in an insurance company contract guaranteeing 9 percent interest for ten years, it would be inappropriate to use that 9 percent interest rate to estimate the present value of all future obligations for a current group of employees. The reason rests with the fact that the plan's future liabilities might be 50 times greater than the current $1 million asset. Future contributions must be invested at investment earnings rates that are not reliably predictable today because the contributions will be received during each of the next 20, 30, or more years.

Those responsible for setting the investment earnings assumption, among other things, must take into account the effect of inflation in addition to current investment earnings rates. However, a rate of interest may be considered to be the sum of three components: that is, pure interest related to the value of holding money, say, 2 percent to 3 percent per annum, as generally considered by economists; a factor that reflects the rate of inflation; and an interest risk premium. The latter premium generally will reflect the risk that interest rates on bonds will rise above current rates—causing a capital loss if a currently purchased bond has to be sold before maturity and also the risk that the principal and interest may not be paid. If the long-term future rate of inflation is assumed to be 5 percent to 6 percent, then the earnings rate expectation may reasonably be 8 percent to 10 percent, the rate of return justifiably expected from the investments of a plan's investment manager. However, the actuary will employ a substantially lower investment earnings assumption in his or her calculations so that reasonable assurance can be given to the plan's trustees that the benefits can be supported by the expected contributions. Therefore, a 5 percent or 6 percent investment earnings rate may be justified. Other considerations include the maturity of the pension plan (i.e., the proportions of active and retired workers) since that relationship governs the plan's expected cash flow, the probable excess of contributions and investment income over benefit payments and expense. In addition, the size of the current pension fund in relation to ultimate plan obligations, the stability of the industry, and current investment earnings rates available under the plan's investment policy should be reflected in the investment earnings rate assumption.

A common rule of thumb is that an increase (or decrease) of

one fourth of 1 percent in the investment earnings rate assumption can produce an increase (or decrease) of 5 percent to 7 percent in the level of initial pension benefits. This common rule can lead to fallacious conclusions under certain circumstances. For instance, if the actuary's projections anticipate an excess of disbursements over income, an increase in the investment earnings rate assumption has the effect of increasing the value of the resulting financial drain on the plan and may actually produce a decrease in the level of benefits that the expected contributions would appear to support. This anomalous result is not likely to arise until a plan has been in effect for many years and the projected benefit payments become substantial. However, awareness of this fact points up the need for forecasting the cash flow of a plan to assist the trustees, the investment advisor, and the actuary in understanding the influence of probable experience on investment policies and practical investment earnings assumptions, and in avoiding misleading actuarial conclusions as to the soundness of plan financing.

In general, if the actuary assumes an investment earnings rate of 6 percent per annum, he or she expects that as much as 65 percent to 75 percent of all benefit costs will be paid from investment earnings. The higher the assumed rate of investment earnings, the greater the proportion of benefits that must ultimately be paid out of cash investment income. As a plan reaches maturity, this substantial demand for cash investment income (dividends, interest, and realized capital gains) will gradually make the trustees' investment policy less flexible because of the need for predictable investment earnings each and every year.

Death Rates

The death rates experienced by a group of participants influence pension costs. In the first place, deaths among the active participants reduce the number of participants who will become entitled to pension benefits. For example, the probability that a worker age 45 will survive to age 65 is 83 percent under a modern mortality table. Thus, the actuarially determined present value at age 45 of the worker's expected pension payable at age 65 is discounted by 17 percent for the probability that the worker will not live until age 65 and receive a pension. Combining this mortality discount with the discount factor developed in the explanation of interest discount, a single sum payment of $10,000 payable at retirement age 65 to a male worker now age 45 is $3,128. In other words, the $3,769 ($10,000, discounted for interest for 20 years) is reduced by 17 percent to $3,128. If lower death rates were assumed, the current value would be somewhat higher because the chance of living until age 65 is greater, and so there is a higher probability that the worker will live to receive a pension. Similarly, for a pension plan, lower death rates mean that more participants will probably live and become eligible for pension benefits, producing a higher cost of their pension benefits. Second, the rate of death among the retired participants determines the duration of the benefits. For each year or month that a group of retired participants lives beyond its life expectancy, there will be an increase in the cost of the pension plan.

The actuary's cost calculations are not based on life expectancies. Calculations are based on probabilities of living and dying. A life expectancy at any age is merely an average number of years that a group of individuals of the same current age will live. Significant numbers of participants will live a greater number of years than their life expectancy. Life expectancy is an index of longevity used to compare different groups of individuals subject to different probabilities of death. In fact, if the plan's obligations to a group of workers retiring at age 65 were to be calculated on a basis that assumed each worker would receive payments for the exact period of the life expectancy, the liability of the plan would be overstated.

Mortality tables showing probabilities of death by age are used as assumptions estimating the future mortality experience of a pension plan. In the recent past, the 1951 Male Group Annuity Table has been used (with an age set back for females), and sometimes provision has been made for mortality improvement since 1951 to reflect improvement in general population mortality which has arisen from medical advancements. Many actuaries have now adopted more modern tables; for example, the 1971 Male and Female Group Annuity Mortality Tables, wherever these tables appear appropriate.

The mortality table used has an important effect on the estimated cost of a pension plan. The choice of mortality table determines the actuary's estimate of the probable future accumulated funds (or reserves) released from time to time when participants die, and, consequently, the funds that will be effectively pro rated among the surviving participants. For example, a change in mortality tables can produce differences in estimated costs ranging from 1 percent to 12 percent, or more if a plan does not include any death benefits. If more funds are released by death, fewer funds will be necessary as contributions for the same level of benefits. In fact, the elimination of the mortality improvement factor from a typical table could reduce estimated costs by as much as 10 percent. (Past studies have shown that mortality rates have tended to decline, and so actuaries have used an improvement factor to adjust a standard mortality table's rates to reflect the anticipated decline.) In other words, one actuary's selection of such a table could effectively assume that about 10 percent more accumulated funds will be released by deaths than another actuary would have projected by using a table that included a mortality improvement factor of that magnitude.

With a joint trust pension plan, if the actuary judges, because of knowledge of the industry or trade, that the group of participants will not experience improved mortality, because of that judgment alone, he or she might recommend pension benefit levels 10 percent higher than another actuary might recommend. The reason might be that another actuary would not have had knowledge of the particular industry or trade. As a matter of fact, mortality rates are significantly different for certain types of crafts, such as asbestos workers because of lung disease and ironworkers because of the heavy and dangerous work involved.

Participant Termination Rates

Obviously, not every participant will remain in covered employment until normal retirement date. Therefore, where the participant group is large enough, the actuary's calculated present value of future benefits will also discount costs in advance for future estimated turnover. The reduction in estimated plan costs by discounting for turnover are substantial and generally will exceed the effect of preretirement mortality. As a very simple example, assume that of a group of workers now age 45, 3 percent terminate employment next year, then, of the remaining group, 3 percent terminate employment the following year, and so forth over a 20-year period. If terminated employees forfeit all benefits, then the present value of a single sum payment due at age 65 to the workers now age 45 who remain in service until age 65 would be discounted by about 46 percent. (This calculation assumes that none of the workers remaining in service die during the 20-year period.) By comparison, the mortality discount for this same period is only 17 percent.

The combined effects of discounting for interest, mortality, and termination is demonstrated approximately as follows, using the simple example of a benefit of a single sum payment of $10,000 to be made at retirement age 65 to a male worker now age 45:

Single sum payment at age 65	$10,000
Less: Interest discount at 5% for 20 years	6,231
Present value of payment discounted for interest	$ 3,769
Less: Mortality discount for 20 years from age 45 (17%)	641
Present value of payment discounted for interest and mortality	$ 3,128
Less: Turnover discount, reflecting an annual rate of employee turnover of 3% applicable to survivors each year for 20 years (46%)	1,438
Present value of payment discounted for interest, mortality, and turnover	$ 1,690

Thus, the effects of (modest) discounts for interest, mortality, and turnover combine to reduce the single sum payment to a present value of about 17 percent of the $10,000 single sum payment due 20 years in the future. In other words, under these assumptions, a present fund of about $1,700 for each worker now age 45 would probably be sufficient *in the aggregate* to provide a $10,000 payment for each worker who does not die or terminate employment before age 65. (A more sophisticated demonstration of the effects of actuarial assumptions on plan costs is provided later in this chapter.)

Present values of future benefits should be calculated to reflect terminations by use of turnover tables based on industry experience. The turnover table used in any particular plan is that which is expected to closely reflect the turnover pattern of the particular group of participants.

Generally, there is little statistically useful information concerning turnover when a plan is first established. Thus, it is the actuary's judgment—based on the available information and knowledge of geographical, industrial, and occupational trends, and so forth—that governs the choice of the turnover table to be employed.

In the same manner as death rates, turnover rates greater than the actuary assumed will release more accumulated funds (or reserves) than expected, allowing a faster buildup of funds for those participants who survive in service and, possibly, benefit improvements with no increase in cost. On the other hand, turnover rates lower than the actuary assumed will release smaller accumulated funds (or reserves) than expected, causing a slower buildup of funds for surviving participants and, possibly, requiring that the deficiency be offset by increased employer contributions or by benefit reductions.

The introduction of a turnover scale can produce a difference in estimated benefit levels ranging up to 30 percent or 40 percent or more. However, the number of terminating participants who will be entitled to vested pensions under the plan has a considerable influence over the effective cost discount on account of turnover. Also, to the extent that a plan may enter into reciprocity agreements with other plans, the discount due to employee turnover is reduced.

Disability Retirement Rates

Disability benefits are often provided under a joint trust pension plan. The disability pension generally is provided for participants who suffer total and permanent disability. To simplify administration of these benefits, trustees often rely on social security disability benefit entitlement as the basis of determining eligibility for pension plan disability benefits. However, because of reliance on social security awards which have been granted whenever the duration of disability is expected to be 12 or more months, social security disability benefits reflect total, not necessarily permanent, disability. Consequently, the actuary's assumptions should reflect this reality if the trustees decide to rely on social security adjudication for the granting of disability pension benefits. It is possible for a participant to be totally and permanently disabled from working at his trade or craft and yet be unable to receive a social security disability award. The reason is that the employee can be rehabilitated to perform other work. In such instance, the trustees may still wish to provide some form of disability pension. In this situation, the trustees may wish to allow only an actuarially reduced pension, rather than the full earned pension benefit to offset the substantially increased cost of this type of benefit.

Where disability benefits are provided under the pension plan, some type of advance funding is usually employed for the anticipated costs of the disability benefits, thus reducing somewhat the level of pension benefits that would otherwise be supported by employer contributions. Here again, the actuary will estimate the annual cost of the disability benefits, usually by employing a standard disability table until adequate experience develops. Disability rates are generally influenced by economic conditions and the industry in which employees work. In recent years, studies have demonstrated a remarkable increase in the level of disability retirement under plans relying on social security entitlement. If a disability pension is allowed when a participant does not receive a social security award, the actuary will anticipate a significantly higher incidence of disability under the plan.

It is imperative that the actuary continually monitor disability retirement experience to advise trustees of the financial impact of the standard employed in the adjudication of total and permanent disability claims. Normally, total and permanent disability rates will be relatively low for most groups, representing only a small proportion of total pension costs. However, in certain high-risk occupations, especially where a disability pension is granted without a social security disability award to a disabled participant, there could be more disability retirements than age retirements.

Age Retirement Rates

The normal retirement age is usually regarded as the earliest age at which all eligible employees are permitted to retire with unreduced benefits.[1] In the past, the actuary often assumed that all employees who survived to the normal retirement age retired at that time, especially in plans that did not provide for post-

---

[1] The age at which benefits commence and the normal, postponed and early retirement provisions of joint trust plans are more fully discussed beginning on page 81.

ponement of retirement or early retirement benefits in excess of the actuarial equivalent value.

Introduction of an assumption that some participants will retire before the normal retirement age makes the actuary's calculations more complex, but some recognition should be given to the possibility of early retirement, especially if unreduced pensions are allowed before the normal retirement age. Such recognition is particularly important at those ages when the number of early retirements may be significant, such as ages when social security benefits would be payable (age 62 and above). Besides the availability of social security benefits, the number of retirements which will occur before the usual normal retirement age 65 reflects (1) the liberality of early retirement benefits; (2) general economic conditions, that is, availability of nonindustry work; (3) inflationary trends; and (4) specific industry work opportunities and related wages.

When a level actuarial cost method is used by the actuary and full actuarial reductions are not imposed on pensions available at an early retirement age, the use of early retirement rates allows the projected cost savings related to the future accruals of benefits that will not be earned, together with the actuarial value of early retirement reductions, to be offset against increased costs resulting from the reduced periods over which benefit costs will be funded. If no provision for early retirement rates is made under such a situation, the actuary underestimates plan costs. When full actuarial reductions are imposed upon early retirement, lack of an appropriate provision for early retirement rates will overstate the plan's cost under level cost methods if a significant number of participants retire early.

In general, whether a level cost or accrued benefit cost method is employed, if substantial numbers of employees are expected to retire early, the actuary's formulas should reflect early retirement rates. The use of early retirement rates will enhance the actuary's ability to develop a "best estimate" of benefit costs and fulfill his or her obligation to do so under ERISA.

Expense Rates

Expense rates are generally expressed as a percentage of expected employer contributions rather than as a percentage of plan assets. However, if the actuary's assumed investment earnings rate is significantly lower than expected earned investment income, the actuary may make no direct, specific provision for expected expenses. The actual expense rates associated with a particular group vary with the number of participants, the amount of pension assets under investment management, the variety of benefits provided by the plan, the type of record-keeping required, the number of participating employers, the number of different employer contribution rates, and the number of beneficiaries receiving benefits. Since the enactment of ERISA, the annual insurance premiums payable to the PBGC and for fiduciary liability insurance have become significant for some joint trust pension plans. Expense also will vary according to the nature and extent of the professional actuarial, administrative, legal, and investment services required. With the advent of ERISA, expense levels are significantly higher than in the past because of the more frequently required and more complex actuarial studies, the increase in the number and frequency of reports to the federal government and to employees, and the increase in the number of legal suits against plan fiduciaries.

In general, expenses heretofore have been as low as 1½ percent or 2 percent of plan contributions on very large plans and 10 percent to 12 percent of contributions for small plans. In a medium-size plan covering 200 to 500 participants, annual expenses probably have averaged about 6 percent to 8 percent of contributions. The ERISA-mandated increased administrative, actuarial, and legal services have increased expenses by as much as 50 percent for large plans and by as much as 100 percent or more for small plans.

In the determination of benefit levels, actuaries usually assume an expense rate that they expect to be appropriate for the particular pension plan over the long term. Of course, deviations in actual expenses incurred from those assumed in the cost calculations are reflected in the future surpluses or deficiencies that develop under the plan. Again, with the advent of ERISA and its requirement that the actuary determine net experience gains and losses for each separate plan year, most actuaries will probably make a specific provision for the expense rate and adjust it frequently, if necessary, to avoid unduly understating or overstating expense rates.

Number of Hours Worked

The assumed average number of hours worked per year by a participant is extremely important in establishing the funding posture of a plan. In general, the greater the assumed number of hours per year worked per participant, the greater the anticipated amount of employer contributions to the fund and, consequently, the greater the portion of employer contributions assumed to be available to amortize any unfunded actuarial present values. It is always important to compare the level of contributions assumed to be received with the contributions actually received to validate any method used to estimate the amount of employer contributions.

To illustrate a fairly reliable estimating method, if a plan allows a full pension credit for participants who work 1,500 or more hours in a plan year and a pro rata pension credit for fewer hours worked in a plan year, the actuary might estimate the average number of hours worked per year, according to records of employees in several "hours worked" groupings. For example, employees who worked 750 hours or less might comprise one grouping; employees who worked 751 to 1,500 hours might form a second grouping; and employees who worked 1,501 hours or more might make up a third grouping. The actuary will then use these employee groupings to project future service pension credits and to estimate employer contributions. Since past service benefits are often the same for different groups of employees who work different numbers of hours, such breakdowns are important in assessing the margins available to amortize the cost of past service benefits (benefits granted for service when no contributions were made).

Some actuaries now use a more sophisticated approach in projecting employee pension credits and in estimating employer contributions. With the ready availability of computer processing, many actuaries now project benefits and related employer contributions according to the exact two- or three-year average number of hours worked by each employee. Using a two- or three-year average smoothes out yearly variations in hours worked and more directly relates the projected cost of benefits to the age/sex/service characteristics of each employee. For instance, an employee with substantial service generally will also work more than the average number of hours and, of course, will usually be older than the average age of the employee group to which he or she belongs.

ACTUARIAL COST METHODS

The mathematical technique that actuaries use to make their actuarial cost and present value calculations is called the "actuarial cost method." The actuary combines various actuarial factors to develop for each participant the annual employer contribution necessary to provide that participant with a specified amount of pension. The total of these annual employer contributions for all participants is called the normal cost of the plan. Also, there is usually a supplemental present value (sometimes called a supplemental liability) at a plan start-up, when the plan is amended, or when experience losses occur. This supplemental present value is calculated for each participant as of the effective date of the plan or the plan's amendment to reflect the cost of benefits (primarily past service benefits) which must be paid in excess of the plan's normal cost. The sum of these supplemental present values for all participants is the total supplemental present value for the plan.

A number of actuarial cost methods are in common use. Usually, for joint trust pension plans, the individual level cost method with supplemental present value (also known as the entry age normal cost method) is used. Sometimes an accrued benefit cost method is used, and occasionally other methods, such as an aggregate level cost method with or without supplemental present value, are used. This discussion is limited to the accrued benefit cost method and the individual level cost method with supplemental present value because the other methods are relatively uncommon for joint trust pension plans.

Under the individual level cost method with supplemental present value, an assumed age at entry for each active employee may be based on an examination of the actual ages of recent new entrants, a study of the actual entry ages of the existing population of employees, or on other judgment factors. The entry age assumption, in conjunction with the individual level cost method, implicitly assumes a future group with the same number of covered employees, but with age and service characteristics that approach a stationary condition (i.e., having the same age and service distribution based on the underlying actuarial assumption). Use of the accrued benefit cost method assumes that each year the flow of new entrants, together with the surviving participants from the prior year, will maintain the same age and service characteristics of the group and that a stationary or stable population already exists. The accrued benefit cost method presents a very difficult conceptual problem for the actuary. If the actuary, in fact, makes any reasonable assumptions concerning the probable flow of new entrants, it is quite unlikely and improbable that future populations will be projected which will have the same age and service characteristics of any current population. For example, if a plan starts out with a very young group, unless the turnover assumptions (and related turnover experience) are very high, the population of employees will age. This fact alone conflicts with the inherent assumption of this method that the population of employees is stationary and will not age.

The following discussion explains how actuaries make their calculations under the two principal cost methods used for joint trust plans.

Accrued Benefit Cost Method

Under the accrued benefit cost method, also called the unit credit cost method, actuarial costs are based directly upon pension benefits accrued under the plan to the date of cost determination. For example, if a participant had accrued 10 years of past service credit when the plan was first established and has earned an additional 5 years of credit immediately prior to the valuation date, the actuary will make calculations on the basis of 15 years of accrued pension benefits. The current value of such accrued pension benefits payable at the participant's normal retirement age will be determined, based on the participant's present age. This value is called the "supplemental present value." The actuary then calculates the current value of the pension credit expected to be earned in the year beginning as of the valuation date. This value is called the "normal cost." By summing the supplemental present value and the normal cost for all participants, the actuary develops the plan's total supplemental present value and normal cost.

The accrued benefit cost method is best adapted to those plans that provide a specified dollar amount of monthly pension for each year of credited service. Although best adapted to such plans, this cost method can also be used for plans which provide a composite benefit based on the participant's total period of credited service. For example, the plan may provide a $100 monthly pension benefit at age 65 for participants with 25 or more years of service. In this instance, the actuarial cost method will assume that the $100 monthly pension will be earned pro rata over a participant's total years of service to age 65.

If a participant would have 30 years of service by the time age 65 is reached, the actuary would assume that the participant earns a monthly pension credit of $3.33 per year of service. A similar approach may be used to apply this cost method to plans with benefits based on final average earnings or final contribution rates. The first step in the calculation of the plan's normal cost under the accrued benefit cost method is to determine the current value of each participant's benefit credit expected to be earned during the year for which costs are being calculated. The cost per dollar of monthly pension reflects the participant's age and sex and the actuary's assumptions of death, turnover, disability, and investment earnings rates.

If the participant has to work, say, 1,500 hours to earn a full pension credit each year, the actuary's cost calculations will incorporate an actual or assumed number of hours worked in the past and the expectation of hours to be worked in the future. Since the calculations are always based on a participant's age on the valuation date, the normal cost for each participant increases each year as the participant gets closer and closer to retirement age. The reason is that the contribution made to pay the normal cost will be invested for progressively shorter periods before pension payments begin; and as a participant gets closer to retirement, there is a decreasing probability that the participant will die, become disabled, or terminate employment before retiring. Also, as a participant gets older, there will be fewer expected forfeitures because more of the participants who terminate will have vested rights to their pensions.

To illustrate how the actuaries make their calculations, assume a male participant is first covered when he is 25 years old and will receive a monthly pension at age 65 of $40, that is, he will earn a $1 monthly pension each year. Also assume that $1 of monthly pension at age 65 has a value of $120. If all actuarial assumptions of death, turnover, and investment income rates are disregarded, the normal cost of the $1 monthly pension earned each year is determined from the following table:

Male Age	Normal Cost
25	$120
30	120
35	120
40	120
45	120
50	120
55	120
60	120

In other words, the normal cost would be the same at every age as it is at retirement age 65.

Since this hypothetical participant would forfeit his pension if he dies before retirement age 65, the normal cost is discounted by death rates which vary with the participant's age. The resulting Normal Costs are as shown in the following table:

Male Age	Normal Cost (discounted for death* only)
25	$ 97.61
30	97.95
35	98.41
40	99.06
45	100.10
50	102.04
55	105.48
60	111.05

* Death rates according to the 1951 Male Group Annuity Table, with mortality improvement projected to 1966 according to scale C.

When an annual investment earnings rate assumption of 5 percent is assumed, the normal cost is further discounted and decreased as follows:

Male Age	Normal Cost (discounted for death and investment earnings)
25	$13.87
30	17.76
35	22.77
40	29.25
45	37.73
50	49.08
55	64.76
60	87.01

By introducing the assumption that participants will terminate employment voluntarily according to the following schedule,

Male Age	Annual Probability of Employment Turnover
25	7.72%
30	7.22
35	6.28
40	5.15
45	4.65
50	4.10
55	3.50
60	2.35

the normal cost by age is again discounted and reduced further as follows:

Male Age	Normal Cost (discounted for death, investment earnings, and turnover)
25	$ 1.95
30	3.69
35	6.76
40	11.74
45	19.44
50	31.81
55	51.13
60	80.80

The dramatic discounting impact of actuarial assumptions can readily be recognized from the effect of moderate factors used in this illustration.

Finally, assuming that the average participant will be 100 percent vested in all of his accrued pension credits after ten years of service, the added cost of vesting increases the normal cost as shown in the next table:

Male Age	Normal Cost*
25	$ 6.55
30	12.44
35	22.77
40	29.25
45	37.73
50	49.08
55	64.76
60	87.01

* Discounted to reflect death, turnover, investment earning rates, and 100 percent vesting after ten years of service.

These accrued benefit normal costs are specifically for a male who enters covered employment at age 25 and is 100 percent vested in pension credits once he reaches age 35. For a participant who enters employment at, say, age 35 the normal costs at age 45 and above would be the same as shown in this table. The rates are the same only at those ages when participants cannot suffer forfeitures of their pension credits if they terminate employment.

Under the accrued benefit cost method the supplemental present value and the normal cost for a participant at any age are determined by use of the same factors if, as is almost always true, the same vesting schedule applies to both past and future service credits. For example, if a male participant entered covered employment at age 25 and the plan was established when he was 30, he would be granted five years of past service credit of $1 monthly pension payable at age 65 and his supplemental present value at age 30 would be $62.60 (= $5 × 12.44). His normal cost for $1 monthly pension payable at age 65 would be $12.44.

The normal cost for the plan as a whole is simply the sum of the separate normal costs for the benefits credited to each participant during a particular year. Although the normal cost for a given participant increases over time under this accrued benefit cost method, the normal cost for the plan as a whole often does not increase as rapidly; sometimes, it may remain fairly constant or even decrease. The reason for this apparent anomaly is that some older participants will die or terminate employment and be replaced by much younger workers. If the distribution of current service benefit credits by age and sex remains constant, the normal cost for the plan as a whole will remain constant.

However, certain pitfalls exist in adopting the accrued benefit cost method. Relatively substantial increases in the average normal cost per employee can occur if the work force gradually declines, such as when an industry or trade declines and fewer younger employees are hired. As a result, the margins available in employer contributions (contributions in excess of the increasing normal costs) required to amortize the unfunded supplemental present value will diminish—weakening the funding posture of the pension plan. Also, this method may not be readily adaptable to developing appropriate costs of ancillary benefits which are deferred, for example, spouse pensions and disability benefits that are available only after 15 years of service or so.

Individual Level Cost Method with Supplemental Present Value

The basic approach used by the actuary under the individual level cost method with supplemental present value (also known as the entry age normal cost method) is to calculate the level annual payments necessary to provide a plan's schedule of benefits. The actuary generally assumes that the level payments begin at entry age (i.e., the age when a participant first entered covered employment) and that the payments continue until the participant's retirement age. On any particular valuation date, the actuary will also calculate a supplemental present value, that is, the accumulated value of the level annual payments presumed to have been made from entry age to the participant's age on the valuation date. To the extent that such normal cost payments were not actually made, there is an "unfunded supplemental present value."

This approach is retrospective in nature. Another way to develop the supplemental present value is to evaluate costs prospectively by calculating the excess of the present value of future benefits over the present value of future normal cost payments. If a plan's schedule of benefits never changes, the two approaches produce the same results.

To illustrate the actuary's cost calculations, consider the same situation treated in the discussion of the accrued benefit cost method. As before, the participant enters covered employment at age 25 under the plan and earns a monthly pension credit of $1 for each year of service. In the 40 years of employment until age 65, the participant will earn a $40 monthly pension. Assuming that each $1 of monthly pension has a single sum value of $120 at age 65, then $4,800 must be accumulated by the time the participant reaches age 65. If assumptions of death, turnover, and investment earnings rates are disregarded, the normal cost payment for the pension is merely $4,800 divided by 40, or $120.

It should be noted that when all actuarial assumptions are ignored, both cost methods produce the same normal cost, that is, the single sum cost, at normal retirement age, of the pension earned during the year. At any point in time after a participant's entry age, the supplemental present value will be $120 times the number of elapsed years as of the date of valuation. After ten years, the supplemental present value would be $1,200 (= 10 × $120).

The effect on the above costs of the various actuarial assumptions can be illustrated by again introducing successively the several actuarial factors previously considered. Introducing mortality (or death) rates, the normal cost of $120 reduces to $102.19 and the supplemental present value of $1,200 becomes $1,027.01. Introduction of a 5 percent investment earnings rate assumption further reduces these costs; that is, the normal cost declines to $31.54 and the supplemental present value becomes $418.70. Again, using the same employment turnover discount factors from the previous example, the normal cost further reduces to $8.85, and the supplemental present value becomes $185.11. Finally, introduction of the assumption that the participant will be 100 percent vested after ten years of service, increases the normal cost to $18.62 while the supplemental present value rises to $389.45. In this situation, the employment turnover discount only affects the number of pension credits that the actuary projects the participant will earn when he or she is 100 percent vested. The participant no longer can forfeit any accrued pension credits when he terminates employment after completing ten years of credited service.

Actuarial assumptions exert a powerful influence on the estimated level of pension costs. Even modest differences in assumptions generate significant changes in estimated costs.

Under both the accrued benefit cost method and the individual level cost method with supplemental present value, the initial unfunded supplemental present value is usually amortized over 30 or 40 years. Under ERISA, the maximum amortization period is initially set at 40 years for joint trust pension plans and the actuary is required to continually examine the experience of the plan to maintain the funding schedule. Experience deficiencies and gains must be amortized (or spread) over a 20-year period, and necessary periodic increases in contributions or reductions in benefits will be required to maintain actuarial balance if deficiencies accumulate.

ACTUARIAL FORECASTS

A traditional actuarial valuation can be considered as a "snapshot" of the future lifetime values of a pension plan. Although the plan's present values and assets are determined at one particular point in time, these present values do *imply* a particular projected stream of payments, both into and out of the pension fund. Therefore, the traditional actuarial valuation can be considered as a single dimensional view of a long-range actuarial projection which takes into account all of the probable future events anticipated by the actuary's assumptions.

Actuarial opinion is now leaning toward the adoption of methods of estimating the costs of pension plans which more directly disclose to trustees and their advisors long-range insights into the implications of the actuary's assumptions. These methods are based on an "actuarial forecast." Today, many actuaries believe that ERISA's imposed fiduciary responsibilities *require* that the trustees and investment advisors understand the *potential* year-by-year financial characteristics of the plan to allow long-term financial planning and to establish investment objectives intelligently. An actuarial forecast can be used as a window to let trustees and investment advisors obtain a multidimensional view of the plan's anticipated population characteristics, benefit payouts, and the actuarial values implied by the actuarial assumptions. By using such a forecast, the following information can be disclosed for each future year or for any specified future period of time:

a. The value of the benefits for retired employees.
b. The value of the benefits for vested employees.
c. The value of all accrued benefits.
d. The supplemental present value (or accrued liability) implied by the cost method.

In a cost method based on an actuarial forecast one of these values at a specific future time might be used as a funding goal.

The forecast can also provide information on the expected year-by-year investment income, benefit payouts and expense, employer contributions, asset size, size of the work force, and other useful statistical information.

One of the great advantages of an actuarial forecast is that it allows the actuary and the trustees to examine the reasonableness of some of the actuary's assumptions. For example, the population characteristics developed by the forecast can be examined in light of trustees' expectations concerning future industry employment. Another equally important value lies in the forecasting of the plan's liquidity or cash flow requirements for investment planning purposes. A significant value of adopting a forecast actuarial cost method is the resulting ability of the actuary to communicate the meaning of actuarial valuation results to trustees. Nonactuaries are unaccustomed to phrases such as present value, normal cost, and other seemingly mysterious actuarial terms. The movement to actuarial forecasts should allow the actuary's valuation results to be explained in a more comprehensible and valuable manner than ever before—allowing joint trust pension plans (as well as other pension plans) to be more effectively and efficiently administered for the benefit of plan participants.

CHOICE OF ACTUARIAL COST METHOD

Whether a traditional or forecast actuarial cost method is employed, the true cost of a pension plan is not known until the last pensioner dies.[1] Consequently, the actuary must estimate the required contributions using mathematical techniques, experience, and judgment. Different actuaries develop different estimated

---

[1] Forecast actuarial cost methods are not currently permitted under ERISA for funding standard account purposes.

contribution levels (and different levels of pension benefits), depending upon their knowledge of and experience with an industry or trade, the accuracy of census data, and the degree of conservatism or liberality in the choice of actuarial factors. However, regardless of an actuary's estimates, the long-term employer contributions to a plan must equal:

Total benefits paid

plus

Cost of administration

less

Investment income on fund assets

Since actuaries cannot determine the true cost of a plan in advance, they can only estimate required contributions and benefit levels. Therefore, the role of the actuary is to determine initial benefit levels so that the portion of the employer contributions used in the early years of a plan to pay pensions to older participants leaves a surplus that can be invested for the younger participants. If the actuary has made reasonably accurate cost estimates, this invested surplus will accumulate and be sufficient to pay pensions and other benefits to those participants who will retire 10, 20, or more years in the future. Regardless of the accuracy of the actuary's estimates of costs and benefit levels, he or she must continually adjust estimated costs and recommended benefits to reflect actual experience as it emerges over the years. For joint trust pension plans, the actuary generally will develop the plan's normal cost payments under either a traditional or forecast actuarial cost method in a manner that will level out the annual payments required for a participant. A cost method that develops a level annual cost is most often employed because the value of each pension credit a participant earns each year increases as the participant approaches retirement age. When a plan covers a group of participants with a young age composition in a growing industry, a level type of actuarial cost method allows a significant growth of assets in the early years because the payments substantially exceed the value of pension credits earned. On the other hand, the normal costs sometimes are developed under the accrued benefit cost method, and the actuary's calculations provide only for the actual value of pension credits earned at each age. Therefore, the assets grow more slowly under the accrued benefit cost method than under a level type of cost method, generating less investment income and increasing the probability that employer contributions will ultimately need to be increased to maintain actuarial balance.

EQUILIBRIUM BETWEEN SUM OF PLAN ASSETS AND EXPECTED EMPLOYER CONTRIBUTIONS AND EXPECTED VALUE OF FUTURE BENEFITS

As stated previously, the present value of benefits and expenses expected to be paid under a pension plan must be equal to the present value of both the contributions expected to be paid into the pension fund and the investment income anticipated to be earned on the pension plan's current and future assets. With a static population and a fixed rate of investment return, the ultimate level of employer contributions will be governed by the size of the pension fund and the level of benefits provided by the plan.

There would appear to be no "absolute" criteria for selecting cost methods or actuarial assumptions. However, there are certain criteria that provide some minimum conditions that must be met in selecting actuarial cost methods when a pension plan is expected to be maintained indefinitely into the future. That is, certain conditions apply when a plan is to be maintained not just for the current generation of employees but also for those future generations of employees who continue to enter the trade or industry as successive generations of employees die, become disabled, retire, or terminate employment for other causes.

With this long-range view of a pension plan's continuation, the actuarial cost method selected by the pension actuary should be one which at least will satisfy the following conditions of actuarial balance between contributions, investment income, expenses, and benefits:

The present value of future contributions for the existing population of participants and the present value of contributions for all future generations of participants, plus the value of the pension fund assets at any time must be equal to the present value of all future benefits and expenses for the current population of participants and the present value of all benefits and expenses for all future generations of participants.

Under this condition of equilibrium, we have an equation involving two perpetuities if the pension actuary assumes that the age and service characteristics of the participants will ultimately stabilize. It can be mathematically demonstrated that under such static population assumption, simplification of the equation of equilibrium develops a minimum annual payment equal to the normal cost of the plan plus the assumed investment income on the unfunded supplemental present value, where both elements have been determined by calculating the normal cost for all participants who will earn benefits under the plan using a level type of cost method on the assumption that the plan always existed in its current form. Therefore, this cost method provides a direct check of the equilibrium condition.

Clearly, the pension actuary should evaluate the condition of equilibrium in terms of the best judgment of the board of trustees concerning the growth or decline of the business or businesses in which the participants work. If the industry is growing, then the actuary's assumption of a static population of participants will produce a conservative basis for annual cost calculations. On the other hand, if the business or industry is declining or may decline, then the assumption of a static population of participants is not valid, and the actuary should attempt to make a reasonable approximation of the rate of decline of the population in order to fix either (1) the level of benefits supportable by the bargained-for contributions under the plan, or (2) the level of increased contributions necessary to maintain existing benefits.

A major problem encountered, especially in large plans, is that of incomplete data. The missing data may be birth dates, sex, or hire dates making direct valuation impossible. The actuary has several options as to how such incomplete data can be properly accommodated and reasonable cost estimates still be developed.

The simplest method would be to assume that the data for those participants with incomplete information is similar to the data for those with complete information. Thus, if complete information exists for 1,000 participants out of a total of 1,050 participants, the actuary may just prorate the cost estimates upward by the ratio 1,050/1,000 = 1.05. Then, if the present value of benefits based on complete data is $2,000,000, that value would be increased by 5 percent to $2,100,000. This prorating technique often may be based on ratios of hours worked instead of number of individuals, if such information is available. Usually, the latter approach will be more accurate if the valuation results for participants with complete information is broken down by "hours worked" categories. As mentioned previously, there is a direct correlation between the number of hours a participant works and job seniority. Consequently, those participants who work the greater number of hours tend to have high cost characteristics.

Sometimes a more sophisticated technique may be used. Suppose the problem is mainly missing dates of birth and a study has been made which shows that age increases significantly with length of service. The actuary could take the data for participants with complete information (i.e., with both hire dates and birth dates) and divide the data first by length of service and then by date of birth. By establishing a correlation between the data with missing birth dates and the complete data according to service, and the data with missing hire dates and the complete data according to dates of birth, the actuary can develop a reasonable estimate of values for the incomplete data and merge the results with the values calculated for participants with complete data.

The actuary's decisions as to which method to use depends on the extent of incomplete data and judgment as to whether or not the refinement of the second method justifies the extra work. Under ERISA, actuaries may have to qualify their opinion if less than complete data are available.

ACTUARIAL VALUATIONS AND THE FUNDING STANDARD ACCOUNT

Periodic Actuarial Valuations

Periodically, the actuary revalues the plan to determine the extent to which the plan is being funded. Under ERISA, valuations must be made at least every three years, but certain technical provisions of ERISA now suggest that actuaries may need to perform annual valuations to certify the funding status of the plan until or unless they believe that the plan's experience is not significantly different from their assumptions.

Generally, the actuary's first valuation after a plan has been established will be performed by using the same actuarial factors employed in the initial work, unless there are obvious reasons for using different assumptions. Consequently, the actuary once again develops the normal cost payment, the plan's supplemental present values, and the value of plan assets. The difference between the expected annual employer contributions and the required normal cost is the amount available to amortize the unfunded supplemental present value (i.e., supplemental present value less the value of plan assets). Using this procedure, the actuary determines the number of years that will be required to pay off the unfunded supplemental present value with the excess of employer contributions over the plan's normal cost. (The normal cost is the estimated cost to pay for all plan benefits if contributions had always been made on behalf of all plan participants.)

Assuming that the original amortization period required to pay off the supplemental present value was 30 years, if the actuary's second valuation develops an amortization period of 29 years, the actuary can conclude that, in aggregate, his or her assumptions were reasonable. However, if the amortization period has reduced to 28½ years, then there have been gains which the actuary did not anticipate. If, on the other hand, the amortization period has not decreased but has increased, then there have been experience losses. In other words, the actuary's assumptions have in some manner fallen short of experience.

Generally, actuaries will perform at least an approximate gain and loss analysis to isolate the source of such gains and losses and will report their conclusions in the actuarial valuation report. If serious losses continue over several years, actuaries change their assumptions to conform to experience and specify the degree to which contribution increases must be bargained or benefit levels decreased to achieve actuarial balance.

Impact of Funding Standard Account

Under ERISA, the aggregate net experience gain or loss must be isolated each year and amortized over a 20-year period as part of a system for measuring experience deficiencies on an accumulated basis under a funding standard account which must be established for every defined benefit pension plan. If an actuary determines that changes in his or her actuarial assumptions are necessary, ERISA requires that the resulting changes in the unfunded supplemental present values must be amortized over a 30-year period. The act also requires that accumulated deficiencies be eliminated as of the next collective bargaining date by increases in contributions or decreases in benefits. Obviously, these legal requirements severely limit a plan's flexibility in dealing with adverse experience.

Since each year's net experience loss contributes to possible future accumulated funding deficiencies under the provisions of ERISA, actuaries have a responsibility to employ those factors and assumptions that they believe will minimize net experience losses. If significant net experience losses occur in successive years, even the amortization of those losses over a 20-year period (as required by ERISA) could cause an accumulated funding deficiency.

The existence of such a deficiency can:

Interfere with the normal bargaining process between the union and employers,

Jeopardize maintenance of future benefit levels, and

Impose special financial liabilities on contributing employers.

On the other hand, the actuary's assumptions should not be so conservative as to regularly generate substantial net experience gains, producing accumulated funding surpluses and deferring increased benefits for many years into the future. Where experience gains have been consistent and substantial, the actuary often recommends improvements in the benefits without the need for additional employer contributions. Alternatively, the actuary may recommend that cumulative experience gains be applied to more rapidly amortize a plan's unfunded supplemental present value.

Experience gains and losses can arise from numerous sources. The sources of gains and losses are from (1) investment income and asset value changes, (2) participant turnover different from the assumed rates, (3) age and/or disability retirement rates different from those assumed, (4) increases or decreases in the number of hours worked, (5) changes in expense levels, (6) fluctuations in the death rates, and (7) corrections to the employee data. Appendix F sets forth a specimen actuarial report for a simple specimen plan and Section F of the report illustrates how actual experience produces gains and losses and, therefore, changes the actuary's cost estimates for the plan.

Funding Deficiencies

The general effect of the funding requirements of ERISA is that contributions to the plan (in the first year to which the requirements apply) must be at least equal to the normal cost for the year and 40-year funding of the plan's unfunded supplemental present value. The funding standard account must be maintained, showing charges and credits, and this account is used to determine funding deficiencies. To the extent that such deficiencies arise, penalties may be imposed on contributing employers.

For subsequent years, the requirement must be met on a cumulative basis starting with the first year to which the requirement applies. Other items enter into the requirement. Increases in the unfunded supplemental present value that arise from plan amendments (or contribution increases) get a new 40-year start. Experience losses first recognized in a given year go on a 20-year track. Any loss from a change in actuarial assumptions gets on a 30-year track. If, instead of increases in the unfunded supplemental present value, there are decreases from the causes just recited, these, too, are amortized over the periods mentioned.

In other words, the funding standard account (FSA) mandated by ERISA will be used to:

Determine annually whether or not funding deficiencies have arisen,

Force a 40-year amortization of unfunded supplemental present values resulting from a new plan or a plan amendment,

Spread the net annual experience gains and losses over a 20-year amortization period (net experience gains and losses will reflect asset value changes), and

Amortize over 30 years, changes in unfunded supplemental present values produced by changes in actuarial assumptions.

To accomplish these requirements imposed by ERISA, the law requires that:

An annual certification of costs be made by an enrolled actuary,

An actuarial valuation be performed at least every three years,

Records be developed and maintained to allow calculation of accrued benefits so that the plan administrator can communicate those benefits to participants upon request, and

The adequacy of benefit records for actuarial valuation purposes be certified by the enrolled actuary. If such certification cannot be made, the enrolled actuary must qualify his or her opinion relative to the plan's actuarial posture.

This FSA is principally an actuarial account because most of the items that go into the account are actuarial in nature. The principal purpose of the FSA is to establish whether or not an "Accumulated Funding Deficiency" exists because if a deficiency exists, it must be eliminated quickly.

ERISA's accumulated funding deficiency is the excess, if any, of accumulated defined charges to the FSA over the accumulated defined credits to the account. Charges and credits to the FSA are of three types:

Actuarially determined items,

Contributions, and

Special adjustments on account of any "waived funding deficiency."

The actuarially determined items charged to the FSA are:

1. The plan's normal cost. This generally is the level annual payment necessary to provide a plan's schedule of benefits.
2. The amount required to amortize over several years the following estimated costs:
    a. The unfunded supplemental present value,
    b. Increases in unfunded supplemental present values arising from plan amendments,
    c. Actuarial losses, and
    d. Any increase in cost on account of changes in actuarial assumptions.
3. Expected annual expenses.
4. An interest adjustment at the actuary's assumed rate for the period between the time each charge is incurred and the end of the year.

The credits to the FSA are:

1. Employer contributions actually paid plus those contributions that are "receivable" at the end of the plan year, provided that they are paid within a specified period of time.
2. The amount required to amortize over a number of years:
   a. Actuarial gains, and
   b. Any decrease in unfunded supplemental present values on account of changes in actuarial assumptions or plan provisions.
3. An interest adjustment at the actuary's assumed rate of investment earnings for the period between the time the contribution or payment is credited and the end of the year.

Although the operation of the FSA involves numerous items of an actuarial nature, its operation is not especially difficult to grasp once the reader has examined how the actuary develops the charges and credits. Section F of the specimen actuarial report in Appendix F develops the FSA for a specimen plan.

Employers who contribute to joint trust pension plans generally negotiate contributions in terms of a specified amount per hour of service, per week of employment, or some unit of output. Without some form of relief from the specific requirements of the funding standard account, contributing employers and plan trustees would be placed in a very difficult situation when the actual contributions in a plan year fall short of the amounts estimated by the actuary. For example, a strike may cause substantial reductions in expected contributions and cause a funding deficiency, or the industry may be financially depressed because of an economic slowdown. In order to minimize the impact of these types of conditions, the Internal Revenue Service proposes to allow joint trust pension plans to adopt a special method, called the "shortfall method," for computing charges to the funding standard account.

Under the shortfall method as proposed by the IRS, the charge to the funding standard account would be based on the actual number of units of production (e.g., hours of service or weeks of employment, etc.) for the applicable year. The difference between the FSA charge determined according to the actuary's estimate (if the shortfall method were not employed) and the charge under the shortfall method can be amortized over a 20-year period. In addition, the amortization of this shortfall and the amortization of other actuarial gains and losses may be postponed for up to five years.

The employment of this shortfall method should give many joint trust pension plans time to take corrective action under the normal collective bargaining process instead of having deficiencies that must be corrected immediately.

Implications of an FSA Funding Deficiency

Any experience gain or loss attributable to a plan year does not affect the FSA for that particular year. A net experience gain or loss for a particular year must be amortized over 20 years and applied to adjust required future pension contributions. The gain or loss does not affect the FSA for any purpose in the year in which it arises.

Without the relief allowed by the IRS through use of the shortfall method, a deficiency determined just before the expiry of a plan's collective bargaining agreement would cause significant problems for trustees since they would probably have to act to eliminate the deficiency by that date, either by reducing (perhaps temporarily) future benefits, by moving to the alternate funding standard account (a method of providing temporary relief allowed under ERISA), or by seeking a waiver. The FSA establishes a rather rigid structure for measuring the funding status of a plan even though relief is granted under the shortfall method previously described. Trustees should adopt amortization periods for supplemental present values short enough to allow margins so that the deviations of actual experience from the actuary's assumptions will not interfere with the normal bargaining process. Also, trustees should demand that census data and records be more complete and accurate to preclude random variations in a plan's estimated cost caused by adjustments in data. In the long run, ERISA should be an advantage to both the trustees and the actuary since the data on which calculations are based will have to be far more accurate than in the past. With actuarial valuations required at least every three years and an actuarial report required annually, trustees will be in a position to continually monitor the overall operation of the plan.

Through an analysis of the actuary's data requirements, the trustees will have to ensure that a long-term program is adopted to secure adequate records. The trustees should then require the actuary to make cash flow projections for at least one to three years to help the trustees visualize whether or not unfavorable experience would cause a funding deficiency. In general, the trustees will have to become more aware of the plan's operations and actively make decisions governing administration, record keeping, and investments, and demand continuing actuarial analysis of experience trends.

A waiver of a funding deficiency can be granted if there is a substantial business hardship, that is, "10 percent or more of the employers are unable to meet the standard" and if application of the minimum standard would be adverse to participants [act Section 1013(a) adding IRC Section 412(d)]. Although any part of a deficiency, except amortization of previous waivers, may be waived, no more than five waivers may be allowed in any 15 consecutive years, and the waived amount must be amortized over 15 years. Hopefully, by use of the shortfall method and adoption of reasonably conservative periods for amortizing unfunded supplemental present values, there will be little need for seeking waivers of funding deficiencies.

The amortization of unfunded supplemental present values may be extended up to ten years by the Secretary of Labor if the purposes of ERISA are maintained, the participants are protected, otherwise the plan might terminate, and so forth. However, the extension of an amortization period from 40 years to 50 years provides very little relief. Also, no benefit increases, accrual rate changes or vesting changes may be made while there is any unamortized waived funding deficiency or while an extended amortization period exists.

Penalties for Noncompliance

There is an initial excise tax of 5 percent of an accumulated funding deficiency imposed on the contributing employers. Also, if such initial excise tax is not paid when due, a 100 percent additional excise tax is incurred. The liability for these nontax deductible penalty taxes is allocated to employers, according to ERISA, "in a reasonable manner not inconsistent with regulations" (which are not yet prescribed). The allocation is to be made first on the basis of contribution delinquencies, and second on the basis of liabilities for contributions under the plan.

ACTUARIAL VALUATIONS AND PLAN ASSET VALUES

A very important element in the actuary's gain and loss analysis is the degree of capital value changes in the pension fund. If assets were valued fully at market, there could be very substantial actuarial gains and losses during unsettled economic conditions. ERISA requires that the actuarial values of equity investments be established to reflect market values, but the amortized cost of debt securities is acceptable for actuarial purposes. Internal Revenue Service regulations are to specify the acceptable methods of implementing the asset valuation provisions of ERISA.

Numerous methods have been used to value the assets of a pension fund for actuarial purposes. The basic objective is to avoid drastic fluctuations in the asset values from year to year while obtaining a reliable indication of both the short-term and long-term true value of the assets.

As a practical matter, under ERISA the actuary must value equity securities in a manner that reflects market values. Bonds can be carried at their amortized value where premiums are amortized over the period to the earliest call date and discounts are spread out over the entire bond period.

A method that has not been very commonly used prior to ERISA is valuation of a plan's assets at full market value. If assets are valued at full market, it means that each particular security's market value is determined on the valuation date. Ordinarily, this practice is simple because the closing price of the stock on the particular exchange where it is sold is readily available. Sometimes securities are purchased on a direct placement basis, investments are made in real estate, and so forth, and there is no readily available market value. In such instances, a value has to be established based upon independent appraisal by one or more investment experts, banks, or other appraisers as appropriate.

Under this market value method, the value of the same asset from one trust fund to another trust fund would be the same for each security, and the value would be the same for identical securities within the same trust. Furthermore, selling the same security and repurchasing it would not result in a new value. Obviously, there would be no reason to do the latter, but it has been done in the past when assets were valued at cost in order to achieve a more realistic valuation of the plan's securities.

As measured against the actuary's criteria (i.e., to establish the most realistic long- and short-term asset values), the market value method is subject to radical fluctuation from year to year and may or may not be a good measure of true value in the short term. Even over the long term, experience has demonstrated that this method probably will not produce a reliable set of security values.

A modification of the market valuation of plan assets (other than amortizable bonds) is to value assets at the average market value for each security. This method has not been commonly used because it is quite complicated and could be time-consuming. It requires valuing each security at the average of its market price for some preceding period of time, such as three or five years.

This type of valuation will produce more constant values for the same security from trust to trust and for the same security within the same trust, and selling the same security and repurchasing it will not result in a new value. It meets the criteria quite well in that values should not fluctuate radically from year to year and it should be a good indicator of true long-term value. This particular method would be a very satisfactory method if it were not for the complexity of determining the values.

There are numerous variations in the methods of reflecting market values in establishing the asset values of a plan's equity investments. One method of achieving a reflection of market values for establishing the actuarial value of assets might be to base the current portfolio's value on the *ratio* of all market values for a period of years to all cost values of an equity portfolio over the same period of years. The ratio would be applied to the plan's current equity portfolio's cost values. The result would represent the actuarial value of equity assets for funding purposes.

THE ACTUARIAL REPORT

The actuarial report is the means by which a plan's actuary informs the trustees of the results of his or her periodic actuarial valuations or special studies. Since the actuarial report is the only formal source of information on the ability of the plan and trust to meet future benefit commitments, its importance to the trustees cannot be overemphasized.

A good actuarial report should contain clear recommendations of possible courses of future action in addition to a statement of the plan's current condition. The report should not stop with a presentation of the static circumstances of the plan's finances. Rather, it should point to existing or prospective plan problems and outline recommended steps to solve the problems. If further analyses or studies are required, the report should so state. In other words, an actuarial report should present results that show the current financial status, and, if possible, projections that give an insight into the future. Also, it should include thoughtful and convincing recommendations for timely action wherever they are needed. Appendix F is a specimen actuarial report illustrating the information which might be supplied to the trustees of a joint trust pension plan.

In general, a good actuarial report should include:

An explanation of the purpose of the report.

An outline of plan benefits.

A description of census data employed in the valuation and an explanation of any special assumptions made.

A summary of statistics of the group and the development of actuarial values of assets, as well as the audited financial asset information on which such values are based.

A summary of the basic actuarial valuation results with a suitable statement of the adequacy of the expected employer contributions.

A statement of actuarial assumptions and methods.

Information concerning the funding standard account maintained for the plan.

Finally, the report should contain, where appropriate, an appraisal of the suitability of assumptions made and reference to factors which were not considered. Changes in assumptions from those used in previous reports should be pointed out and their effect noted.

The actuary's statement should not merely list the explicit assumptions but should also mention the presence or absence of other factors which the actuary believes significant in the valuation of future costs or the incidence of future costs. Such factors could include inflation, margins for fluctuations in experience, the effect of possible plant shutdowns, and so on.

The appraisal of the suitability of actuarial methods or assumptions should include an evaluation of whether the conclusion reflects the long-term cost implications for the plan. For example, if the accrued benefit cost method is used, the actuary should not imply that the calculated pension costs are a measure of the long-term cost unless the actuary has, in fact, based his or her opinion on a positive evaluation of the present circumstances and future probable changes of significance which bear on the participant population and the future of the trade or industry. Also, if the actuary believes that inflation will continue or that the covered work force will decline, he or she should test the financial effects of such events on a reasonably likely hypothetical basis, hopefully chosen with the help of the trustees.

Since actuaries are responsible for the reasonableness of their assumptions, they should be verified by periodic studies of the plan's experience. Ideally, the actuarial report should regularly include a gain and loss analysis and a discussion of the effects of the current gains and losses on the financial status of the plan. The likelihood of similar gains and losses in the future should also be discussed. The actuarial report (Appendix F) does, in fact, incorporate a discussion of the plan's experience gains and losses. In addition, the report demonstrates the development of the funding standard account information for the year under study and an estimated account for the following plan year.

WITHDRAWAL OF CONTRIBUTING EMPLOYERS

The withdrawal of contributing employers can have significant actuarial implications as regards the ability of a joint trust pension plan to continue in the future. In addition, effective July 1, 1979, a withdrawing employer may have residual plan liabilities if there are any unfunded vested present values attributable to the withdrawing employer. Some actuarial implications relating to an employer's withdrawal from a joint trust pension plan have been previously discussed.[2] Subtitle D of Title IV of ERISA imposes a contingent employer liability if a joint trust pension plan terminates in its entirety and imposes certain financial requirements upon the withdrawal of a substantial employer. This contingent employer liability has probably had the greatest conceptual impact on the contributing employers associated with joint trust pension plans.

The following discussion considers (1) the distinction between substantial employers and other employers that contribute to joint trust pension plans; (2) the conditions that can cause an employer to become a withdrawn employer, subject to residual plan liabilities; and (3) the nature of the contingent employer liability which arises on account of the termination insurance provisions of ERISA.

Definition of a Substantial Employer

In general, ERISA defines a substantial employer for any plan year as an employer that has contributed 10 percent or more of the employer contributions made to a joint trust pension plan during each of the immediately preceding two plan years, or during each of the second and third immediately preceding plan years. Within 60 days of the withdrawal from a plan by any substantial employer, notice must be filed by the plan administrator with the PBGC. As of the effective date of the employer's withdrawal, the PBGC shall establish the employer's share of the plan's unfunded vested present values, if any. If any unfunded vested present values are attributed to the employer, the employer must either post a bond with the PBGC in an amount equivalent to 150 percent of the amount of the PBGC determined unfunded vested present value or transfer funds under trusteeship to the PBGC in an amount equal to the unfunded present value (but not in excess of 30 percent of the employer's net worth). The amount of the bond or the transferred funds are applied to provide for the

---

[2] See page 65.

unfunded vested present value if the plan is terminated within the five-year period commencing with the employer's withdrawal. If an employer that is not a substantial employer withdraws from the plan, any unfunded vested present values relating to the employees of such employer must be borne by the plan and the remaining contributing employers. As a consequence, the joint trust pension plan may wish to have specific provisions requiring the forfeiture of past service benefits in such circumstances in order to limit the extent of the unfunded vested present values relating to the employees of a withdrawn employer.[3]

The employer's contingent liability depends on its share of the excess of the actuarial present value of the insured vested benefits over the assets of the plan, as determined by the PBGC. Therefore, the trustees of a joint trust pension plan may restrict the amount of potential liability by limiting, as much as possible, the vested benefit to the extent allowed under ERISA. For example, a plan may not provide for the accrual of past service benefits and restrict benefit accruals to a level allowed under ERISA's minimum accrual rules. Under such an arrangement, past service benefits may be allowed only to participants who achieve retirement eligibility. It is also noteworthy that the contingent liability is limited to 30 percent of the employer's net worth, which means that financially healthy employers can be penalized when compared to employers near or in bankruptcy, and this offends many individuals' sense of equity.

As is apparent, the contingent employer liability arises only when (1) a pension plan is terminated, and (2) at the time of termination, the plan assets are not sufficient to provide the guaranteed vested benefits. Even though this liability is contingent on these events, it can be significant. If a substantial employer withdraws from a plan, other employers may decide to withdraw from the plan to force a plan termination before the end of the five-year period following the substantial employer's withdrawal. This action might relieve such employers from the financial burden which might be imposed by the withdrawing substantial employer whose liabilities would be abated if the plan does not terminate before the end of the five-year period following withdrawal.

---

[3] See page 65 and the discussion of suggested limits which should be imposed on the past service liability of an employer which withdraws from the plan.

Conditions Causing Withdrawal of an Employer

Employers who contribute to joint trust plans generally do not unilaterally join the plan, set the level of benefits, or withdraw from the plan. Employers usually join such a plan as a result of entering into a collective bargaining agreement that specifies the basis for determining the amount of the employer contributions to the plan. Also, the employer does not fix the level of plan benefits: the board of trustees adopts a plan benefit structure after receiving alternate recommendations by an actuary. Finally, the employer does not necessarily control the conditions governing withdrawal from a plan.

The withdrawal of a contributing employer can be caused by many factors unrelated to the employer's interest in or desire for terminating contributions to a joint trust plan. For example, a bargaining agreement requiring contributions to the plan may not be renewed because the union is de-certified as the representative of the employees or the employer may go into bankruptcy. On the other hand, the union membership may demand the termination of pension contributions because the union membership is comprised of young employees who are not interested in pension contributions. Finally, the employer may merely determine to terminate the business for basic profit reasons.

From an actuarial viewpoint, the contingent employer liability problems of joint trust plans can be minimized (but not eliminated) by a judicious selection of a cost method and amortization schedule for a plan's unfunded supplemental present values. For instance, the actuary should seriously consider adoption of an amortization schedule substantially shorter than the 40-year period allowed under ERISA for benefit improvements and, possibly, to amortize experience losses over a shorter period than experience gains. In addition, the actuary should actively monitor plan and industry experience trends and revise actuarial assumptions, as needed, not only to add assurance that the plan participants will receive the expected benefits but also to provide that the contributing employers will have reasonable assurance that the bargained contributions will, in fact, fund all expected benefits.

CHAPTER 10

REPORTING AND DISCLOSURE

PRE-ERISA

Prior to 1958, federal regulation of pension plans rested in the hands of the Internal Revenue Service (IRS) as the tax collecting agency and enforcer of the Internal Revenue Code. Under the Code, a pension plan could enjoy substantial tax advantages, including (1) the deductibility of employer contributions, (2) tax-free investment income, and (3) the deferral of the income taxation of plan beneficiaries until benefits are actually paid to them.[1] To achieve these tax advantages, a plan had to be found to be qualified by the IRS. The IRS examined pension plans to prevent the discrimination prohibited by the Code in favor of shareholders, officers, supervisors, and highly compensated employees and to protect against excessive tax deductions that would reduce the amount of revenue collected. In general, the supervision exercised by the IRS had little effect on the operation of joint trust pension plans and little impact on the protection of individual benefit rights. In fact, with the emphasis on tax collection, the IRS may have discouraged adequate funding of pension plan obligations.

The Labor-Management Relations Act of 1947 (often referred to as the Taft-Hartley Act) did impose certain restrictions on union negotiated pension trusts, especially the requirement that such trusts be jointly managed by an equal number of employer

---

[1] In addition there are certain other estate and gift tax considerations related to pension plans.

and union trustees. Employer contributions could not be made directly to the union or its representative but had to be made to such a jointly administered trust, or to a life insurance company under a contract issued to the employer making the contributions. The Taft-Hartley Act offered some general protection, especially with respect to the assets of a plan, but no specific protection of the rights of individuals.

In 1958, Congress passed the Federal Welfare and Pension Plans Disclosure Act (WPPDA). The act was the response of Congress to the uncovering, by the Senate Subcommittee on Labor, of unsavory practices of some employee benefit plans. The investigation brought to light speculative investments, excessive commissions, and fraudulent conversion of plan funds. While the act required the filing of certain reports with the Department of Labor, the thrust of the law was to provide covered employees with general information on the benefit provisions of a plan and its financial operations so that they could watch over their own plan. In other words, the burden of protecting their rights was basically on the shoulders of plan participants themselves.

Under the WPPDA, the administrator of a plan covering more than 25 employees had to report to the Secretary of Labor information concerning the provisions of the plan and to file copies of plan documents. The administrator was also required to file with the Secretary annual reports on the financial dealings of the plan. These documents were to be made available to plan participants only upon their request. In 1962 the act was amended to give the Secretary of Labor broader but still limited responsibility and authority. The act made embezzlement and kickbacks with respect to employee benefit plans federal crimes. The Secretary of Labor was authorized to conduct investigations to uncover violations of the act. However, the scope of the Labor Department's responsibility was basically limited to protecting the assets accumulated by the plan. For example, bonding of persons handling plan funds was required. But there were no standards for the proper conduct of the plan's affairs in areas other than asset management. The courts found that cases charging improper conduct of plan trustees in, say, changing the plan's eligibility rules, had no standing under the WPPDA.

In the absence of federal minimum standards for plan

provisions relating to benefit rights, the Labor Department had no responsibility to protect the benefit rights of individual participants. In fact, prior to ERISA, requirements to protect participants were very limited. For example, the Internal Revenue Code did not require the vesting of accrued pension benefits after a certain number of years of service or the attainment of a specified age. The IRS often did require vesting provisions, but only as an extension of their obligation to prevent the bulk of pension plan contributions from going to an employer's highly compensated employees. Generally, these requirements were imposed only on smaller pension plans.

Eventually, the inadequacies of federal regulation became apparent, and the seeds of comprehensive reform were planted by the report of the President's Committee on Corporate Pension Funds completed in 1964, to come to fruition in the Employee Retirement Income Security Act of 1974 (ERISA). ERISA substantially improves the protection of participant rights not only by broad requirements for disclosure to participants but also by setting minimum standards for eligibility, vesting and benefit accrual provisions and for funding. In addition, the act vastly increases the responsibilities of the IRS and the Department of Labor for the proper operation of plans. The Department of Labor is charged with very specific duties in the enforcement of the requirements of ERISA and is empowered to intervene or bring suit to protect the rights of participants with or without the action of the participants themselves.

POST-ERISA

One of the aspects of ERISA that makes actual compliance with the law so difficult is the dual jurisdiction of the Department of Labor and Treasury Department. This dual jurisdiction is the result of the involvement in ERISA's drafting by both the labor and the tax committees of both houses of Congress. Congress declared in ERISA Section 2(c) that it was the policy of the act to protect both the "Federal taxing power, and the interests of participants in private pension plans. . . ." While everyone recognizes that both the tax consequences of plans and participant benefit rights are of great importance, dual jurisdiction by two federal agencies has resulted in the creation of a substantial federal bureaucracy and long delays in the issuance of regulations in significant areas of ERISA.

In early 1977, Representatives Dent and Erlenborn, ranking members of the House Labor Committee and two of the architects of ERISA, introduced a bill to establish a single federal agency to regulate benefit plans to simplify such regulation. Dual regulation is seen to be especially cumbersome for smaller pension plans which cannot afford the added expense of overlapping federal regulation. Since dual regulation has also caused delays in the issuance of regulations and the approval of exceptions, it has also been a burden on larger plans. Under ERISA, administrative costs have increased as much as 50 percent to 100 percent, according to many professional observers. In joint trust pension plans, increases in administrative costs reduce the funds otherwise available to provide benefits. Thus, it is in the long-range interest of participants as a whole to reduce expenses related to federal regulation to the minimum level possible, while maintaining the ability to effectively protect the rights of participants to information and benefits.

Title I of ERISA, "Protection of Employee Benefit Rights," basically sets forth the duties of plan administrators with respect to disclosure, participation, vesting and funding, fiduciary responsibility, and the related duties of the Department of Labor for administration and enforcement. The provisions relating to participation, vesting and funding essentially duplicate similar provisions of Title II of ERISA, which are amendments to the Internal Revenue Code. The basic obligation of the Labor Department with respect to participation and vesting are to provide regulations relating to determination of hours of service for purposes of the application of the rules embodied in the law. Regulations on minimum standards for employee pension benefit plans with respect to participation and vesting were published in the *Federal Register* on December 27, 1976.[2]

In ERISA, Part 3, "Funding," of Title I is a counterpart of Section 1013 of Title II which adds Section 412, "Minimum Funding Standards," to the Internal Revenue Code. While the new

---

[2] Details on these rules will be found in pages 50–57 and 76–99.

minimum funding standards are set forth in the Labor Department's title because of the history of the legislation, the Labor Department has no specific duties with respect to enforcement of funding standards, which is left in the hands of the Internal Revenue Service. The annual certification by the enrolled actuary of the compliance of the plan with the minimum funding standards of ERISA is to be reported to the IRS on Schedule B of Form 5500, the annual report. However, the extent to which the Labor Department will examine compliance with the minimum funding standards is unclear at this time. It appears that if participants wish to question the funding security of their benefit program, the Department of Labor would assist participants in getting their questions answered.

Part 1, "Reporting and Disclosure," Subtitle B of Title I of ERISA, deals with reporting and disclosure with respect to both participants and the Department of Labor. By enforcing compliance with this portion of ERISA, the Department of Labor can oversee the information participants receive about their benefit programs. Subtitle B provides for a repeal of the limited reporting requirements of the Welfare and Pension Plans Disclosure Act and replaces them with substantial requirements for reporting directly to participants as well as to the Department.

Summary Plan Description

The summary plan description is the basic document required by ERISA to inform participants of the significant provisions of the pension plan which provide and protect benefit rights. Basically, the law requires that the summary plan description be distributed within 120 days after a new plan becomes subject to the reporting and disclosure requirements, and to each new participant within 90 days after the covered employee becomes a participant. Because the underlying collective bargaining agreements often require employer contributions to begin with the first covered hour, joint trust pension plans that do not require any hours of service prior to participation must provide for immediate participation by covered employees. Thus, the administrator must provide a system for the prompt distribution of the summary plan description after notice is received of a new covered employee.

Material modifications in the plan must be reported to the participants and the Department of Labor within 210 days after the end of the plan year in which the change is adopted. The summary plan description must be republished every five years, if changes have occurred within that period. Even if there are no changes, the document must be republished within ten years.

The Labor Department does not prescribe a form for the summary plan description but by regulation has established substantial requirements as to what must be included. A primary requirement is that the summary plan description be written in a manner calculated to be understood by the participants. It is not clear to what extent the Department of Labor will actually examine the filed summary plan descriptions to see how this requirement is met. However, a plan still has substantial freedom in preparing the format and style of the summary plan description. The Department of Labor has issued regulations concerning the duties of the plan administrator to communicate in a language other than English for those plans where a substantial number of participants have another primary language. This issue may have a substantial impact on joint benefit plans, especially among plans covering employees in the food processing and agricultural industries where a substantial number of participants speak primarily Spanish.

Another requirement for the summary plan description that will be significant for joint trust pension plans is the requirement that a participant "bill of rights" be published in the summary plan description. This requirement provides for clear notification of the protective rights under ERISA for participants with respect to obtaining information and documents concerning the plan, including documents filed with the Department of Labor. The bill of rights must contain a statement that documents will be provided upon written request and at a reasonable charge. The statement must indicate the place where documents may be examined without charge. The bill of rights must also include a statement of the rights of participants to file suit in a federal court if any of the required materials are not received within 30 days of the request, unless the materials were not sent for reasons beyond the control of the administrator. A court may require the plan administrator to pay up to $100 for each day's delay until the materials are received.

The bill of rights must also discuss the duties of the plan's fiduciary to act solely in the interest of the plan participants, and with prudence. Fiduciaries who violate requirements under ERISA may be removed, and they may be required personally to make good any losses they may have caused the plan. Furthermore, the employer may not take any action against participants to prevent them from obtaining pension benefits or from exercising any rights under ERISA. Finally, participants are advised that they may file suit in a state or federal court if they are improperly denied a pension benefit in full or in part. If a plan's fiduciary is misusing the pension fund, participants have a right to file suit in a federal court or request the assistance of the Department of Labor. If participants are successful in the suit, the court may decide to require the defending party to pay the legal costs incurred by the participants. Also, if participants have any question about the bill of rights, they are encouraged to contact the plan administrator or the nearest Area Office of the Labor Management Services Administration, Department of Labor. Thus, ERISA gives the Department of Labor substantial power to provide active assistance to an employee who has been wrongfully deprived of benefits or plan information.

The summary plan description must also include a general statement with respect to the coverage of the plan's benefits by the PBGC. The participant must be told that more information on the PBGC's insurance protection and its limitations is available from the plan administrator or the PBGC.

The summary plan description must explain to a participant how to present a claim for benefits or appeal a denial of benefits and also where to contact the plan administrator. Finally the trustees of the plan must be listed as well as the agent for service of legal process, the IRS Employer Identification Number of the Plan, and the Plan Number.

Plan Description

ERISA also requires that a formal plan description be prepared on the Form EBS-1 designed by the Department of Labor. In general, the plan description is to be filed within 120 days after the plan is established. The description need not be distributed to participants but must be made available upon request. Previously the EBS-1 was required to be refiled within 60 days after the adoption of a material modification; current regulations delete this requirement. However, material modifications to the plan reported to participants as discussed above must be reported to the Department of Labor.

In any event, the formal plan description on Form EBS-1 must be updated to reflect changes since the last plan description was filed and must be filed with the Department of Labor but no more frequently than once every five years.

The initial version of the Form EBS-1 was long and required answers in narrative form to questions on plan provisions. In February 1976 the Department published a revised form that is shorter and simpler to complete because answers to the questions are indicated by checking the appropriate preprinted answer.

Annual Report

The new annual report mandated by ERISA for plans with at least 100 participants requires information concerning the financial operations of the plan, similar to the information required by Form D-2 under the Welfare and Pension Plan Disclosure Act. However, the amount of information disclosed has been greatly increased. The annual report form has been prepared jointly by the Department of Labor, the IRS, and the PBGC and is designated "Form 5500." A Schedule A requests information concerning any insurance contracts used to fund the benefits of the plan. A Schedule B, "Actuarial Information," embodies the certification of the plan's enrolled actuary with respect to the compliance of the plan with the minimum funding standards. In addition, a Schedule SSA reports any vested deferred benefits of terminated participants. The annual report form for joint trust benefit plans together with the schedules described above must be filed with the IRS on or before the last day of the seventh month following the close of the plan year, subject to any extensions. Only a single annual report form must be filed with respect to a multiemployer plan and the contributing employers need not file a report with respect to such a plan.

Form 5500 stipulates that information must be included with respect to compliance with various provisions of ERISA. The form for the annual report requires information as to any decreases in the number of active participants in order to reveal whether a reportable event has occurred with respect to a substantial decline in the number of active participants. The form also asks whether the plan has terminated or whether a resolution to terminate the plan or merge with another plan has been adopted. It also requests information concerning the payment of compensation from the plan, directly or indirectly, to any person who rendered service to the plan. Details of any transaction involving plan assets with a person known to be a "party-in-interest" is requested. The form also questions whether there has been any change since the last report with respect to the plan's trustees, accountant, insurance company, enrolled actuary, administrator, investment manager, or custodian. If so, the changes must be explained in space provided in the form. Presumably, this information is to be examined by the Department of Labor and the Secretary of the Treasury to determine whether the interests of the plan participants have been adversely affected.

There has traditionally been much difficulty in developing accurate updated census data for joint trust pension plans. This is especially true where covered employees work for numerous participating employers as in the construction industry, and where a plan has perennial problems with delinquent reporting by employers. Consequently, joint trust pension plans will have to expend a great deal of administrative effort and incur substantially increased expenses to develop accurate information for inclusion in the annual report within the deadlines established by the federal agencies.

Another significant requirement of the annual report is the requirement that for plans covering at least 100 participants, there must be attached an accountant's opinion as to the fairness of presentation of the financial statements made with respect to the operations of the pension plan. This requirement is intended to protect the participants by requiring a certification as to the assets and income statement reported by the plan administrator. At this date the Financial Accounting Standards Board (FASB) has published a discussion paper on the accounting principles and practices for pension plans. Among other things, the proposed rules would require a plan's assets to be valued at market, even though the resulting asset values may be substantially different from the actuarial value of assets used by the plan's enrolled actuary as he or she measures the funding status of plans. In addition, the proposed rules would establish a standard for the mortality and investment earnings rate assumptions which would be based on the PBGC's published tables and the use of the accrued benefit cost method. No provision for employee turnover discount would be allowed for measuring the value of earned benefits for nonvested participants. These accounting rules, if adopted, will undoubtedly create great confusion among those plan participants who discover that the funding of the plan's benefits will be measured quite differently by the accountant and the actuary.

Summary Annual Report

While the complete annual report is to be filed with the federal government and must be made available to plan participants upon request, ERISA requires that the rather voluminous annual report be summarized for participants and distributed to them. For 1976 and later, the summary annual report is to be distributed within nine months following the end of the plan year. Preferably, the summary annual report will be sent to participants by first-class mail; or, if first-class mail is not used, the administrator must guarantee return postage and remail, first class, any reports returned with address corrections. Alternatively, the report may be distributed by the contributing employers to active participants in person or with payroll checks. The report may also be published in a union or employer newsletter or paper if the distribution list is comprehensive and maintained on an up-to-date basis. In any event, the method of distribution must be reasonably calculated to reach all participants and beneficiaries to whom it is required to be distributed.

One of the great problems encountered to date by joint trust pension plans with these several requirements is the difficulty of the trustees in ensuring delivery of all the information required to be distributed to participants. Often, especially in seasonal employment situations, an address file of employees is difficult or impossible to maintain. Many seasonal employees are almost nomadic in nature; they work a short time in one location and then move on to other employment. Although regulations allow trustees to request the contributing employers to deliver summary plan descriptions and summary annual reports to employees, it is questionable that the trustees can actually force employers to do so, especially without compensation to the employers for the special services rendered on behalf of the joint trust pension plan. However, the local unions which represent the participating employees may be helpful in assisting the trustees in the distribution of information to employees—through the union newsletter, by making summary plan descriptions available at local union offices, and by their distribution at local union meetings.

Recognizing the difficulties that joint trust pension plans face in mailing summary annual reports to participants, the Labor Department modified, at least temporarily, the original distribution requirements for these reports. Basically, the temporary regulation required, for the plan year beginning in 1975, that the plan make good faith efforts to distribute the summary to participants not receiving benefits—the administrator is expected to have available a complete mailing list of those persons receiving benefits. For the summary report for plan year 1975 (for calendar-year plans), the deadline was February 15, 1977. By that date, the plan administrator was either to use one of the basic methods of distribution, or, alternatively, to provide sufficient copies to the contributing employers, the unions, or both, for personal distribution to active participants. While it is to be hoped the special recognition of the distribution problems of joint trust plans will be continued in the future, it appears that in the long run plan administrators will have the burden of maintaining up-to-date address files of active and terminated participants and beneficiaries.

Reporting of Individual Benefit Rights

The four documents that were briefly described above are required by ERISA to give general information to participants concerning plan provisions and the financial operations of the plan. In addition, ERISA provides for the right of participants to receive specific information as to their individual benefit rights under the plan. Participants are entitled to receive, upon request, not more than once every 12 months, a statement of accrued pension benefits and either the amount of benefit in which they have a vested right or the date by which they would achieve vested status. The plan administrator is obligated to respond within 30 days of the written request. Section 105(d) of ERISA states that this requirement will be applicable to multiemployer plans as provided in regulations to be issued by the Department of Labor in coordination with the Department of the Treasury.[3]

While ERISA Section 105(a) does provide that the information is to be provided on the basis of the latest available information, it is hoped that the regulations to be issued will recognize the special problems of joint trust pension plans in meeting the requirement.[4] It would be very helpful if regulations will allow the reporting of individual participant benefit rights based upon reasonable but unverified data, such as the date of union membership or the past service reported by the participant, with the proviso that the actual past service benefit according to the terms of the plan will be determined only upon vested termination or retirement. It would seem desirable that joint trust pension plans be permitted to avoid the needless expense of verifying past service history for the many participants who will terminate service without any vested right to a benefit.

ERISA (Section 1031) also requires that upon a participant's separation "from service covered by the plan," any vested deferred rights must be reported to the IRS and the participant. The IRS is to transmit this information to the Social Security Administration for inclusion with the participant's social security records. This requirement provides substantial protection to terminated participants in that when they apply for social security benefits, they will be reminded of the amount of their vested deferred benefit and the name of the plan that owes it to them. This provision makes it more likely that vested participants will actually receive the benefits to which they are entitled.

While the reporting of deferred vested benefits has a very worthwhile purpose, the limitations on the quality of information available from the records of joint trust pension plans should be

---

[3] See page 118 for additional discussion.
[4] See pages 123–25 for a discussion of these special problems.

recognized.[5] In particular, it is often difficult to determine on a timely basis whether, in fact, a participant has actually terminated service or is merely temporarily absent from covered employment. For example, a participant for whom no covered hours are reported in the latter part of a year may have transferred to employment with another participating employer who has not reported the employee by the end of the plan year. Also, a covered employee could have been promoted out of the bargaining unit to a noncovered supervisory position with his or her employer. Even though this contiguous employment with the same employer has to be counted for vesting purposes, the plan administrator may have been notified that the employee terminated.

ERISA's break-in-service rules also cause difficulties in this area. These rules provide that an employee who is a vested participant has an unlimited time to return to covered employment and be 100 percent vested in all benefits earned after reemployment. If a vested participant were to terminate service several times and a report of total vested benefit were to be filed each time, the Social Security Administration may have a confusing record of the vested benefit to which the participant is entitled. IRS regulations recognize some but not all of these administrative difficulties under joint trust pension plans.

---

[5] See pages 122–25 for more information on the notification of vested benefit rights and the related problems.

CHAPTER 11

INVESTMENT OF PLAN ASSETS

The investment practices being established by the trustees of joint trust pension plans· in the current ERISA environment are significantly different from those of past years. The impact of many factors is tending to orient investment decisions of trustees to more conservative practices. For example,

The impact of ERISA's mandatory funding standard account and the possibility of funding deficiencies resulting from sharp decreases in the values of common stock or real estate have caused trustees in many plans to reconsider their policy with respect to equity investments.

The fiduciary responsibilities of trustees require that investments be made solely in the interest of plan participants and beneficiaries and that they exercise prudence in diversifying investments to minimize losses. Consequently, many trustees are compelled to limit or eliminate investments in "socially desirable" investments (e.g., community projects, investments in the industry covered by the plan, and so forth) if other investments have a lower risk or higher rate of return.[1]

The contingent liability imposed by ERISA on contributing employers has caused employer trustees to demand faster funding of plan benefits and related assurance of adequate funding through use of more conservative investment practices, thereby minimizing the risks of contributing employers.

---

[1] See pages 20–29 for details of fiduciary responsibilities.

ERISA requires the establishment and carrying out of a funding policy, whereby the cash flow needs of the plan can be monitored so that an investment policy will be designed to reflect those needs.

ERISA's prudent man rule and the provision for shedding investment responsibility have caused greater reliance on professional investment managers.

In addition to these obvious influences that bear on the trustees' decisions concerning investment policies, a joint trust pension plan has the unique characteristic of being a defined benefit plan with a defined contribution formula since the contribution rates are set forth in the collective bargaining agreements. These characteristics, when viewed in the light of ERISA's minimum funding standards, tend to encourage trustees to establish relatively conservative investment practices because investment losses can require either reductions in benefits or increases in employer contributions, serious consequences which trustees must strive to avoid.

The following sections of this chapter discuss the development of a plan's investment policy, the methods by which trustees select investment managers, and the process of monitoring investment performance.

INVESTMENT POLICY

As trustees have become more aware of their accountability for investment results, they are seeking to improve investment performance by clearly defining an investment policy. Having a written investment policy has substantial advantages for the trustees, the investment manager, and the other professional advisors. A written policy provides a vehicle for setting forth the investment goals of the trustees. The goals can be communicated to the managers who will know the standard by which their performance will be measured. If the trustees have engaged more than one manager, the fund is more likely to achieve consistent results if all managers know what is expected of them. A written policy also is helpful in selecting managers and in determining the types and number of managers needed. For example, if the trustees determine that a range of 25 percent to 50 percent of fund assets are to be invested in bonds, they may decide to avoid a manager whose expertise is limited to stocks or they may decide to hire two managers, one to buy and hold long-term bonds and another manager to invest in common stocks and to more aggressively manage a bond portfolio. Clearly, the preparation of a written investment policy will avoid confusion and may assist in any defense the trustees may have to mount to protect themselves from personal liability. Finally, the existence of a written policy will help to explain why one type of investment was made instead of another if the investments of the trust are questioned by a participant or other interested party.

In order to develop an investment policy, the trustees must understand the unique features of their plan. For example, they must recognize the basic benefit design and whether benefit improvements are made automatically by the plan's benefit formula as contributions are increased or only after a deliberate decision to improve benefits has been made by the trustees. In the former situation, the potential cash flow demands of the plan will tend to accelerate as the plan matures. In the latter instance, the trustees exert a stronger control over the cash flow requirements of the plan. The trustees must understand the effect on investment policy of (1) the maturity of the plan and (2) the growth or decline prospects for the industry or industries covered by the plan. If a plan is 20 or 30 years old, the yearly benefit payouts may equal or exceed all employer contributions. In this situation, the fund needs a dependable flow of investment income, and the trustees are less able to make investments which might result in fluctuating portfolio values and investment income. In other words, the investment policy must reflect the cash flow position of the plan.

If a plan is relatively new, the usual actuarial cost method will result in a relatively rapid buildup of assets for investment, and the cash flow posture of the plan will allow considerable investment flexibility. Whether a given joint trust pension plan is new or mature, if short-term and, possibly, long-term cash flow projections are developed by the actuary, the trustees will be in a position to define a logical investment policy. This investment policy must be set forth in clear and concise written form before the trustees can develop a successful investment program.

As stated above, the written statement of investment policy is the vehicle by which the trustees communicate their philosophy to the investment manager and should be considered a vital, living document which may, and probably should, change from time to time as investment market conditions and the benefit payment pattern of the plan change over time.

A useful investment policy should resolve questions concerning:

The philosophy of the trustees regarding the long-range orientation of investments towards equity or fixed-income securities, or some specified ratio of bonds and stocks to be included in the plan's investment portfolio.

The discretion to be granted to the investment manager to execute portfolio decisions within the broad philosophical guidelines established by the trustees.

Limitations, if any, on real estate, mortgage, bond, or stock investments. For example, the need of the plan's actuary to reflect market value changes of equity type investments in each year's funding standard account may impose a practical limit on a plan's share of equity investments. Again, investments in stocks with a high degree of volatility may be strictly limited for these reasons alone even though such investments may offer the promise of a significant long-range increase in the portfolio's rate of return.

Requirements that the bond or stock holdings be listed on a national exchange; that stocks have a minimum period of continuous dividend payments; that bonds have a minimum yield rate, a maximum premium, or discount at purchase.

For bond investments: certain maturity schedules, credit ratings, types of issues, and use of convertibles.

For stock investments: the desirability of growth, cyclical, and "special situation" stocks, together with a position concerning the use of bank commingled funds, insurance company separate accounts, or mutual funds.

Portfolio diversification. For example, the number of issues and the maximum/minimum positions to be achieved in any single security or industry might be specified.

Limitations, if any, on security turnover rates.

The liquidity needed to hedge against market declines and to reflect the plan's cash flow requirements.

The generally expected level of performance of the investment manager and the frequency of performance measurement.

An integral part of an investment policy is the *performance goal*. Typically, the performance goal should be established on a basis which is related, over a reasonable time frame, to the general investment return of the market as measured by one of the broad market indices such as the Standard and Poor's Index of 500 stocks. The marketplace cannot be ignored. It is not reasonable to expect any investment manager to achieve a growth rate of 15 percent per year in common stocks in a year in which the general market goes down 10 percent! In addition, the measurement of the extent to which a performance goal is achieved requires a minimum exposure period of at least several years.

The goal, in theory, should not be related directly to the actuary's investment return assumption unless the plan's combined contribution and investment income is reasonably close to or approaching the combined level of benefit and administrative expense payments. The reason is that the actuary's investment assumption usually relates to expected long-term returns, not the current level of return on investments, and also because invested assets are often only a small fraction of the plan's actuarial liabilities. At all times the performance goal must fit a particular plan's risk tolerance: if the plan is mature and a significant portion of the investment return is needed for benefit/expense payments, the performance goal cannot be as high as for a plan with a substantial positive cash flow. In this situation, the rate of return must be highly predictable and the performance goal must be set accordingly; that is, lower, since a more conservative investment policy will be established.

If the investment policy allows substantial bond, stock, and convertible security investment, separate goals should be set for bonds and equities. For example, the bond performance goal perhaps may be geared to a return of, say, 1 percent above the average return of bank fixed-income commingled funds *or* the guaranteed rate of interest of an insurance company guaranteed investment contract. Then again, for common stocks, the goal may be set at a minimum return in excess of the Standard and Poor's 500, but perhaps not more than 15 percent to 25 percent in excess of the return of that index. To some extent, if the investment manager has full discretion to change the proportion of assets invested in bonds, stocks, and cash equivalents, the trustees may well establish a minimum average goal for realized investment return (dividends, interest, and capital gains) at an annual rate of return of 6 percent to 7 percent during any performance measurement period.

There are, of course, other approaches to setting portfolio goals; that is, comparing the fund's performance results with similar funds and, consequently, judging the manager's effectiveness according to the fund's performance rank in a comparative survey. There are numerous investment measurement firms who will prepare regular periodic comparisons of the results of a client fund with those of a universe of trust funds. However, the differences in the investment policies of different plans may invalidate the use of this technique because of different cash flow considerations, varying degrees of manager investment discretion, and so forth.

If a board of trustees gives careful thought to each of these matters and sets down in writing its policy concerning each area, an excellent foundation is established as the basis for selecting an investment manager and, once selected, for measuring and evaluating his or her performance against the established criteria.

SELECTING THE INVESTMENT MANAGER

Having established a basic investment policy, the trustees will generally request the administrative manager or one of the plan's advisors to screen prospective managers whose track record imply that they can effectively carry out the established policy. On the other hand, they may employ a firm whose principal business consists of assisting in the selection of investment managers. Regardless of the approach employed, the selection process is not very easy because experience has shown that a good past record is no *guarantee* of future success. It is important to have done well in the past, but past experience has proven that a good record alone is not sufficient. As with the selection of all other plan advisors, the reputation of the individual advisor or firm, the objective evidence of professional credentials and experience with joint trust plans, the basic policies of the firm, and the firm's continuity of professional staff and organizational backup are paramount.

There is simply no way that a professional investment manager can achieve success for a joint trust pension plan (or any other type of pension plan) unless there is a high ratio of professional talent to the funds under management, combined with a well-conceived and effectively implemented investment philosophy. Naturally, the organization should have a capacity for timely research, security trading, information processing, portfolio selection, and, consequently, client service. However, unless the organization can skillfully and efficiently motivate capable professionals to continually carry out the firm's philosophy and objectives, the investment manager will not achieve the performance the trustees desire. For example, a firm may have achieved significant success in managing an investment portfolio with an investment policy similar to that of a given joint trust pension plan, but the firm may recently have undergone a major changeover in personnel, investment practices, and basic organization. In this situation, a firm's past track record may mean little as a guide to future performance. The selection process should first involve decisions as to which firms have a good track record, a stable professional organization, and a consistent investment philosophy. Once the organizations with these characteristics have been determined, those firms which appear most compatible with the policies and philosophy of the trustees should be selected for interview.

Personal interviews are critical because they allow the trustees an opportunity to evaluate each prospective investment manager's awareness of ERISA's impact on investment policies and his or her ability to communicate investment ideas, philosophies, and practices to the trustees in a meaningful, practical manner. Besides compatibility of investment policies and practices, the compatibility of the investment manager with the board is exceedingly important.

Selection of the investment manager is merely the first in a continuing series of steps which the trustees must take to accomplish their investment goals. If the statement of the plan's investment policy is written and explicit, then the agreement with the investment manager will ensure that investment experience data will be collected in such a manner that the investment manager's performance can be monitored and evaluated in terms of compliance with the stated investment policy. Initially, the monitoring procedures may be established on a fairly frequent basis, for example, through monthly or quarterly meetings of the investment manager with the trustees or a designated trustee investment committee. Frequent initial meetings will assure that the statistical content of reports will be satisfactory and will assist in the timely elimination of any misunderstandings of investment policy. The frequency of meetings will, of course, be influenced by the size of the pension fund and by whether or not significant changes in investment strategy are being initiated. In any event, after the initial investment policy criteria have been fully understood by the investment manager and an effective communications program with the trustees has been implemented, regular meetings may be set on a quarterly or semiannual basis.

The investment manager may be a bank, an insurance company, an independent investment counselor, a management organization affiliated with a mutual fund, the investment department of a brokerage firm, or some other form of investment management firm. If the manager is other than a bank or insurance company, it must be registered under the Investment Advisors Act of 1940. A board of trustees may wish to select more than a single investment manager where there are various types of investments. For example, a large fund may have a manager specializing in real estate, an insurance company managing a guaranteed return contract, and also a professional manager of a bond and stock portfolio.

In recent years, many joint trust pension plans have moved to select insurance company guaranteed investment contracts to assure the fund of a specific minimum level of return—and some contracts have guaranteed rates as high as $9^{1}/_{2}$ percent for a period of years. This technique is being used for a portion of the assets of plans with funds in the $15–$20 million bracket and above. However, many smaller sized funds have shifted almost entirely to guaranteed investment contracts as trustees have attempted to eliminate or minimize their investment management responsibilities. Under a guaranteed investment contract, trustees can secure very substantial guaranteed rates of return and a guarantee of principal as part of the commingled general account assets of an insurance company.

Some larger pension funds have shown interest in investing in an index fund in which investments are made in a broad spectrum of common stocks such as those comprising the Standard and Poor's Index. In an index fund, the weighting of the various issues is adjusted to reflect the relative price changes of the included securities. The use of an index fund presupposes a desire to have a portion of the fund achieve exactly the investment performance of the market rather than the ability to "beat the market." Investment in an index fund for a portion of a fund may be appropriate for a fund which has a policy of long-term investment in common stocks but which would have too large a commitment to be able to get out of the market even if a downturn in common stock prices is anticipated.

Another new approach to increasing a fund's investment return is to sell call options or "calls" against stocks in the portfolio. In brief, a call involves selling the right to purchase a specific block of owned securities at a set price within a limited period of time. In return for the right to buy the stock, the purchaser pays the fund a premium which often has ranged between 5 and 10 percent of the current market value of the securities involved.

For example, suppose the fund owns 1,000 shares of a stock worth $34⅝ per share. It may be able to sell a call on the 1,000 shares at $35 per share within 90 days. The fund receives a premium of, say, $3,875 and continues to receive any dividends as long as the stock is owned. In order for the buyer of the call to make a profit, the price of the stock must rise to $38⅞ per share (i.e., the call price plus the premium). If the fund actually does sell the stock at the stated price, it breaks even. If the value of the stock rises further, the fund does not participate in the gain; however, if the manager believes the stock will rise still further, the securities can, of course, be repurchased. Usually, the fund would not sell options against stock which the manager believes in holding, but rather against a position which the manager wants to eliminate or reduce. For example, if 2,000 shares of a security are owned and the manager believes a position of only 1,000 shares would provide a more favorable portfolio mix, a call against 1,000 shares might be sold.

In practice, most options are never exercised since buyers of calls are frequently takers of large risk against the chance of a large profit. In the example cited, if the stock rises to $40 per share, the purchaser would make about a 30 percent gain within 90 days on the premium paid. If the option is not exercised, the premium represents additional income to the fund. But the risk in purchasing or holding the security has not been eliminated. The stock could fall in value below the value on the date the option is sold less the premium received, causing a paper loss to the fund. On the other hand, the stock could rise too rapidly for the position to be restored after the call is exercised and the fund would not participate in the additional gain. Nevertheless, some funds may find it advisable to sell options, especially since Congress clarified in 1976 the tax-exempt status of the premium income earned by pension funds using this additional investment avenue.

Sometimes a board may select more than one manager for the same type of investment in an attempt to stimulate competition and to obtain a greater overall portfolio performance. The concept that multiple managers are useful presumes that a fund with portfolios under separate management will receive a greater level of attention from the competing investment firms. Other groups of trustees may find it prudent to engage multiple managers to diversify investment management among firms of different philosophies or strategies. Whatever the trustees decide, they can expect each type of organization to promise performance, but within each organization there are important differences of policy, quality, and performance, and only practical experience can validate an investment manager's claims.

Some of the deficiencies of using multiple investment managers are:

If firms have differing investment strategies, their year-to-year performance comparisons may show substantial comparative differences with each other and with the general market, yet their long-term performance may be similar, making the evaluation of performance difficult.

If managers understand that their performances will probably be based on a comparison of numerical investment results, they may modify their investment strategies as the end of an observation period approaches. If a manager judges that his or her performance has been "good," decisions might not be made that would otherwise be made because of the possible decline the portfolio could suffer from a short-term market swing. On the other hand, the manager who has not done too well may change the portfolio radically in an attempt to improve apparent performance.

Each investment manager will impose investment management fees according to a schedule which declines with the size of the fund under management. Consequently, the plan will incur additional investment management costs because the fees of each separately managed portion of the fund will start at the top of the fee schedule.

MONITORING INVESTMENT PERFORMANCE

The key to effective performance monitoring is (1) timely periodic statistical analysis to disclose to trustees the effect of recent economic events and investment decisions, and (2) an annual report which provides a trail of past events for comparison with the current year's experience. The latter report should be sufficiently comprehensive for the current year results to be evaluated in relationship to historic performance, the fund's investment policy and goals, and the manager's investment strategies. Usually, these results are compared with general market trends, insurance company separate accounts with similar investment policies, the similar commingled funds of banks, and to the extent possible, with other pension funds with similar characteristics and investment objectives.

In evaluating these broad-gauge comparisons, certain basic points should be considered, for example:

Rates of return for periods of less than a single year should not be annualized to avoid confusing comparisons due to overemphasis of the effects of short-term investment performance.

The *internal rate of return* for longer time intervals should be developed to reflect the effect of capital changes during the time period under study. The internal rate of return is a level equivalent rate of return on the investment portfolio which takes into account all dividends, interest earned, and realized and unrealized capital gains and losses over the period of time being observed. Separate rates of return may be developed for stocks, bonds and other segments of an investment portfolio. This rate of return will measure the consistency of the investment manager's performance with the plan's long-term actuarial funding requirements.

The fixed income returns should be compared with, say, the returns of bank commingled bond funds because tax-exempt bonds and convertible securities will generally be excluded. Comparisons with other bond funds may be difficult because they may include few issues, and the issues themselves may change from year to year. Also, the credit rating and maturity schedules of investments held by fixed income security funds vary widely. Finally, trading volume of other than bank commingled bond funds may be light and, consequently, performance may not truly be indicative of market trends.

The common stock performance should probably be best related to the Standard and Poor's 500 Stock Index. (The Dow Jones Industrial Average reflects too limited a spectrum of companies, especially if growth stocks are emphasized in a fund's portfolio.)

The total rate of return on a pension fund, in general, has no correlation to the size of the fund, but pension plans must be categorized by their essential characteristics to develop meaningful comparisons: for example, the experience of joint trust pension plan investments should only be compared with experience of other joint trust plans with reasonably similar investment policies.

In analyzing these resulting comparisons, the actuary or an independent investment performance measuring service may apply various mathematical techniques to measure volatility patterns of common stock returns and to analyze the quarterly equity investment rates of return relative to a market index. This information, in return, can be used to develop measures of the relative deviations of the fund's performance from the index. Whatever technical methods are applied, they cannot be used to *predict* the fund's performance or to isolate in any mathematical way, the absolute impact of market risk, the portfolio's inherent risk characteristics, and the manager's skill in timing and security selection. The reasons are that no investment manager maintains a static portfolio structure and strategy in all market conditions. Therefore, the performance of any manager will fluctuate as market values rise and fall.

CONCLUDING OBSERVATIONS

Since the enactment of ERISA, trustees of joint trust pension plans have an increased awareness of their fiduciary responsibilities to perform the investment management function professionally or to hire others to do it, to formulate clear investment policies and to monitor investment performance results.

Certainly, trustees have raised the level of their understanding of how to measure investment performance. Unlike the past, the invalid comparisons of "cash yield to book value" for either stocks or bonds have been replaced by the total return principle of measuring investment performance, that is, including the effects of unrealized changes in value. Many sophisticated techniques have been developed for measuring performance and making comparative studies. But no techniques have adequately been established to identify portfolio volatility as an indicator of investment risk.

The professionalism with which trustees oversee the investment management process will be gradually improved as trustees reach out for more understanding of the financial needs of their funds through use of the actuary's cash flow projections of the fund under alternative assumptions of future investment yield possibilities.

A cash flow or population forecast study will project estimated contributions to the fund, anticipated annual expenses, and expected benefit payments. This forecast, developed from the projection of the actuary's assumptions into the future, will give the trustees and the investment manager a picture of the funds available for investment each year and the cash needs for payments out of the fund. A *population profile* will depict the changes in the age and service characteristics of the participants over a span of years, the gradually changing proportion of retirees to active participants, and the progression of the number of vested participants and their vested benefit values. If the cash flow projection also reflects the probable trends in total industry hours worked, the average yearly hours worked per plan participant, and the numbers of nonvested terminations, disability retirements, and age retirements, the future cash needs of the fund can be properly evaluated. A *financial profile* portrays the effects of investment diversification among equities, bonds, real estate, and other types of investments, and trends in the rate of return of each class of investment and of the fund as a whole. Comparison of the financial profile with other funds and general market indicators can provide a valuable indicator of the fund's ability to respond to the investment objectives of the trust.

The future offers substantial hope of using existing tools and developing new methods to provide trustees with more knowledge and insights in maintaining effective investment policies. However, neither mathematical tools nor elaborate investment performance studies and comparisons will ever be an adequate substitute for the intelligent commonsense judgments of trustees as they perform their duties of reviewing their investment policies and the performance of their investment managers.

CHAPTER 12

CRITIQUE: A LOOK INTO THE FUTURE

The reader has undoubtedly concluded that the subject of joint trust pension plans encompasses a wide range of concerns that are interwoven into the collective bargaining process, the design of the trust agreement and plan, the administration of the plan, trustee investment responsibilities, and actuarial considerations in the funding of the plan. Within this framework, ERISA has brought about revolutionary changes, exemplified by the following examples:

Some plans have operated while seriously underfunded. Under ERISA, a funding standard account must be maintained and the funding sufficiency of the plan and the costs of all benefit improvements must be certified by an enrolled actuary.

Administrative records often have been substantially incomplete, especially with regard to past service, so that statements of accrued benefits could not be readily prepared for plan participants. Today, every plan participant has a right to receive, upon request, a statement of accrued benefits and the portion of the accrual that is vested, or, if the participant is not vested, the earliest date by which benefits could become nonforfeitable.

Great numbers of employees have participated in plans for many years and never achieved vesting status. Now, every plan must have a vesting schedule at least as liberal as one of the three statutory vesting standards, and employees will always have some vested benefit rights after ten years of qualifying service.

The operations of numerous plans were essentially controlled by the union trustees because the employer trustees tended to believe that the contributing employers' responsibilities ended for all practical purposes with the making of the bargained-for contributions. ERISA's fiduciary standards have prompted employer trustees to develop a keener awareness of their continuing responsibilities to the plan participants. Also, the concern of employers regarding contingent employer liabilities has caused some employer trustees to take a more active role in trust fund management.

Plan funds often were invested, without professional advice, to create jobs for the employees in the covered industry and, sometimes, to achieve union organizing goals. In this ERISA environment, most trustees recognize the need to obtain professional investment counsel, to diversify investments and to be prudent in all their actions and authorizations of fund expenditures.

With these major changes in trust fund operations brought about by ERISA, it would be wise to pause and consider the probable future of joint trust pension plans. The near future may see a decline in their growth. A large portion of the past growth has been due to the coverage of newly organized groups because the existence of joint trust plans has provided labor unions with an effective organizing tool.

However, the proportion of workers who are unionized has been declining for many years. Furthermore, large numbers of the newly organized employee groups come from the public sector where most employees already are covered by governmental plans and, therefore, are not candidates for private plan coverage. Also, the effectiveness of a joint trust pension plan as an organizing tool has diminished, at least in the short run. The reasons rest with both the new minimum funding standards of ERISA and the problems of contingent employer liability which tend to discourage the granting of significant past service benefits to newly eligible employee groups.

In view of these considerations, perhaps the first point to consider in evaluating the probable near term future of joint trust pension plans is the entirely new climate created by ERISA. Then, several likely future influences and legislative changes can be considered which may alter the long-term development of these plans.

CLIMATE CREATED BY ERISA

Employers who become "organized" in the immediate future may argue steadfastly against participation in the type of joint trust pension plan discussed in this text, primarily because of concern over the contingent employer liability imposed by Title IV of ERISA. The employers may press for either (1) a money-purchase (or defined contribution) pension plan under joint union-employer trusteeship, but for which there is no contingent employer liability, or (2) a defined benefit corporate plan instead of a joint trust plan, under which benefits, not contributions, are negotiated, and both the operations and the investments of the plan will be controlled by the employer.

Under a defined contribution plan, the rate of employer contributions are fixed by the terms of the collective bargaining agreement, and the retirement benefits become a variable, depending on each participant's account balance, age, and sex. Under such an arrangement, each participant has an individual account established on his or her behalf and investment earnings are periodically credited to this account. This approach is simple since funds are accumulated for all active participants, and there is no actuarial complexity. However, the older union employees in the bargaining unit would recieve little or no past service benefits, and the plan would be oriented principally to the younger employees who would have rapid vesting and substantial future benefit expectations. This alternative would be unfortunate because it would foreclose opportunities for adequate retirement income for the many workers whose pension coverage does not commence until they are older and relates the retirement benefit to the level of employer contributions, the period of time during which the contributions have been made and the trust fund's investment earnings. Thus, a "money-purchase" plan precludes adequate pensions to employees who reach their normal retirement age soon after a plan is established, unless supplemental past service benefits are provided for the older employees on a defined benefit basis at the plan's inception. However, the latter technique would result in contingent employer liability which this money purchase arrangement was intended to avoid.[1]

Under a defined benefit corporate plan, unlike a joint trust pension plan, the plan's experience, especially investment performance, is directly reflected in the employer's costs, not in the levels and types of plan benefits. In other words, the employer maintains the level of benefits, not the level of contributions. Therefore, if experience is more favorable than the actuary's estimates, the effect is to reduce the employer's costs rather than to provide benefit improvements. On the other hand, of course, less favorable experience would increase employer costs since the benefit levels must be maintained. With this "maintenance of benefits" arrangement, there is a substantial lessening of the involvement of the employees in the decision making related to plan design and administration. As a modification of this approach, the union could negotiate with the employers for a jointly managed trust to provide a defined benefit plan for which the employers would agree to "maintain benefits." Under this special form of a jointly managed trust with benefits maintained by employer contributions, the union trustees remain personally involved with the plan design and administration. However, benefit levels, not contribution rates, become the subject of collective bargaining between employers and the union. The bargaining emphasis would thus be on benefit goals rather than on increases in the level of employer contributions. Unlike the situation under a single employer corporate plan, the union trustees in such a joint trust would have direct knowledge of the extent to which plan experience is more or less favorable than the initial actuarial assumptions as certified by the actuary retained on behalf of the participants. The union trustees would then knowledgeably participate in any decision regarding a decrease or increase in the level of employer contributions needed to maintain the bargained benefits.

---

[1] A comprehensive analysis of money purchase pension plans can be found in Dan M. McGill, *Fundamentals of Private Pensions* 3d ed., published for the Pension Research Council (Homewood, Ill.: Richard D. Irwin, Inc., 1975).

The immediate future also points to an increase in the number of plan mergers among existing joint trust plans. Many trustees probably will consider merging plans to accomplish several goals, some of which might be to:

Decrease the number of employers who would be classified under ERISA as "substantial employers" and, consequently, would reduce the worries over contingent employer liabilities, and

Lower the administrative expense as a percentage of the bargained-for contributions since the increased revenue base of the merged plans could allow the new administrative duties imposed by ERISA to be performed more efficiently.

One result of mergers will be a diminished influence of local unions over the design and operation of the plan. Consequently, mergers will tend to weaken the local union leadership in the eyes of the union members. (Some critics of joint trust plans may see this as a favorable trend if coupled with more active participation by management trustees.)

In addition to these possible movements away from defined benefit plans or towards the merger of plans, joint trust plans in the immediate future may adopt ultraconservative practices in many areas to reduce the risk of lawsuits against the trustees: that is, in establishing benefit levels and conditions for entitlement, in the management of the plan's investments and in the selection and retention of professional advisors. For example, in order to minimize any increase in the contingent liabilities of substantial employers, there may be a movement to (1) eliminate or measurably curtail past service benefits allowed to newly participating employee groups, or (2) restrict increases in the levels and types of plan benefits by adopting periods for funding plan liabilities that are significantly shorter than the 40 years allowed under ERISA. If this tack is followed, joint trust plans will be more conservative financially, but will not be as attractive to newly organized employee groups, and the growth of joint trust plans will decline. To make matters worse, if ultraconservative practices in other areas are adopted, there could be substantial increases in trust expenses. For example, the trustees may urge the trust's auditor to retain another actuary to independently audit the enrolled actuary's assumptions and methods or the trustees may request a periodic peer review of all professional advisors to obtain a greater degree of insulation from possible claims that the trustees have not acted prudently. Certainly, the trustees have a responsibility to monitor the performance of their investment advisors, but it does not require much imagination to foresee that some trustees will generalize this responsibility and monitor all professionals.

FUTURE INFLUENCES

There have been criticisms of joint trust pension plans by union members, the federal government, and others. There have been calls for fundamental changes in existing laws or additional federal laws and regulations to eliminate the alleged abuses. For example, suggested changes include amending the Taft-Hartley Act to require independent trustees, representing neither the unions nor employers; changing federal law to impose even more rigid fiduciary responsibilities than ERISA requires; and action by the federal government to take over the operations of these plans.[2]

There can be little question about the motives behind federal involvement with joint trust pension plans. Some plans have been badly underfunded and have verged on collapse. Record keeping has often been extremely weak, and there is widespread knowledge of some breaches in trustee fiduciary responsibilities. ERISA has provided tools for stopping and preventing abuses, but the public and Congress are acutely aware of past sins and that knowledge will continue to influence future attitudes.

It is the author's opinion that ERISA provides ample protection of participant rights, especially since the Department of Labor is empowered to assist participants in lawsuits or to investigate and act to eliminate discovered abuses. Since the passage of ERISA, there have been numerous examples of the Department of Labor acting to institute legal proceedings or impose penalties where abuses have been discovered. These actions and future court decisions provide a foundation on which both existing financially sound joint trust plans and newly formed plans can construct

---

[2] See Richard Blodgett, *Conflicts of Interests: Union Pension Fund Asset Management* (New York: The Twentieth Century Fund, Inc., 1977).

their future practices and procedures. There undoubtedly will be continuing improvement in the funding, administration and investment practices of these plans as trustees, aware of their *personal* fiduciary responsibilities, assume a more effective role in fulfilling their duties and apply more objective criteria in the selection and retention of professional advisors:

There is no doubt that private pension plans will eventually be forced to include more liberal vesting rights than ERISA now mandates. Even with the improvement in vesting provisions required by ERISA, there is pressure for still earlier vesting, if not full and immediate vesting, of all benefit credits. Some commentators see the ERISA minimum vesting conditions not as a final solution to the need to protect benefit rights, but a first step toward eventually providing immediate vesting. Some have proposed a federal clearing house or "bank" where the value of even very small amounts of previously nonvested benefits would be deposited for eventual distribution to the former participants of a plan. More liberal vesting would tend to weaken the historic ties between continued union membership and adequate retirement benefits. Joint trust pension plans, by providing continuity of coverage if an employee transfers among participating employers or to another area plan with a reciprocity agreement, have provided more benefit protection for workers than single employer plans. However, if plans were required to provide immediate vesting of all pension credits, then the trustees would be forced either to reduce the level of future benefits, and perhaps eliminate valuable ancillary benefits provided upon death or disability, *or* to obtain substantial increases in contributions to maintain current pension benefit levels.

If and when more liberal vesting standards are required for pension plans, the pressure may build to change existing joint trust plans to money purchase type plans since it may seem impractical to continue defined benefit plans. However, even though future legislation may require further liberalizations in vesting, joint trust pension plans with defined benefits will survive: these plans will still be able to provide some form of past service credits to older employees of newly organized groups and will continue to contain features that protect earned benefits in a manner that is not possible under other forms of private pension plans. Because joint trust plans cover employees of many employers in a wide geographical area and often have reciprocity arrangements with plans in other areas, many employees can change jobs within the same industry without ever losing their pension benefit credits. The reciprocity agreements can assist employees in retaining past service benefit rights which might otherwise be lost, and in achieving early retirement and other benefit rights which might not otherwise be available.

It is the author's opinion that the simplistic approach to resolving perceived problems by switching to money purchase pension plans will never adequately meet the needs of unionized employees for flexible and adequate retirement programs. Mergers may solve certain financial problems, but they will reduce the effective voice of many union leaders, producing unsatisfactory results. Joint trust defined benefit pension plans, with some legislative relief, will demonstrate the flexibility to weather the many storms created by ERISA and to accommodate future legislated liberalizations in vesting standards and will continue to be one of the prime thrusts in the development of private pension plans in this country.

LEGISLATIVE CHANGES NEEDED

However, the problems facing joint trust plans are great and legislative changes will be necessary. Among several legislative changes needed, the following appear to the author as paramount in assisting joint trust pension plans more effectively to provide workers with the pension coverage they must achieve:

1. *Contingent employer liability.* Employers participating in joint trust plans must be able to insulate themselves from burdensome potential liabilities over which they may have little or no control. Perhaps this goal can be achieved through federal insurance at reasonable cost; private insurance does not appear to be practical under any circumstance. Perhaps the resolution of the employer concerns could be minimized if pre-ERISA unfunded liabilities could be insured by governmental funds. Of course, this type of government insurance involves problems. First, it involves potentially enormous federal expenditures at a time when most people want to stabilize or

even reduce the federal budget or to limit new federal programs. Secondly, if funds for this insurance were to come out of general revenue, individual and corporate taxpayers, some without pension plans of their own, would be subsidizing the pensions of others and might view the resulting taxation to be inequitable.

Perhaps a solution to the problem of the contingent employer liability would be to limit the PBGC insurance of unfunded benefits to those benefits that have been earned after the effective date of ERISA. Thus, the potential claim on employer net worth would be limited to increases in liabilities which the employers agreed to with knowledge of the new contingent employer liability provisions of ERISA which have so radically changed the nature of the employers' responsibility for pension benefits.

The most logical solution to the contingent employer liability problem would be to eliminate this onerous form of liability entirely, by restructuring the vested benefits which are guaranteed by the PBGC. Some current proposals would involve revision of the PBGC benefit guarantees so that they relate to the funding policy of a joint trust pension plan. If the unfunded actuarial liabilities were being funded over, say, a ten-year period (the shortest period for which employer contributions are tax-deductible) the plan's vested benefits might be fully guaranteed. However, if the unfunded liabilities were being funded over a longer period (the maximum period is 40 years), the PBGC guarantees would be scaled down. If this tack were adopted, the PBGC would have to establish consistent and uniform sets of actuarial assumptions and methods to measure the extent of the vested benefit guarantees, but the contributing employers would be relieved of liabilities over which they often have no control. On the other hand, the trustees would continue to control all facets of the plan's operation, and the funding policy would strongly influence the extent to which the vested benefits would be guaranteed if the plan terminates.

2. *Trust fund investments.* Investments in the same industry in any form of security, real estate, and even with "parties-in-interest" should be possible if the investment is per se "prudent." ERISA should be amended to allow greater investment

flexibility, subject to federal regulation on a streamlined basis. Such investment flexibility would allow the investment manager of a joint trust plan to appraise investment opportunities purely on merit, without the artificial restrictions imposed by "parties-in-interest" concerns. Consequently, the investment manager would be more readily able to carry out effectively the plan's investment policy.

3. *Pension contributions as a priority item in bankruptcy proceedings.* Employer contributions should be considered as a form of employee wages so that the benefits earned and vesting rights accrued can be secured, to the extent possible, by the contributions expected by the plan. If an employer participating in a joint trust plan goes bankrupt while owing contributions to the plan, the plan should have a priority claim on the net worth of the employer to the extent of the unpaid contributions. The reason is that the plan may be obliged to continue providing benefits for the employer's former employees with respect to service rendered with the employer even though contributions would otherwise not be received. The bankruptcy laws would need revision to accommodate this important financial protection for joint trust plans. This type of change would assist joint trust plans in maintaining the sound funding of earned benefits and would also strengthen the power of the plans to collect delinquent employer contributions.

4. *A consolidation of federal regulation.* The Department of Labor, the Treasury Department, and the Pension Benefit Guaranty Corporation have established reporting requirements and have published implementing regulations. Action must be taken soon to reduce the resulting administrative burden. As required by ERISA, the various independent agencies have made substantial efforts to coordinate their overlapping responsibilities. For example, there is now a single annual report form (Form 5500) which is filed with the IRS but which is used by the DOL and PBGC. This form replaces separate pre-ERISA reports for the IRS and DOL. However, further steps must be taken to reduce the burdensome and confusing administration and paperwork which results from having separate federal agencies with overlapping responsibilities. Some

legislators and experts have urged the establishment of a single regulatory agency. Critics claim that this solution is not practical. The significant tax aspects of pension plans requires the continued IRS responsibility for tax qualification purposes. In any event, in order to simplify the administration and regulation of pension plans, at least a realignment of regulatory responsibility should be considered as well as a minimization of dual regulation. Legislative action modifying ERISA would be required. In addition, the *Daniel* case[3] has introduced the possibility of regulation by the Securities and Exchange Commission of additional aspects of pension plan operations. Legislation may be necessary to eliminate the intrusion of another federal agency into an already overly complex regulatory process.

SUMMARY

The enactment and implementation of ERISA clearly have brought about significant improvements in participant benefit rights and protections, but, for the numerous reasons cited, enactment of this law has stunted the growth of joint trust defined benefit pension plans. Congress is just awakening to an understanding of the great administrative burdens imposed by ERISA and also the serious flaws in the structure of plan termination insurance. The tragic impact on joint trust plans of this "insurance scheme" is not limited to employer concerns over contingent employer liabilities. The annual per capita premium rate charged for this insurance may also have to increase to $10, $20, or even $50 to enable the PBGC to meet its obligations. Fundamental legislative changes must be made.

In its rush to pass ERISA and simultaneously solve all the problems of private pension plans, Congress dealt a crippling blow to the growth potential of all private defined benefit pension plans. Hopefully, after recognizing the mounting evidence of the problems resulting from this act, Congress will legislate the changes required to allow the continued development and growth of private defined benefit plans, and especially joint trust pension plans.

---

[3] *John Daniel, for himself and on behalf of all others similarly situated* v. *International Brotherhood of Teamsters, et al.* United States District Court, Northern District of Illinois, Eastern Division No. 74 C 2865, March 1, 1976.

APPENDIX A

SPECIMEN TRUST AGREEMENT

XYZ WORKERS PENSION FUND AGREEMENT AND DECLARATION OF TRUST

Contents

I. INTRODUCTION

    A. *Name.* The official name of the Trust created hereby, which is generally referred to hereafter as the "Trust," is: XYZ WORKERS PENSION FUND AGREEMENT AND DECLARATION OF TRUST. It was originally established on December 15, 1965.

    B. *Purpose.* It is the purpose of this Trust to use and invest the contributions received by it for the exclusive purpose of providing benefits to Participants and their Beneficiaries and defraying reasonable expenses of administration. This purpose shall be accomplished in accordance with all applicable laws, specifically including the Employee Retirement Income Security Act of 1974 (ERISA), as amended from time to time. The Trust shall be irrevocable (although it may be terminated as hereafter provided), and no part of its corpus or income shall ever revert to or inure to the benefit of any contributing employer except for the return of erroneous contributions as provided hereafter.

    C. *Benefits.* The type of benefits to be provided, which are referred to hereafter as the "benefits," are pension benefits and other benefits incidental thereto.

        The specific benefits from time to time provided, and the eligibility requirements, therefore, are set forth in one or more documents entitled: "XYZ WORKERS PENSION PLAN," referred to hereafter as the "Plan." The Plan may include more than one set of benefits and eligibility rules to take account of different contribution rates or other pertinent factors. The Plan, as amended from time to time, is incorporated herein by reference and is a part of this Trust Agreement.

II. DEFINITIONS

    The following words and phrases have the special meanings indicated. Other words and phrases with special meanings are defined where they first appear unless their meaning is apparent from the context.

A. "Board of Trustees" means the group of individuals appointed to administer the Trust as provided below. As a group they are referred to as the "Joint Board." The individual members, including any alternates when acting in place of regular members, are referred to as "Trustees."

B. "Union" means XYZ Workers International Association Local Unions No. 2, No. 22, and No. 42 and any successors thereto. It shall also include any other labor organization affiliated with the XYZ Workers International Association whose participation as a "Union" hereunder is approved by the Joint Board.

C. "Association" means each of the following: XYZ Contractors National Association, Greater Los Angeles Area Chapter; XYZ Contractors National Association, Sacramento Chapter; and XYZ Contractors National Association, San Francisco Metropolitan Area Chapter.

D. "Employer" means any business entity which is required by a collective bargaining agreement between the Union and an Association to make payments into this Trust. It also includes any of the following which agree to make contributions equivalent to those required of other Employers hereunder:

1. The Union or any labor council or other labor organization with which it is affiliated if it elects to provide benefits hereunder for its employees.

2. A qualified exempt Trust approved by the Trustees which provides for payment to this Trust when an employee is unemployed or underemployed and otherwise would lose his eligibility for benefits.

3. Any other business entity which contributes to the Trust pursuant to a written agreement with the Union and with the approval of the Joint Board.

4. Any governmental unit whose participation on behalf of its XYZ workers is approved by the Joint Board.

5. Any other business entity whose participation is

required by a final judgment of any court of competent jurisdiction.

The Joint Board may condition its approval in such manner as it deems necessary to assure the financial integrity of the Trust and equity among Employers and Participants; but failure of the Joint Board to grant such approval or agree on such conditions shall not be subject to arbitration. The Joint Board may also require any Employer to sign a subscription agreement acceptable to it before crediting the Employer's contributions or benefits attributable thereto.

E. "Pension Agreement" means any collective bargaining agreement, subscription agreement, or other written agreement approved by the Joint Board requiring contributions hereto.

F. "Participant" means any person on whose behalf contributions have been properly payable to the Trust and who either (1) is currently eligible for benefits or (2) has contributions and/or employment credited to his account by the Trust to be used in determining his or his Beneficiaries' eligibility for benefits; also any other person who may qualify as such under ERISA. "Beneficiary" means any person related to a Participant or designated by a Participant in accordance with the Plan who is or may become entitled to benefits thereunder.

G. "Plan Year" means the fiscal year on which the records of the Plan and Trust are kept.

(Note: Whenever any words are used herein in the masculine gender, they shall be construed as though they were also used in the feminine gender in all cases where they would so apply and vice versa, and wherever any words are used herein in the singular form they shall be construed as though they were also used in the plural form in all cases where they would so apply and vice versa.)

III. OBLIGATIONS OF EMPLOYERS

A. *Payment of Contributions.*   All employer contributions required by a Pension Agreement shall be payable not later than the 20th day of the month, for the immediately preceding month, and shall be payable at such place in the county where the Trust's principal place of business is located as the Joint Board may from time to time specify; payment elsewhere shall be permitted only with the Joint Board's prior written approval. Payments shall be accompanied by complete reports on forms furnished by the Trust so that the contributions can be allocated accurately. For any report period for which an Employer fails to file a report, until the proper report is filed by the Employer and accepted by the Trust, the amount due from the Employer for the report period for which the Employer has failed to file shall be deemed to be not less than the amount due pursuant to the most recent complete report filed by the Employer. The Employer may be compelled by the Trust or its assignee, by way of subpoena, civil discovery, or other legal proceeding, to prepare, submit, and file with the Trust proper reports for any period for which the Employer has previously failed to file.

B. *Delinquent Contributions.* Any Employer contribution shall be deemed delinquent if not received on or before the due date specified above. The Joint Board may, in the event of repeated delinquencies by the same Employer, make special rules applicable to the due date of said Employer's contributions and may require the Employer to post a bond or other security against further delinquencies.

It is recognized and acknowledged that the regular and timely payment of Employer contributions is essential to the efficient and fair administration of the Trust and the maintenance of Plan benefits. If Employers do not make timely payments, the Trust loses the investment return it should have received, and incurs additional administrative expense in the form of letters, telephone calls, and other collection expenses. The Trust is also delayed or prevented from processing claims by employees for benefits under the Plan. The Trust's collection expenses, loss of return on investment, and inability to pay benefits constitute damages arising from an Employer's default in making timely payments; and these damages cannot be allowed to deplete the contributions promptly paid by other Employers. It would be extremely difficult and impractical to fix the actual expense and damage to the Trust, over and above attorney's fees, for each Employer's default. Therefore, the amount of damages to the Trust resulting from any Employer's default, over and above attorney's fees, shall be presumed to be the sum of $20 per delinquency or ten percent (10%) of the amount which is delinquent, whichever is greater. Such amount shall become due and payable to the Trust as liquidated damages, and not as a penalty, on the first day of the month following the month in which the delinquency occurs, but may be waived by the Joint Board if received before that time or where the Joint Board determines there was reasonable cause for the delinquency which is not likely to recur.

Contributions and liquidated damages unpaid by the first day of the month following the month in which they are due shall bear interest from such date at the rate of seven percent (7%) per annum.

C. *Record Keeping and Audits.* Each Employer shall maintain weekly timecards, checks, and check stubs, and such other records relating to employment for which contributions are payable hereunder, sufficient (1) to determine whether it has satisfied all obligations to the Trust and (2) to permit compliance with all applicable laws. These records shall be maintained for a period of not less than seven years following the end of the calendar year in which the employment occurs. If an Employer fails to keep records adequate to determine its obligations, it shall be conclusively presumed, at the option of the Trust, that all sums paid to Participants by such Employer were wages for work for which contributions were payable to this Trust.

The Joint Board, or its authorized representatives,

may require any Employer to submit to it any information relevant to the administration of the Trust. Upon notice in writing, an Employer must permit an accountant or other authorized agent of the Trustees to enter upon the premises of such Employer during regular business hours to examine and copy such books, records, papers, timecards, tax records, and copies of Employer's State and Federal Quarterly Tax Returns as may be necessary to determine whether the Employer is making full and prompt payment of all sums required to the Trust. In the event that an examination of the Employer's records reveals that full and prompt payment of all sums due is not being made, then such Employer shall reimburse the Trust, upon demand, for the costs of said examination in addition to any other obligations it may have hereunder.

D. *Collection Actions.* The Trust may institute legal proceedings to recover or collect delinquent Employer contributions, audit costs, liquidated damages, interest, and attorney's fees, and to require the filing of required reports. Such proceedings may be instituted in the name of the Trust or the Joint Board, or the claim may be assigned to a third person for collection. The judicial district in which the particular Employer contribution is payable shall be a proper one in which to institute legal proceedings to collect all sums owing by the Employer.

The Employer shall reimburse the Trust, or its assignee, for all reasonable attorney's fees, court costs, and all other reasonable expenses incurred in connection with such suit or claim, including any and all appellate proceedings therein. It is recognized that the extent of legal services necessarily incurred in the collection of required Employer contributions may in certain cases have no relation to the fact that the amount of the delinquency is relatively small.

E. *Return of Contributions.* Employer contributions made to the Trust may not be returned to the Employer unless made as a result of a mistake of fact, and then only if the Employer requests repayment within one year after the date of the contributions. (This one-year limitation is to comply with ERISA, and should a longer period become permissible under ERISA, it shall automatically replace said one-year limitations.) If a contribution is made on behalf of a person for whom contributions are not required under the Employer's Pension Agreement, the Trust's sole obligation with respect thereto shall be to return the erroneous contribution, subject to the time limitation just set forth; provided, however, that the trust shall have the option of retaining any contributions based upon which benefit eligibility has been provided. The Trust shall not be obligated to provide benefits dependent upon such erroneous contribution and may recover from the Employer any losses resulting from benefits paid as a result of the latter's error by assigning to it any right of recovery against the recipient.

F. *Cooperation with Joint Board.*   Whenever requested by the Joint Board, the Employer will distribute to all Participants currently in its employ such information as the Joint Board deems necessary to carry out its obligations. That distribution shall be made in such manner as the Joint Board may specify and without charge to either the Participants or the Trust. Any Employer which willfully fails to comply with any such reasonable request of the Joint Board shall be liable for any penalties or damages which are thereby incurred.

G. *Limitation on Liability of Employers.*   Employers and their bargaining representatives shall have only such liabilities to the Trust as are set forth or authorized hereunder or under their Pension Agreements. They shall have no other liabilities for the operation or obligations of the Trust, nor for the failure of other Employers to fulfill their obligations to the Trust, except as specifically imposed under ERISA or other applicable laws.

IV. FIDUCIARIES

A. *General Rules.* The Joint Board and the individual Trustees who are its members shall be the "named fiduciaries" required by ERISA. Any other person shall be a fiduciary only to the extent he has discretionary authority or discretionary control respecting management of the Trust or Plan; or exercises any authority or control respecting management or disposition of Trust assets; or has any discretionary authority or discretionary responsibility in the administration of the Plan; or renders investment advice for a fee or other compensation, direct or indirect, or has any authority or responsibility to do so. Any person or group of persons may serve in more than one fiduciary capacity with respect to the Plan and Trust.

It is not intended that either the Union, or any Employer or its bargaining representative, or any attorney, accountant, broker, actuary, office personnel, professional administrator, or consultant (other than an Investment Manager) shall itself be a "fiduciary" simply as a result of performing services for the Trust pursuant to agreement with the Joint Board. Therefore, such persons shall not perform acts of the type set forth above which would make them fiduciaries except as specifically authorized by the Joint Board.

B. *Fiduciary Standards.* All fiduciaries with respect to the Plan (whether or not "named fiduciaries") shall discharge their duties solely in the interest of the Participants and Beneficiaries in furtherance of the Trust's purpose as set forth in Article I above and in accordance with the requirements of this Trust Agreement, the Plan, and ERISA. In so doing, they shall use the care, skill, prudence, and diligence under the circumstances then prevailing that a prudent man acting in a like capacity and familiar with such matters would use in the conduct of an enterprise of a like character and with like aims.

C. *Allocation of Fiduciary Responsibilities.* Fiduciary responsibilities may be allocated or delegated as follows, so long as the allocation or delegation meets the fiduciary standards set forth above and is evidenced by an appropriate resolution of the Joint Board:

1. Any responsibility to manage or control Plan assets may be allocated only among the Trustees, except insofar as such responsibility is delegated to an Investment Manager as provided hereafter.

2. Other responsibilities may be allocated or delegated to any person, but any Participant or Beneficiary whose claim for benefits is denied shall have the right to have the denial ultimately reviewed by the Joint Board itself.

D. *Liability of Fiduciaries.* In no event will a fiduciary be liable with respect to a breach of a fiduciary duty if such breach was committed before he became a fiduciary or after he ceased to be a fiduciary. Furthermore, to the fullest extent permitted by law, no fiduciary shall be liable for any act or omission of any other person. Specifically:

1. If a specific responsibility, obligation, or duty relating to control or management of Plan assets is allocated among the Trustees or any Investment Manager, then one to whom such a function has not been allocated shall not be liable either individually or as a trustee for any loss to the Trust arising from any acts or omissions on the part of those to whom such function has been allocated.

2. Upon the proper allocation or delegation of any other fiduciary responsibility, no Trustee shall be liable for the acts or omissions of the person or persons to whom such responsibility has been allocated or delegated, provided that there has been no violation of the fiduciary standards set forth above with respect to such allocation or delegation, nor with respect to the establishment or implementation of procedures relative thereto, nor in continuing the delegation.

Nothing herein shall be construed as limiting a fiduciary's liability for a breach of fiduciary responsibility of another fiduciary with respect to the Plan if (i) he knowingly participates in or undertakes to conceal an act or omission of such other fiduciary knowing it is a breach, (ii) by his failure to comply with fiduciary standards in the administration of his responsibilities making him a fiduciary, he has enabled such other fiduciary to commit a breach, or (iii) he has knowledge of a breach by such other fiduciary and he fails to make reasonable efforts under the circumstances to remedy the breach.

E. *Compensation and Expenses.* To the extent approved by the Joint Board, fiduciaries may receive reasonable compensation for services rendered by them. However, no fiduciary who already receives full-time pay from an employer or an association of employers whose employees are Participants in the Plan, or from an employee organization whose employees are Participants in the Plan, shall receive compensation for his services unless ERISA is amended to allow such payment.

To the extent authorized by the Joint Board, all fiduciaries may be reimbursed for expenses actually and properly incurred in accordance with the performance of their duties hereunder, or given an appropriate advance against such reimbursement subject to immediate repayment if the advance should exceed the amount to which they are entitled hereunder. Expenses for which reimbursement may be authorized shall include, without limitation, those incurred in attendance at meetings and other functions of the Joint Board or its committees, or in attendance at institutes, seminars, conferences, or workshops relating to matters of common interest to trusts such as this, or in defending against legal actions which do not result in a judgment that the Trustee has violated any ERISA-imposed responsibility, obligation or duty.

F. *Bonds and Insurance.* No bonds or other security shall be required of any fiduciary or other person except as required by law, but the Joint Board may direct that such other bonds be obtained as it deems appropriate for itself or others. The Joint Board may also direct that such insurance be purchased as it deems appropriate to protect itself, the Trust, or others. The cost of such bonds or insurance shall be paid by the Trust; provided, however, that any bonds or insurance purchased with Trust funds which insure against liability or losses occurring by reason of the act or omission of a fiduciary shall permit recourse by the insurer against the fiduciary in the case of a breach of a fiduciary obligation by such fiduciary. In addition, any fiduciary may acquire such additional insurance as it deems appropriate to protect itself (including, if available, a waiver of the carrier's retained right of recourse in any insurance policy purchased with Trust funds) so long as the cost of such insurance is not paid by the Trust.

V. APPOINTMENT AND PROCEDURES OF JOINT BOARD

  A. *Number of Trustees.*   The Joint Board shall be composed of an even number of individuals, half of whom shall be known as "Union Trustees" and half of whom shall be known as "Employer Trustees."

   The total authorized number of Trustees is six (6), but this number may be changed from time to time by the Joint Board, so long as the positions open to Employer Trustees and Union Trustees remain equal in number.

  B. *Method of Appointment of Union Trustees.*   Each Union which is and remains party to a collective bargaining agreement requiring contributions hereto shall appoint one Trustee to serve at its pleasure, but if it fails to do so within sixty (60) days after receiving notice of the vacancy, the remaining Union Trustees shall fill the vacancy. Furthermore, if at any time the number of Unions entitled to appoint Trustees are fewer than the number of Associations entitled to appoint Trustees, a majority of the Union Trustees shall appoint sufficient additional Union Trustees, to serve at said majority's pleasure, so that there will always be an equal number of Employer and Union Trustees. If a vacancy is not filled within ninety (90) days after it occurs, any Trustee or participant may petition the appropriate federal court to fill the vacancy. Any person appointed by the Union Trustees or a court due to failure of a Union to fill the vacancy shall serve at that Union's pleasure the same as though appointed by it.

C. *Method of Appointment of Employer Trustees.* Each Association which is and remains party to a collective bargaining agreement requiring contributions hereto shall appoint one Trustee to serve at its pleasure, but if it fails to do so within sixty (60) days after receiving notice of the vacancy, the remaining Employer Trustees shall fill the vacancy. Furthermore, if at any time the number of Associations entitled to appoint Trustees is fewer than the number of Unions entitled to appoint Trustees, a majority of the Employer Trustees shall appoint sufficient additional Employer Trustees to serve at said majority's pleasure, so that there will always be an equal number of Employer and Union Trustees. If a vacancy is not filled within ninety (90) days after it occurs, any Trustee or participant may petition the appropriate federal court to fill the vacancy. Any person appointed by the Employer Trustees or a court due to failure of an Association to fill the vacancy shall serve at that Association's pleasure the same as though appointed by it.

D. *Alternates.* If alternate Trustees are authorized by the Joint Board, the party appointing a Trustee may also appoint an alternate for such Trustee to serve at the pleasure of the appointing party. Any such appointment shall be made by written instrument delivered to the Joint Board. In the event that a Trustee is absent from a meeting of the Joint Board, or is not readily available to sign any written consent authorized hereunder, his alternate may act for him.

E. *Term of Office.* Each Trustee shall begin serving at the time specified in the instrument appointing him (or upon receipt of that instrument if it does not specify a time), but not before signing a written acceptance of his appointment. The Trustee shall serve until his successor assumes office, but shall have the right to resign at any time by written instrument delivered to the Joint Board.

F. *Officers.* The officers of the Joint Board shall be a Chairman and a Secretary, one of which offices shall always be held by an Employer Trustee and one of which shall always be held by a Union Trustee. The Joint Board may provide for such additional officers as it deems appropriate.

G. *Meetings.* The Joint Board shall determine the time and place for regular periodic meetings, which shall be held at least semiannually. Special meetings may be called by either the Chairman or Secretary or by any two Trustees upon at least five days' written notice to all other Trustees. A meeting shall be valid even if proper notice is not given if all Trustees then serving or their alternates are present or if all absent Trustees, not including absent alternates, waive notice in writing either before or after such meeting. The Joint Board may also act without a meeting by written instrument executed by all Trustees.

H. *Quorum.* To constitute a quorum, there must be present at least two of the Employer Trustees then serving and two of the Union Trustees then serving.

I. *Method of Voting.* The Employer Trustees present at any meeting shall share equally as many votes as there are authorized Employer Trustees, and the Union Trustees present at any meeting shall share equally as many votes as there are authorized Union Trustees. Any Trustee may give a written proxy to any other Trustee who is a member of his group, but the proxy may not be used if the Trustee's alternate is present at the meeting. Each group's total authorized voting power shall be cast by majority vote of the members of that group present and voting.

J. *Deadlocks and Arbitration.* A deadlock shall be deemed to have occurred with respect to any matter voted upon by the Joint Board which results in a tie vote. A deadlock shall also be deemed to have occurred if there is a tie vote among the members of either group on any matter.

In the event of a deadlock, the matter shall be submitted to arbitration upon the request of any Trustee. The Joint Board shall agree upon a person to serve as arbitrator. If an agreement is not reached within thirty (30) days of the request for arbitration, any Trustee may petition the United States District Court with jurisdiction over the area where the Trust has its principal office to appoint the arbitrator. The arbitrator shall determine the procedures to be followed in the arbitration.

All expenses incurred by the Joint Board in connection with the dispute, including legal fees, shall be paid by the Trust. No other party who may participate in the arbitration may recover his costs of advocacy unless specifically allowed by the arbitrator or required by law.

Unless otherwise prohibited hereunder, any matter within the jurisdiction of the Joint Board may be submitted to the arbitrator as provided above, but unless specifically provided elsewhere hereunder the arbitrator shall have no power to add to or subtract from, alter, or change the provisions of this Trust Agreement, the Plan, or any Pension Agreement. The decision of the arbitrator, so long as it does not go beyond the scope of his authority, shall be final and binding upon all parties to the dispute.

K. *Establishment of Administrative Office.* The Joint Board shall establish an administrative office and shall staff such office in such manner as it deems appropriate, either with its own employees or by contract with such business entity as it may select. It may also establish such additional offices as it may from time to time deem necessary.

The administrative office and personnel and costs related thereto (as well as other appropriate administrative services and costs) may be shared with other trusts subject to ERISA to reduce the expenses of administration, achieve greater efficiency, and/or provide better service to participants and their beneficiaries; the basis of sharing shall be such reasonable method as the Joint Board may approve.

L.   *Execution of Instruments.*   The Joint Board will authorize one or more of its members to execute checks drawn on any bank accounts maintained by it, or to issue checks bearing facsimile signatures of such persons. Furthermore, any two Trustees, one of whom is an Employer Trustee and one of whom is a Union Trustee, may execute any contracts or other legal documents on behalf of the Trust if so authorized by the Joint Board.

Instructions to any Custodian of Funds or Investment Manager, or other communications, shall be similarly executed or may be executed in such other manner as the Joint Board may have previously authorized.

Any person may rely on any documents executed in accordance with this provision as having been duly authorized by the Joint Board and executed in accordance with the terms of this Trust Agreement.

VI.   AUTHORITY OF JOINT BOARD

A.   *General Authority.*   Subject to its powers of allocation and delegation set forth elsewhere hereunder, the Joint Board shall have exclusive authority to control and manage the operation and administration of the Trust and its assets, and shall be the "Administrator" required by ERISA.

B. *Establishment of Plan and Claim Procedures.* The Joint Board shall establish the benefits to be provided, the eligibility requirements therefor, and all other matters appropriate to the Plan, including procedures for applying for benefits and remedies for the redress of claim denials which comply with the requirements of ERISA. It may from time to time amend any or all of the provisions of the Plan in the manner set forth hereafter.

C. *Records and Reports.* The Joint Board shall keep on file at the principal administrative office, and in such other places as may be necessary to make available all pertinent information to Participants and Beneficiaries, a copy of this Trust Agreement, the Plan, and all annual and interim reports made in connection therewith; and shall cause to be furnished to each Participant and Beneficiary all descriptions and information required by ERISA. It shall also file with the appropriate governmental agency all forms, reports, and other information required by ERISA.

Insofar as required by ERISA, the Joint Board shall make copies of all documents described above, and other documents under which the Plan is established or operated, available for examination by any Participant or Beneficiary and shall furnish copies of such documents to any Participant or Beneficiary upon written request, and may in its discretion charge such reasonable amounts therefor as are permissible under ERISA.

The Joint Board shall engage, on behalf of all Participants, an independent qualified public accountant to prepare an annual audit and give his opinion as to whether the financial statements of the Trust are presented fairly and in conformity with generally accepted accounting principles applied on a consistent basis with that of the preceding year.

The Joint Board shall also engage, on behalf of all Participants, a person enrolled as an actuary pursuant to ERISA who shall be responsible for preparing the actuarial statements required by ERISA. The actuary shall utilize such assumptions and techniques as are necessary to enable him to form an opinion as to whether the contents of the actuarial statement (1) are in the aggregate reasonably related to the experience of the Plan and to reasonable expectations and (2) represent his best estimate of anticipated experience under the Plan.

D. *Miscellaneous Powers.* The Joint Board may exercise all other lawful powers appropriate to the exercise of its authority hereunder, including the following:

1. To pay all Trust expenses;
2. To establish such rules and regulations as may be necessary in the administration of the Trust;
3. To borrow money to carry out the purposes of this Trust and to pledge, assign, or hypothecate any of the Trust assets to secure such loan;
4. To sue or be sued on behalf of this Trust. The Joint Board shall be the only necessary party plaintiff or defendant in any legal action, and service of process upon it may be made upon any Trustee;
5. To accept, compromise, arbitrate, or otherwise settle any obligation, liability, or claim involving this Trust, including, but not by way of limitation, any claim for contributions or other sums payable hereto, and to enforce or contest any other obligation, liability, or claim by appropriate legal proceeding if, in its sole discretion, it is in the interest of the Trust to do so, or to assign any such claim and allow the assignee to institute legal or arbitration proceedings in its own name to enforce collection;
6. To require any person with obligations or rights hereunder to furnish, or permit an audit of, any reasonable information, data, and documents which are pertinent in verifying the accuracy of

contributions and acting upon claims for benefits, or which are otherwise pertinent in administering this Trust.

7. To publish, file, and distribute all reports required by law;

8. To construe any of the terms or provisions of the Trust or Plan; and any such construction shall be binding on all persons concerned;

9. To determine all questions relating to eligibility for benefits, how they will be provided, and similar questions, including the establishment of rules relating to the extent, if any, for which credit will be given for required contributions not actually received by the Trust, and the Joint Board's decisions on such questions shall be binding on all persons, except as may be otherwise specifically provided herein or in regulations duly adopted by the Joint Board;

10. To retain or employ attorneys, accountants, actuaries, office personnel, professional administrators and consultants, and other suitable agents and employees; and unless otherwise provided by ERISA, it shall be immaterial that the persons so retained or employed have been retained or employed by anyone else with rights or obligations hereunder. Any agreement with such persons may be for any period of time the Joint Board deems appropriate, but it may terminate any such agreement at any time, even if by so doing this Trust might be liable for breach of contract;

11. To establish such reserves as it deems appropriate or as may be required by ERISA;

12. To enter into reciprocal agreements with joint boards of other trusts providing similar benefits, so that persons may move from one trust's jurisdiction to another's without loss of benefits, and to agree to the transfer of funds from one such trust to another if necessary or advisable in con-

nection therewith; but failure of the Joint Board to agree on any such action shall not be subject to arbitration.

13. To provide Plan benefits either directly from Trust assets or through one or more contracts with organizations legally qualified to enter into contracts providing Plan benefits (including insurance companies), or partly by direct payment and partly through such contracts. The Joint Board shall exercise all powers granted to contractholders under any such contract except and until it relinquishes them in writing. (Nothing in this Trust shall be construed as making any organization with which this Trust contracts a party to this Trust Agreement, nor as imposing any obligations on it; instead, such organization's obligations shall be only such as are contained in its agreements with the Joint Board.)

E. *Limitation on Liability.* Each Trustee shall discharge his duties hereunder in accordance with the provisions and standards set forth herein. It is to be noted, however, that trusts of this type are relatively recent in origin, and their management presents problems concerning which there has been only limited experience. Also, individuals serving as Trustees hereunder generally do so by virtue of their regular employment and without compensation. For these reasons, the parties desire to limit the obligations of the Trustees, and to hold them harmless against any liabilities hereunder, to the fullest extent permitted by law. Therefore, subject to the ERISA-imposed limitations set forth below, a Trustee shall not be liable for any act or omission to act, so long as it is not committed intentionally or with indifference to the best interests of Participants or their Beneficiaries, and the Trust shall exonerate, defend, reimburse, and hold him harmless against any such act or omission to act. As examples, a Trustee shall be protected:

1. In acting upon any papers, documents, data, or information reasonably believed by him to be true and accurate and to be made, executed, delivered or assembled by the proper parties;
2. For any act concerning which he reasonably relies upon the opinion of legal counsel
3. For the act of any agent, employee, consultant, or attorney chosen and retained with reasonable care; or
4. For any act or omission of another Trustee in which he does not join.

If any of the foregoing provisions should be held by a court of competent jurisdiction to go beyond what is legally permissible, the remaining provisions shall nevertheless be given effect insofar as the law permits, it being the intention that any invalid provisions be severable from the others. Furthermore, except insofar as specifically permitted by ERISA, the foregoing exculpatory provisions shall not apply to relieve a Trustee from responsibility or liability for any responsibility, obligation, or duty established by ERISA, but shall only apply to such additional responsibilities, obligations, or duties as may be performed by him hereunder in good faith and with reasonable care.

VII. FUNDING AND INVESTMENTS

A. *Funding and Investment Policies.* The Joint Board shall establish and carry out funding and investment policies and methods consistent with the objectives of the Trust and the requirements of ERISA, shall review such policies and methods at appropriate intervals, and shall communicate them to the Investment Manager.

B. *Investment Decisions.* The Joint Board may itself invest and otherwise manage Plan assets, or it may delegate all or some of these management powers (including the power to acquire and dispose of Plan assets) to an Investment Manager which qualifies as such under ERISA and acknowledges in writing that it is a fiduciary with respect to the Plan and Trust. The appointment, selection, and retention of any Investment Manager shall be solely the responsibility of the Joint Board, and shall be revocable by it at any time. Any person to whom management powers are delegated shall exercise its powers in accordance with the funding and investment policies established by the Joint Board, but shall have no responsibility for the establishment or adequacy of such policies.

C. *Investment Standards.* Investments shall be prudent ones and shall be diversified so as to minimize the risk of large losses unless it is clearly prudent not to do so. They shall not be in conflict with ERISA's "prohibited transactions" provisions or its limitations with respect to acquisition and holding of "employer securities" or "employer real property" (as those terms are defined in ERISA). No fiduciary shall cause the Trust to engage in transactions which violate these requirements.

D. *Investment Powers.* The Trust assets, or any part thereof, may be invested in securities issued by the United States government; in bonds; in common or preferred stocks; in other securities listed on any exchange or traded in any over-the-counter market, including shares of mutual investment companies; in pooled investment portfolios managed by insurance companies; in improved real estate; in notes; in mortgages; in certificates of deposit of any bank, including any bank acting as custodian of trust funds; in commercial paper; in bankers' acceptances or in any other properties in which this Trust may lawfully invest. If any assets are ever held in which this Trust may not properly invest, they shall be disposed of as promptly as is prudent under the circumstances. Except as otherwise authorized by the Department of Labor, the indicia of ownership of Trust assets shall at all times be held within the jurisdiction of the District Courts of the United States. Whoever holds title to Trust assets shall have all rights and powers with respect to investing the Trust property that an absolute owner would have, subject only to any written directions previously received from another fiduciary authorized hereunder to give such directions. These investment powers shall include, without limitation, the following powers in addition to those set forth elsewhere hereunder and others given by law:

1. To hold in cash in a noninterest bearing account such portion of the Trust assets as may be reasonably required for the day-to-day administration of the Trust and disbursement of benefits, and to deposit the same in any bank (including any bank acting as custodian of trust funds) subject to the rules and regulations governing such deposits. Additional cash shall be placed in interest-bearing accounts and/or obligations (which may be with the custodian of trust funds) until such time as it is otherwise invested;

2. To participate in any plan of lease, merger, consolidation, exchange, foreclosure, or reorganization affecting securities held hereunder at any time;

3. To deposit stocks under voting agreements;

4. To subscribe for stock or bond privileges;

5. To vote with respect to all securities or other assets in person or by proxy, except that where an Investment Manager has been appointed and is acting, proxies and other shareholder material with respect to assets under its supervision will be forwarded to the Investment Manager if it so requests.

6. To register securities in the name of a nominee, or to hold the same unregistered and in such form that they will pass by delivery;

7. To lease, repair, alter, or improve real estate or other assets;

8. To sell any securities, real estate, or other assets at public or private sale for such prices and

upon such terms as it may deem proper, without liability on the part of the purchasers to see to the application of the purchase money;

9. To borrow money and to secure the repayment thereof by mortgage on real estate, pledge of securities, or otherwise, without liability on the part of the lenders as to the application of the assets loaned;

10. To invest Trust assets collectively with funds of other trusts in one or more of the investment funds for employee benefit trusts established by any bank or trust company or any other common or commingled fund now or hereafter maintained by any bank or trust company as the same may be amended from time to time; and if any portion of the Trust is so invested, the declaration creating such funds shall be deemed to be incorporated into this Trust Agreement the same as if fully set forth herein.

VIII. AMENDMENT AND TERMINATION

A. *Amendments.*   The Trust or Plan may be amended at any time by the Joint Board. It may amend them in whole or in part, and at any time, and all persons with rights or obligations hereunder shall be bound thereby. However, no amendment shall alter or negate the Trust purpose set forth in Article I or any applicable and lawful provision of a Pension Agreement which has been approved or accepted by the Trustees. Failure of the Trustees to agree upon a proposed amendment shall not be subject to arbitration as a deadlock, except as provided hereafter in the case of mandatory amendments. Amendments shall be made by written instrument signed by a majority of the Union Trustees and a majority of the Employer Trustees.

B. *Mandatory Amendments.*   Amendment of the Trust or Plan shall be mandatory in the following situations:

1. When necessary to assure compliance with ERISA or other applicable laws;
2. When necessary to assure the tax-deductibility of contributions hereto under federal and state income tax laws;
3. When necessary to assure (if possible) that this Trust remains tax exempt; that contributions to this Trust will not be deemed part of the "regular rate" at which an employee is employed for purposes of the Fair Labor Standards Act; and that such contributions will not be subject to deductions for purposes of any State Unemployment Insurance Act, the Federal Unemployment Tax Act, the Federal Insurance Contributions Act, or any similar legislation.

   If the Trust or Plan is not amended when so required, the matter shall be submitted to arbitration as provided above, and, notwithstanding any other provision hereof, the Joint Board shall be bound to execute such amendment of the Trust or Plan as the arbitrator deems necessary to satisfy the requirements of this provision.

C. *Termination.* The Joint Board may terminate the Plan or this Trust at any time. The Trust shall not be terminated without terminating the Plan, but the Plan may be wholly or partially terminated without terminating the Trust. Termination shall be accomplished in the same manner as amendment.

   Upon termination of the Trust, all obligations shall first be satisfied. The Joint Board shall thereupon use the remaining Trust assets to provide Plan benefits in such manner as the Plan may provide, or in the absence of a Plan provision, to continue to provide Plan benefits in a manner permitted by ERISA for so long as Trust assets permit.

D. *Transfer of Assets to Another Benefit Trust.* Notwithstanding anything above to the contrary, the Joint Board may transfer the Trust assets or any portion thereof to the Trustees of any other trust or trusts which provides similar benefits. However, failure of the Joint Board to agree on any such action shall not be subject to arbitration.

Neither the Trust nor the Plan shall be merged or consolidated with, or transfer its assets or liabilities to, any other plan or trust unless each Participant in the Plan would (if the Plan terminated) be entitled to receive a benefit immediately after the merger, consolidation, or transfer which is equal to or greater than the benefit he would have been entitled to receive immediately before the merger, consolidation, or transfer if the Plan had then terminated.

E. *Withdrawals by Individual Employers.* To the extent permitted by ERISA and subject to approval by Internal Revenue Service, the Joint Board may establish regulations to protect the Trust in the event any Employer ceases contributing hereto, which regulations may provide for the curtailment, in whole or in part, of benefits attributable to or dependent upon employment with the terminating Employer before such Employer was required to contribute to the Plan. Neither the terminating Employer, its employees, nor their representatives shall have any right to the return of any monies contributed to the Trust by the terminating Employer, all of which monies shall continue to be held hereunder.

IX. MISCELLANEOUS

A. *Employer-Employee Relationship Not Affected.* Nothing in this Trust shall give any employee the right to be retained in the employment of any Employer, and any employer-employee relationship relating to this Trust shall continue in the same manner as though this Trust had not been executed.

B. *Rights and Remedies Limited.* No person shall have any right, title, or interest in or to Trust assets except as otherwise required by law or otherwise specifically provided hereunder. Furthermore, except insofar as otherwise required by ERISA's prohibition of forfeitures, no person shall have any right to payments barred by the Statute of Limitations unless payment is requested by the person during his lifetime and the Joint Board, in its sole discretion, determines that there are extenuating circumstances justifying payment.

C. *Rights Not Transferable.* Unless permitted by ERISA and approved in advance by the Joint Board, all benefits provided to persons under the Plan shall be paid directly to them; the plan shall not be liable for their debts or other obligations; the benefits may not be assigned, alienated, or used as security by such persons; and the benefits shall not be subject to attachment, execution, or other legal proceedings. Notwithstanding the foregoing sentence, if at any time any person entitled to receive future payments from the Trust has already received from the Trust payments in excess of what he was entitled to receive as of that date, then, except to the extent prohibited by ERISA, the Joint Board may withhold from future payments due to him or his Beneficiary such amounts as are necessary to reimburse the Trust for such excess payments.

D. *Payments during Incapacity.* Notwithstanding any other provisions hereof, if, in the judgment of the Joint Board, any mental, physical, or other incapacity prevents a person entitled to benefits from properly handling his own affairs, and until any benefits to which he is entitled have been claimed by a legally appointed representative, these benefits may, in the discretion of the Joint Board, either be held for his benefit or paid to any one or more persons or institutions responsible for providing for his care and maintenance. The person entitled to the benefits shall promptly be sent notice of any such action.

E. *Governing Law, Severability of Provisions, and Interpretation.* The provisions of this Trust Agreement shall be interpreted, administered, and enforced according to applicable federal law, and to the extent that federal law is not applicable, according to the laws of the place of execution. If any such provision is held by a court of competent jurisdiction to be invalid or unenforceable, the remaining provisions shall continue to be fully effective. When interpreting the provisions of this Trust Agreement, the intention that the Plan and Trust fully comply with the requirements of such laws shall be taken into account, and any ambiguities shall be resolved in favor of compliance therewith. If any provision unambiguously conflicts with any such law, the provisions of the law shall apply instead of the conflicting provision until such time as the conflicting provision can be appropriately amended.

APPENDIX B

SPECIMEN JOINT TRUST PENSION PLAN

XYZ WORKERS PENSION PLAN

Amendment No. t

Effective January 1, 1976, the Plan is hereby amended and restated in its entirety by the attached document.

Signed at _____ , California on _____

BOARD OF TRUSTEES, XYZ WORKERS PENSION PLAN

UNION TRUSTEES   EMPLOYER TRUSTEES

_____   _____

_____   _____

_____   _____

_____   _____

Plan Amendment No. t, effective January 1, 1976.

XYZ WORKERS PENSION PLAN

Contents

ARTICLE 1.   DEFINITION OF TERMS USED IN THE PLAN

1.1 "Actuarial Equivalent" means the dollar value on any specified date computed on the basis of appropriate mortality, interest, and other actuarial factors employed by the actuary in his most recent actuarial valuation or, otherwise, as appended to this Plan.

1.2 "Covered Employee" means any Employee in Covered Employment.

1.3 "Covered Employment" means employment with an Employer in a position subject to a Pension Agreement.

1.4 "Covered Hour" means an hour worked by a Covered Employee for which an Employer Contribution has been made, or was required to be made.

1.5 "Credited Future Service" means the sum of a Participant's Future Service Credits, as determined under this Article 1.5, for Covered Employment rendered with one or more Employers after:

   a. December 31, 1965, for Participants affiliated at the effective date of their coverage with XYZ Workers Local No. 2; or

   b. July 31, 1967, for all other Participants represented by XYZ Workers Locals No. 22 and No. 42.

An Active Participant shall be credited with a Future Service Credit of one fifteen hundredth (1/1,500) of one year for each Covered Hour.

No Future Service Credit will be granted for Covered Hours prior to the first day of the Plan Year immediately preceding the Plan Year during which the Participant first becomes an Active Participant or again becomes an Active Participant after a forfeiture under Article 2.1(*b*).

1.6 "Credited Past Service" means the sum of a Participant's Past Service Credits, as determined under this Article 1.6. A Participant shall be entitled to Past Service Credits if he worked at least 600 Covered Hours during the following periods:

   a. January 1, 1966, through December 31, 1967, for Participants affiliated at the effective date of their coverage with XYZ Workers Local No. 2; or

b. August 1, 1967, through December 31, 1968, for Participants represented by XYZ Workers Locals No. 22 and No. 42;

always provided, however, that the Trustees acting in any case where the circumstances appear to warrant such action may, but need not, liberalize the foregoing conditions.

A Participant entitled to Past Service Credits shall be credited with one quarter of one year's Past Service Credit for each calendar quarter of employment in which the Participant is paid at least $200 of wages, if such employment was or would have been Covered Employment had a Pension Agreement been in effect at such time. Credited Past Service is granted only for employment rendered during the period July 1, 1948, through:

a. December 31, 1965, for Participants represented at the effective date of their coverage by XYZ Workers Local No. 2; or

b. July 31, 1967, for all other Participants represented by XYZ Workers Locals No. 22 and No. 42;

all dates inclusive, up to a maximum of 15 years of Credited Past Service.

However, a Participant who does not meet the above requirements shall nevertheless be entitled to Past Service Credits, if such Participant was, in any period from:

a. January 1, 1966, through December 31, 1967, for Participants affiliated at the effective date with XYZ Workers Local No. 2; or

b. July 31, 1967, through December 31, 1968, for Participants represented by XYZ Workers Locals No. 22 and No. 42;

in any of the following categories:

a. Military absence, provided that the Participant returns to Covered Employment within ninety (90) days after the end of the period in which his reemployment rights are protected by law, and further provided he reports the facts of such military absence within ninety (90) days of his return to Covered Employment; and *b.*   A period of disability as approved by the Trustees.

1.7   "Credited Vesting Service Years" means, for a Participant, the total number of Vesting Service Years completed by the Participant except for any Vesting Service Years which have been forfeited as provided in Article 2.1(*b*).

1.8   "Divesting Service Year" means a Plan Year during which a Participant earns less than 435 Vesting Hours. However, if a Participant fails to earn 435 Vesting Hours in a Plan Year during which he had at least six months of Special Service, then such Plan Year shall not cause a Divesting Service Year.

1.9   "Employee" means any Employee who works for an Employer.

1.10   "Employee Contribution Date" means the date of a Covered Employee's first Covered Hour, or, if the provisions of Article 2.1(*b*)(3) apply, the Covered Employee's first Covered Hour subsequent to his reentry into Covered Employment.

1.11   "Employer" means any Employer (including any Union) which has agreed to be bound by the terms and provisions of the Trust Agreement and is obligated to make Employer Contributions to the Pension Fund in accordance with a Pension Agreement.

1.12   "Employer Contribution Date" means the first date for which an Employer was or shall be obligated by a Pension Agreement to make contributions to the Fund. The Employer Contribution Date to be applied to each individual Covered Employee shall be the one applicable to the first Employer who makes contributions on his behalf.

1.13   "Employer Contributions" means contributions made irrevocably to the Fund by an Employer on account of the Covered Employees of such Employer, in accordance with a Pension Agreement, for the purpose of providing benefits under the Plan.

1.14   "Grace Period" means a period following the date on which a Covered Employee becomes an Active Participant and prior to the date he first becomes eligible to retire pursuant to Article 3 during which the Active Participant fails to work at least 435 Covered Hours in each of two consecutive Plan Years.

    a. If an Active Participant completes a Grace Period, his Normal Pension which has accrued to the end of the Grace Period, but only with respect to Service since the completion of the most recent prior Grace Period, if any, shall be calculated as of his most recent Covered Hour.

    b. Upon any subsequent reentry into Covered Employment after completion of a Grace Period, a Participant's Normal Pension accrued as a result of Past or Future Credited Service completed prior to such Grace Period may not be increased as a result of such return to Covered Employment.

1.15 "Industry" means the XYZ industry of California.

1.16 "Interest" means the amount determined by applying to the single sum Actuarial Equivalent payment specified in Article 10.12 an annual rate of 5 percent after December 31, 1975, subject to change as may be required by federal law or regulation.

1.17 "Participant" means a person who is participating in the Plan in one of the categories of participation specified in Article 2.1 or a Pensioner pursuant to Article 3.

1.18 "Pension Agreement" means an acceptable written agreement between a Union and an Employer which requires payments to the Fund on behalf of Employees of such Employer who are represented by such Union. "Pension Agreement" also means a written agreement providing for payments to the fund on behalf of Employees of a Union.

    The term Pension Agreement shall include any extension, renewal, or replacement thereof. A Pension Agreement shall be considered as being in effect on any date if it provides for Employer Contributions to be made to the Pension Fund with respect to employment on such date.

1.19 "Pension Fund" or "Fund" means the XYZ Workers Pension Trust Fund, and shall include the total of contributions made under the Plan, increased by income and decreased by Plan benefits and by expenses incurred in the establishment and administration of the Plan.

1.20   "Plan" means the plan of pension benefits established effective January 1, 1966, as the XYZ Workers Pension Plan, as evidenced in the following pages, including any amendments hereto. The Plan shall be considered to be attached to and made a part of the Trust Agreement.

1.21   "Plan Administrator" means the administrative manager employed by the Trustees pursuant to the Trust Agreement.

1.22   "Plan Year" means the period from January 1, 1966, through December 31, 1966, and each succeeding twelve-calendar-month period,

1.23   "Special Service" means the following:

    a.   Military absence, provided that the Participant returns to Covered Employment within ninety (90) days after the end of the period in which his reemployment rights are protected by law, and further provided he reports the facts of such military absence within ninety (90) days of his return to Covered Employment;

    b.   Continuous employment in the industry, within the collective bargaining area of the Union, in a class not subject to the jurisdiction of the Union excluding such employment in Uncovered Vesting Employment; or

    c.   Such other circumstances as may subsequently be specified by the Trustees, always provided, however, that any such specification must be on a like and nondiscriminatory basis.

One month of Special Service will be earned for a calendar month if the Participant was in Special Service for any portion of such month.

1.24   "Total Service" means the sum of a Participant's Credited Vesting Service Years and the number of years for which Past Service Credits are granted under Article 1.6.

1.25   "Trust" means that Trust created and established under the Trust Agreement.

1.26   "Trust Agreement" means the XYZ Workers Pension Fund Agreement and Declaration of Trust, executed December 15, 1965, as amended.

1.27   "Trustees" means the Board of Trustees designated and acting under the Trust Agreement.

1.28 "Uncovered Vesting Employment" means an Employee's employment with the Employer after the Employer Contribution Date, in a position not subject to a Pension Agreement, provided the Employee was employed with the same Employer and was a Covered Employee immediately preceding Uncovered Vesting Employment or immediately following Uncovered Vesting Employment. In cases where the Employer is a partnership or sole proprietor, Uncovered Vesting Employment does not include employment as a partner of such Employer or a sole proprietor, respectively.

1.29 "Union" means the XYZ Workers, Union Locals No. 2, No. 22, and No. 42 and any other union affiliated with Locals No. 2, No. 22, and No. 42 and engaged in the XYZ industry and whose participation in this Plan is authorized by the Board of Trustees.

1.30 "Vesting Hour" means the following:

a. A Covered Hour;

b. An hour worked by a Covered Employee for which the Covered Employee is paid by or entitled to payment from the Employer, either directly or indirectly;

c. An hour worked with the Employer in Uncovered Vesting Employment as reported by the Employer;

d. An hour of temporary or total and permanent disability approved by the Trustees. An Employee shall be credited with 35 Vesting Hours for each week of disability; and

e. An hour for which back pay from an Employer is awarded to a Covered Employee or an Employee in Uncovered Vesting Employment, or an hour for which an Employer agrees to pay back pay to a Covered Employee or Employee in Uncovered Vesting Employment, to the extent such award or agreement is intended to compensate the Employee for periods during which the Employee would have been engaged in the performance of duties for the Employer.

There shall be no duplication of hours for which credit is available under more than one of the preceding rules.

1.31 "Vesting Service Year" means, a Plan Year after December

31, 1965, during which an Employee earns 870 or more Vesting Hours.

1.32   "West Coast Trusts" means the following Pension Plans involving Unions and Employers in the XYZ industry on the West Coast:

    a.   Western XYZ Workers Retirement Fund;

    b.   XYZ Workers Retirement Trust of Washington and Oregon; and

    c.   XYZ Workers Pension Plan of Nevada.

ARTICLE 2. PARTICIPATION

2.1   *a.   Active Participant.*   Each person who becomes a Covered Employee after December 31, 1975, shall become an Active Participant in the Plan on the first day of the month during which his total Vesting Hours accrued during the current Plan Year and the preceding Plan Year first equal 870. However, if the Employee's first Covered Hour is on the date his Employer is first obligated to contribute to the Pension Fund with respect to the bargaining unit of which the Employee is then a member, such Employee becomes an Active Participant on such date. Each person, other than a Pensioner or a former Employee entitled to a vested benefit, who was covered under the Plan as it existed on December 31, 1975, shall be covered under this Plan as an Active Participant. A Participant's status as an Active Participant shall cease immediately following the earliest of (1) death, (2) retirement under the Plan, or (3) completion of a Grace Period.

    b.   Inactive Participant.   At the completion of a Grace Period, each Active Participant shall become an Inactive Participant, provided he is not entitled to a vested deferred pension benefit pursuant to Article 6. A Participant's status as an Inactive Participant shall cease immediately following the earliest of (1) death; (2) the date he becomes a Vested Participant, or again becomes an Active Participant; or (3) the date as of which he forfeits his

Credited Vesting Service Years. An Inactive Participant shall forfeit his Credited Vesting Service Years and all rights to a benefit under this Plan at the end of the Plan Year when the accumulated number of his consecutive Divesting Service Years first equals the number of his Credited Vesting Service Years.

If the Inactive Participant has not completed a Divesting Service year during or following his last Grace Period, he shall again become an Active Participant upon completion of a Covered Hour. Any other Inactive Participant shall become an Active Participant on the first day of the month following the date he again becomes a Covered Employee and his total Vesting Hours accrued during the current Plan Year and the preceding Plan Year first equal 870.

c. *Vested Participant.* An Active Participant who completes a Grace Period, or an Inactive Participant, shall become a Vested Participant provided he fulfills the requirements of Article 6.1. Each Participant, who was a former Employee entitled to a vested benefit under the Plan as it existed on December 31, 1975, shall be covered under this Plan as a Vested Participant with no change in his benefit rights. A Participant's status as a Vested Participant shall cease immediately following the earliest of (1) death, (2) retirement under the Plan, or (3) the date he again becomes an Active Participant.

2.2 *Participant Bound by Terms of Plan.* Each Participant shall be deemed conclusively and for all purposes to have assented to the terms of the Plan and shall thereby be bound with the same force and effect as if he had executed it as a party thereto.

ARTICLE 3. RETIREMENT DATE

3.1 *The Normal Retirement Date* for a Participant shall be the first day of the month coincident with, or next following, the later of:

a. His 65th birthday, or

b. The date as of which a Participant has accumulated ten

years of Total Service, of which at least five years are Credited Vesting Service Years but in no event later than the tenth anniversary of his Employee Contribution Date.

The Normal Pension Benefit payable to a Participant shall be as determined under Article 4.

3.2 *Early Retirement of an Active or Vested Participant.* Any Active Participant or Vested Participant who has completed ten Credited Vesting Service Years may elect to retire and receive an Early Pension Benefit at any time after the attainment of age 55. In this event, payment of Early Pension Benefit shall commence at said Participant's Early Retirement Date, which shall be the first day of the month coincident with, or next following, the date stipulated by the Participant as his retirement date, provided he has complied with the provisions of Article 10 with respect to application for pension benefits. The Early Pension Benefit payable to said Participant shall be as determined under Article 4.4 for Active or Vested Participants.

3.3 *Postponed Retirement of an Active Participant.* With the consent of the Employer, any Active Participant may elect to postpone his retirement and to remain in the service of his Employer after his Normal Retirement Date. Such Active Participant shall continue to accrue Credited Future Service pursuant to Article 1.5. In this event, payment of postponed pension benefits to said Active Participant shall commence at his postponed retirement date, which shall be the first day of any month coincident with, or next following, the date stipulated by the Participant as his retirement date, provided he has complied with the provisions of Article 10 with respect to application for pension benefits.

The Active Participant's postponed pension benefits shall be as determined under Article 4.3.

ARTICLE 4. NORMAL PENSION BENEFIT

4.1 The Normal Pension Benefit to which a Participant shall be entitled under the Plan shall be a monthly pension on the Normal Form of Pension described in Article 5.2. A Participant shall be eligible to receive the first monthly payment of his Normal Pension Benefit on his Normal Retirement Date, if he is then living and, if married, he has elected to receive this form of pension pursuant to Article 5.4.

4.2 *Normal Pension.* Subject to Articles 1.14, 4.5, and 4.6, the amount of monthly Normal Pension credited to any Participant shall be equal to $10 multiplied by the sum of the Participant's Credited Future Service and Credited Past Service. Credited Past Service shall be subject to a maximum of 15 Past Service Credits which have not been forfeited pursuant to Article 2.1(b)(3) under the Plan prior to January 1, 1976.

4.3 *Normal Pension Benefit.* The monthly Normal Pension Benefit payable to an Active Participant at his retirement on or after his Normal Retirement Date shall be equal to the amount of monthly Normal Pension credited to the Participant. The monthly Normal Pension Benefit payable to a Vested Participant at his Normal Retirement Date shall be determined under Article 6.

4.4 *Early Pension Benefit for an Active or Vested Participant.* The monthly Early Pension Benefit payable to an Active Participant or Vested Participant at his Early Retirement Date under Article 3.2 shall be equal to the amount of monthly Normal Pension credited to an Active Participant at his Early Retirement Date, or the amount of monthly deferred retirement benefit credited to a Vested Participant under Article 6.2, reduced by 0.5 percent per month for the first 60 months and 0.3 percent per month for each additional month, if any, by which his Early Retirement Date precedes the first of the month coincident with or next following his 65th birthday.

However, the amount of the monthly early retirement benefit payable to a Vested Participant whose break in service occurred prior to January 1, 1976, will be determined based on the Plan provisions in effect prior to January 1, 1976.

4.5 *Modifications.* Notwithstanding any provision of the Plan to the contrary, if a Participant ceases to be credited with Covered Hours because the Pension Agreement requiring contributions on his behalf is not renewed, his Normal Pension shall be equal to the product of (1) and (2) where (1) is $10 and (2) is the number of years and fractions of years of the Participant's Credited Future Service.

4.6   *Limitations.*   The total monthly benefits to be received by an individual under this Plan and all other plans sponsored by an Employer shall not exceed the lesser of:

a. $6,706 per month.

b.   100 percent of the highest monthly average of the individual's compensation during any three consecutive Plan Years.

If the sum of the individual's Credited Future Service and Credited Past Service is less than ten, the maximum monthly benefit specified above shall be reduced by multiplying such maximum by a fraction, the denominator of which is the sum of the individual's Credited Future Service and Credited Past Service and the numerator of which is ten. If the individual is receiving benefits under this Plan or any other affected plan under a form other than a life pension or joint and survivor pension, such individual's monthly benefits shall be adjusted to the level monthly life pension which has an Actuarial Equivalent equal to that of the monthly benefit payable to the individual in order to determine whether or not such individual's monthly benefits exceed the maximum specified above. If the Trustees determine that the maximum specified above will be exceeded, the individual's Normal Pension Benefit shall be reduced to the extent required pursuant to regulations published by the Internal Revenue Service so that, with any reductions imposed by the other affected plans, such excess is eliminated. Any reduction under this plan will be determined in accordance with uniform rules established by the Trustees.

ARTICLE 5.   AUTOMATIC, NORMAL, AND OPTIONAL FORMS OF PENSION BENEFIT

5.1   *Automatic Joint and Survivor Pension Form.*   A married Participant who has been married for at least one year on the date his pension commences and who has not elected otherwise shall receive the Actuarial Equivalent of his pension benefit as determined under Article 4 on the Automatic Joint and Survivor Pension Form described in this Article 5.1, subject to the provisions of Article 5.4. The Automatic Joint and Survivor Pension Form shall become effective on the date of the first monthly payment.

A married Participant who has not been married at least one year on the date his pension commences shall receive the Normal Form of Pension as described in Article 5.2, or if he so elects, the Automatic Joint and Survivor Pension Form described in this Article 5.1, or an Optional Form of Pension described in Article 5.3, subject to the provisions of Article 5.4.

A Participant who is not married on the date his pension commences shall receive the Normal Form of Pension as described in Article 5.2.

Payments under the Automatic Joint and Survivor Pension Form shall be actuarially determined, based on the ages of the Pensioner and his spouse. The actuarially determined monthly pension shall be payable to the Participant as long as he survives. If at his death his spouse survives him, monthly payments will continue to his spouse during her remaining lifetime in an amount equal to 50 percent of the monthly pension payable to the Pensioner under this Automatic Joint and Survivor Pension Form.

A married Participant who has been married for at least one year on the date his pension commences may elect the Normal Form of Pension or an Optional Form of Pension as hereinafter described subject to the provisions of Article 5.4.

5.2 *Normal Form of Pension.* The Normal Form of Pension under the Plan shall be a life pension with 36 monthly payments guaranteed. Monthly payments shall be made to the Pensioner on the first day of each month commencing on his retirement date, if he is then living, terminating with the last payment due immediately preceding the Pensioner's death or with the last guaranteed monthly payment, whichever is later. Any payments to be made after the Pensioner's death shall be made in accordance with Article 7.3.

5.3 *Optional Forms of Pension.* A married Participant may elect to receive the Actuarial Equivalent of his pension benefit on one of the Optional Forms of Pension permitted under this Article 5.3, subject to the provi⸱ ⸱ns of Article 5.4.

The Optional Forms of Pen⸱⸱on are as follows:

a. *Joint and Two-Thirds Survivor Pension.* The Joint and Two-Thirds Survivor Pension option contains the same provisions as the Automatic Joint and Survivor Pension Form as described in Article 5.1, except that the reduced monthly payments to the Participant's surviving spouse shall be equal to two thirds of the monthly pension payable to the Pensioner under this Joint and Two-Thirds Survivor Pension option.

b. *Joint and 100 Percent Survivor Pension.* The Joint and 100 percent Survivor Pension option contains the same provisions as the Automatic Joint and Survivor Pension Form as described in Article 5.1, except that the monthly payments to the Participant's surviving spouse shall be equal to the monthly pension payable to the Pensioner under this Joint and 100 percent Survivor Pension option.

5.4 If a Participant is married, election of the Normal Form of Pension or an Optional Form of Pension must be made within the applicable election period and must be elected jointly by the Participant and his spouse. The applicable election period shall be a period of at least 90 days following the date the Participant and his spouse are furnished with a written explanation of the effect of an election not to effect the Automatic Joint and Survivor Pension as provided in Article 5.5. The applicable election period shall commence at least 90 days prior to the date benefit payments commence and shall end on the date benefit payments commence. In the event the information described in Article 5.5 is furnished to the Participant less than 90 days prior to his retirement date, benefit payments may be postponed until 90 days following the date such information is furnished, in which case, benefit payments will be made retroactive to the Participant's retirement date.

Such written explanation shall be in accordance with the

rules and regulations established by the Trustees. The election of any form of pension shall, in any event, be subject to any conditions imposed by the Trustees with respect to the granting of such form of pension.

5.5 *Information to Participants.* On the later of (1) the date the Participant becomes an Active Participant or (2) the date on or about nine months prior to the Participant's earliest retirement date under the Plan, the Participant and his spouse, if any, will be furnished with the following information:

a. A general description or explanation of the Automatic Joint and Survivor Pension, and the Preretirement Benefit to Spouse Option to provide benefits upon the death of Vested Participants, the circumstances in which these benefits will be provided unless the Participant and his spouse elect not to have benefits provided in this form, and the availability of such an election;

b. A general description of the Preretirement Benefit to Spouse Option to provide benefits upon the death of Active Participants, the circumstances under which it will be paid if elected, and the availability of such election;

c. A general explanation of the financial effect on a Participant's retirement benefit of an election under (a) or (b) above.

ARTICLE 6. VESTED PENSION UPON TERMINATION

6.1 If an Active Participant completes a Grace Period prior to his Normal Retirement Date and he has completed ten or more Credited Vesting Service Years, then in such event he shall become a Vested Participant.

Each Inactive Participant shall become a Vested Participant at the completion of the Plan Year in which he accrues ten Credited Vesting Service Years.

6.2 *Normal Pension Benefit for a Vested Participant.* A Vested Participant shall be entitled to a deferred monthly Normal Pension Benefit. Subject to the provisions of Article 5, the amount of Normal Pension credited to such Participant while he was an Active Participant up to the date he left

Covered Employment shall be payable commencing at his Normal Retirement Date.

6.3   *Early Pension Benefit for a Vested Participant.*   A Vested Participant may elect an Early Retirement Date in accordance with Article 3.2 and receive an Early Pension Benefit as stated in Article 4.4 subject to the provisions of Article 5.

ARTICLE 7.   PRERETIREMENT BENEFIT TO SPOUSE OPTION AND DESIGNATION OF BENEFICIARY

7.1   An Active Participant may elect this Preretirement Benefit to Spouse Option. The death benefit under this option shall be payable only if, at the Active Participant's death, the following conditions are met:

a.   Three months have elapsed since his written election of this option has been received by the Trustees;

b.   He has been legally married to his spouse for at least one year; and

c.   He is at least age 55 and is eligible for Early Retirement pursuant to Article 3.2.

The condition specified in (*a*) above shall not apply if his death is caused by an accident which occurs after such election. For an Active Participant who postpones his retirement pursuant to Article 3.3, this option shall become effective automatically on the later of the Active Participant's 65th birthday or the date he has been legally married to his spouse for one year, unless the Active Participant and his spouse elect in writing not to effect this option. The death benefit under this option shall be a life pension, payable to the Participant's spouse, in the amount which would have been provided if the Automatic Joint and Survivor Pension Form had become effective on the day before the Active Participant's death and 50 percent of the reduced monthly payment were to be continued to his spouse. The election of this option will cause an actuarial reduction in any pension benefit to which the Participant, his spouse, or his beneficiary may eventually become entitled. An election under this Article 7.1 may be revoked or reelected at any time. A revocation shall take effect three months after the Trustees have received written request for a revocation, and any reelection shall be treated as a new election as provided in this Article 7.1. If the spouse dies before the Participant dies, the option will be cancelled. Upon any subsequent remarriage of the Participant, the option must be reelected as provided above. The Preretirement Benefit to Spouse Option will also cease to be in effect upon the Participant's retirement.

7.2 The Preretirement Benefit to Spouse Option is provided to Vested Participants under the following conditions:

a. *Eligibility.* The death benefit provided under this Article 7.2 shall be payable to the surviving spouse of a Vested Participant, who, at the time he became a Vested Participant, was at least age 55 or who became a Vested Participant prior to age 55 and remained in Uncovered Vesting Employment until at least his 55th birthday provided:

   i. The death of such Vested Participant occurs prior to his retirement date, but subsequent to the effective date of this coverage; and

   ii. The Participant and his spouse do not elect otherwise prior to the effective date of this coverage.

b. *Effective Date.* If the Participant and his spouse do not elect otherwise prior to the effective date, then the coverage provided under this Article 7.2 shall become effective on the later of:

   i. The date the Participant becomes a Vested Participant;

   ii. The Participant's 55th birthday;

   iii. The date the Participant and his spouse have been married one year.

If the spouse dies before the Participant dies, the coverage provided under this Article 7.2 shall cease. Upon any subsequent remarriage of the Participant, this coverage will be reinstated automatically on the date the Participant and his spouse have been married one year, unless the Participant and his spouse elect otherwise.

c. *Amount of Benefit.* The death benefit under this Article 7.2 shall be a life pension, payable to the Participant's spouse, in the amount which would have been provided if the Automatic Joint and Survivor Pension Form had become effective on the day before the Vested Participant's death and 50 percent of the reduced monthly payment were to be continued to his spouse.

d. *Election Not to Receive Preretirement Benefit to Spouse.* An election not to receive the Preretirement Benefit to Spouse may be made at any time prior to the Participant's retirement date. Such election may be made subsequent to the effective date, in which case the coverage under this Article 7.2 will cease and the actuarial reduction described in (*e*) below will be based only on the period that the coverage provided in this Article 7.2 is in effect. Such election may be revoked or reelected at any time prior to the Participant's retirement date.

e. *Reduction of Pension Benefit Payable to Participant.* If the death benefit coverage provided under this Article 7.2 becomes effective, then, pursuant to the rules of the Plan, it will cause an actuarial reduction in any pension benefit to which the Participant, his spouse or his beneficiary may eventually become entitled.

7.3 If the death of a Pensioner who is receiving the Normal Form of Pension occurs before the number of guaranteed monthly payments has been made, as defined in Article 5.2, the remaining guaranteed monthly payments shall be made to the Pensioner's designated beneficiary. At the discretion of the Trustees, the Actuarial Equivalent of the remaining guaranteed monthly payments may be paid in a single sum to the Pensioner's designated beneficiary. Upon the death of a Pensioner who is receiving a Joint and Survivor Pension, the death benefits, if any, shall be paid in accordance with Article 5. Such Joint and Survivor benefits shall only be payable to the spouse to whom the Participant was married on his retirement date.

7.4 Each Participant, upon request by the Trustees, shall specify the name and social security number of his spouse, if any, and shall designate a beneficiary to whom benefits, if any, other than under one of the Joint and Survivor Pension

Forms or the benefits described in Articles 7.1 and 7.2, shall be paid in the event of his death. Any beneficiary so designated may be changed by the Participant by filing with the Trustees a written notice of change of beneficiary in such form as is satisfactory to the Trustees. A Participant may designate a new spouse at any time before retirement by filing with the Trustees a written notice in a form satisfactory to the Trustees.

7.5 If no beneficiary has been designated by a Participant or if the designated beneficiary predeceases the Participant, payment shall be made to the surviving person or persons in the first of the following classes of successive preference beneficiaries in which a member survives the Participant:

 a. The Participant's spouse;
 b. The Participant's children, including legally adopted children;
 c. The Participant's parents;
 d. The Participant's brothers and sisters.

In determining such person or persons, the Trustees may rely upon affidavit by a member of any of the classes of preference beneficiaries. Payment based upon such affidavit shall be in full acquittance of any benefit payable under the Plan unless, before the payment is made, the Trustees have received written notice of a valid claim by some other person. If two or more persons become entitled to benefits as preference beneficiaries, they shall share equally. If no preference beneficiaries survive the Participant, then no death benefit shall be payable, except to provide for necessary funeral expenses.

7.6 The interest of any beneficiary who predeceases the Participant shall vest in the Participant unless otherwise specifically provided by the Participant in a written notice received by the Trustees.

7.7 Any death benefit payable to a minor may be paid to the legally appointed guardian of the minor or, if there be no such guardian, to such adults as have, in the opinion of the Trustees, assumed the custody and principal support of said minor.

ARTICLE 8.   RECIPROCAL BENEFITS

8.1   Reciprocal Benefits are provided under this Plan for a Participant who would otherwise be ineligible for a benefit because his years of employment have been divided between Covered Employment creditable under this Plan and employment creditable under the West Coast Trusts, or who, though otherwise eligible, could receive a larger pension by utilization of a Related Credit.

8.2   By resolution duly adopted, the Board of Trustees may recognize another pension plan as a Related Plan.

8.3   The term "Related Hours" means hours of employment which are creditable under a Related Plan.

8.4   The term "Related Credit" means years of vesting service, or portions thereof, creditable to a Participant under a Related Plan.

8.5   The term "Combined Pension Credit" means the total of a Participant's Related Credit plus Total Service accumulated under the XYZ Workers Pension Plan (hereinafter referred to as "XYZ Pension Credit").

8.6   It is specifically recognized that a Participant may have Past Service employment that would have been creditable under this Plan except for his failure to be entitled to Past Service Credit as set forth in Article 1.6 of the Plan. However, such past employment may be creditable:

   a.   If the Participant had Related Hours which, in combination with his Covered Hours under this Plan, would have satisfied this rule; and

   b.   If his Past Service employment that would have been covered by the Plan, except for his failure to be entitled to Past Service Credit as set forth in Article 1.6, were continuous (as defined by either this Plan or the Related Plan) with creditable employment in the area of the Related Plan.

8.7   A Participant shall not receive double credit for the same period of employment. No more than one year of Pension Credit or Related Credit shall be given for all employment in any given calendar year.

8.8   A Participant who, because of his Combined Pension Credits, is eligible to retire in accordance with Article 3 of the Plan shall be eligible for Reciprocal Benefits if he meets the following requirements:

      a.   He would be eligible for a benefit under this Plan were his Combined Pension Credits treated as XYZ Pension Credits; and

      b.   He has accumulated at least one year of Past Service Credit, as defined in Article 1.6 and determined without regard to this Article 8, or 870 Vesting Hours under this Plan.

8.9   Related Hours shall be considered in determining whether a Participant has failed to accumulate sufficient Vesting Service Years to avoid a forfeiture of Credited Vesting Service Years and consequent loss of Pension Credits which had been credited to him pursuant to the conditions of Article 2.1(*b*)(3) of the Plan.

8.10   The amount of the Reciprocal Benefit payable by the XYZ Workers Pension Plan, for a Participant retiring for age, shall be determined based on the Credited Past Service and Credited Future Service earned under the XYZ Workers Pension Plan, as modified by Article 8.6, excluding any years of Credited Service forfeited pursuant to Article 2.1(*b*).

8.11   If the Actuarial Equivalent of the monthly Reciprocal Benefit is less than $1,750, then the Actuarial Equivalent of the Reciprocal Benefit shall be paid to the Pensioner in a single sum.

8.12   Payment of a Reciprocal Benefit shall be subject to all of the conditions applicable to the other types of benefits under this Plan.

8.13   The XYZ Workers Pension Trust Fund shall incur no liability because of the failure of a Related Plan to provide data or to make payment of benefits related to credits earned in the area of the Related Plan. The obligation to determine and report credits earned in the area of the Related Plan shall rest on the Related Plan of the Participant and not upon the XYZ Workers Pension Plan.

ARTICLE 9. FUNDING OF PLAN BENEFITS

9.1 All benefits under the Plan shall be paid from assets held in Trust for the exclusive purpose of providing benefits to Participants and beneficiaries and defraying reasonable expenses of administering the Plan as authorized by the Trustees pursuant to the Plan or the Trust Agreement. Such assets shall be held in Trust under a custodial agreement with a bank or under any other contractual arrangement authorized by the Trustees pursuant to the Trust Agreement.

9.2 No Covered Employee shall be required to make any contribution to the Fund. The sole source of contributions to the Fund shall be Employer Contributions made in accordance with the applicable Pension Agreement.

9.3 The Trustees may delegate investment responsibilities, pursuant to the Trust Agreement and Article 10.1 of this Plan, and appoint an investment manager or managers which shall be an investment advisor registered under the Federal Investment Advisors Act of 1940, a bank as defined in that act with respect to assets of the Plan which are not held under an insurance contract, or an insurance company with respect to assets deposited under an insurance contract. Such advisors shall not act until they have delivered to the Trustees written acknowledgement that they are fiduciaries with respect'to the Trust and the Plan.

9.4 The Trustees from time to time shall determine the immediate and long-term financial requirements of the Plan and on the basis of such determination, establish a policy and method of funding which will enable the Trustees or the investment manager or managers, if any, to coordinate the investment policies of the Plan's funds with the objectives and financial needs of the Plan.

9.5 In no event, will any part of the Plan funds revert to any Employer or the Union or be used for or diverted to any other purpose other than for the exclusive purpose of providing benefits to Participants and beneficiaries and for defraying reasonable expenses of administering the Plan as authorized by the Plan or the Trust Agreement. However, a contribution made by an Employer as a mistake of fact may be refunded by the Trustees within one year after the payment of such erroneous contribution.

9.6 No person shall have any claim for benefits with respect to this Plan against the Trustees, the Union, an Employer, or any insurance company except specifically as may be set forth in this Plan, any applicable insurance contract or as provided by applicable law. The only persons who shall be entitled to participate in the Plan and receive benefits from the Fund will be those Employees who have performed Covered Employment. It is expected that Employers will submit contributions only on behalf of such Employees. The receipt by the Fund of contributions that may be submitted on behalf of persons who may not be eligible to participate in the Plan shall not estop the Trustees from declining or terminating the participation of such persons nor shall it constitute a waiver of any of the provisions of this Plan.

9.7 Neither the Union, the Employer, nor the Trustees guarantee the payment of any benefits under this Plan. It shall be understood specifically that benefits shall be paid under the Plan only to the extent that funds are available therefor under the Trust. No Employer shall have any liability for the obligations under the Plan of any other Employer, except as provided by applicable law. Each Employer shall be discharged of all obligations to contribute under the Plan upon making the contributions required of such Employer under the applicable Pension Agreement, except as provided by applicable law.

ARTICLE 10. ADMINISTRATION OF THE PLAN

10.1 The Trustees shall be the named fiduciaries for the Plan, and, as such, shall administer the Plan according to the powers and duties granted them in accordance with the Trust Agreement. The Trustees shall make such rules and regulations consistent with the orderly administration of the Plan as they deem necessary, desirable, or appropriate. Any rules and regulations and any exercise of discretion or other action by the Trustees will be equitable and nondiscriminatory and will be uniform in application to all Covered Employees, Participants, or beneficiaries in similar circumstances. The Trustees may employ such advisors and providers of service such as accountants, actuaries, administrative personnel, attorneys, or other qualified persons as may be deemed necessary for the proper administration of the Plan. The Trustees may delegate, to the extent authorized by law, any of their powers and duties as provided in the Trust Agreement. Any Trustee or other fiduciary with respect to the Plan may serve in more than one fiduciary capacity with respect to the Plan.

10.2   No Participant, beneficiary, or other payee shall have the right to anticipate, alienate, sell, transfer, assign, pledge, encumber, or charge any benefit or payment under this Plan.

10.3   To the extent permitted by law, no benefit or payment under this Plan shall be subject to any claim or process of law by any creditor of a Participant, beneficiary, or other payee.

10.4   This Plan shall be construed, administered, and enforced in accordance with the Employee Retirement Income Security Act of 1974, as amended, and, to the extent not superseded thereby, the laws of the State of California, fairly, equitably, and in accordance with the purposes of the Plan.

10.5   Nothing contained in this Plan shall be construed as conferring any rights upon any person for a continuation of his employment, or as in any way affecting such employment, nor shall the Plan be construed as limiting in any way the right of any Employer to terminate the employment of, or to retire, an Employee.

10.6   Each Employer shall provide the Trustees or the Plan Administrator with such personnel data as is required to carry out the provisions of the Plan.

10.7   An actuarial valuation shall be made at intervals not to exceed three years. Upon the basis of the recommendation of the actuary, the Trustees may make such changes in benefits as they consider necessary, desirable, or appropriate, subject to limitations of Article 11.1.

10.8   All applications for benefits under this Plan, whether on account of retirement or death, and all elections and designations made by Participants or beneficiaries under this Plan shall be made in writing to the Trustees in the form and manner prescribed by the Trustees. Any misrepresentation by the applicant shall constitute grounds for the denial, suspension, or discontinuance of benefits, in whole or in part, for such applicant, or for the cancellation or recovery of benefit payment made in reliance thereon.

10.9 The Trustees shall have the right to require submission of all necessary information before any benefit is paid, including records of employment; proofs of date of birth, disability, or death; and evidence of existence and marriage. No benefit dependent in any way upon such information shall be payable unless and until the information so required has been furnished. Upon receipt of such information, the Trustees shall determine the eligibility of the applicant for such benefit, and shall notify the applicant of their determination and the amount of any benefit payable.

10.10 No benefit payments will be made under the Plan until an application or claim is made therefor to the Trustees as provided by Article 10.8 and all information required by Article 10.9 has been submitted.

However, the Trustees acting without discrimination in any case where the circumstances appear to warrant such action may liberalize, but need not, the foregoing conditions.

10.11 The Trustees shall provide adequate notice in writing to any Participant or beneficiary whose claim for benefits under the Plan has been denied, setting forth the specific reasons for such denial. The Participant or beneficiary shall be given an opportunity for a full and fair review of the decision denying the claim. The Participant or beneficiary shall be given 60 days from the date of the receipt of the notice within which to request such review, in accordance with rules adopted by the Trustees and promulgated in accordance with applicable laws and regulations.

10.12 If the Actuarial Equivalent of any future monthly benefits payable under the Plan under any benefit is less than $1,750, the Actuarial Equivalent of such benefit shall be paid to the payee in a single sum. Said payment shall be in full settlement of all liability to the payee under the Plan. In the event a Vested Participant reenters Covered Employment prior to his retirement date, he may reinstate the benefit with respect to which a single sum distribution was made provided he repays the single sum distribution with Interest from the date of distribution to the date of repayment.

10.13   To be considered retired, a person must refrain from more than 50 hours per month of employment or work for wages or profit in the Industry, in the same trade or craft, and in the same geographic area covered by the Plan as was the case immediately before benefits commenced. If a Pensioner violates this requirement while in receipt of pension benefits under this Plan, then the pension benefit shall be suspended for each month during which he is engaged in such employment or work, except as provided by applicable law. If suspended, pension benefit payments shall recommence the first day of the month following the cessation of such employment in an amount without adjustment with respect to such employment or cessation of employment.

10.14   A Pensioner who reenters Covered Employment as a Covered Employee and whose pension benefits are suspended during such Covered Employment, as described in Article 10.13, neither shall be entitled to any additional Future Service Credits as a result of such employment, nor shall the monthly pension benefits of such Pensioner be adjusted in any way with regard to such employment on subsequent cessation of such Covered Employment.

10.15   The Trustees or the insurance company, if any, which is providing benefits under the Plan to the Pensioner, shall have the right to require satisfactory evidence that a Pensioner is living on each and every date when a pension benefit is due such Pensioner. In the absence of such evidence, when required, any payments due shall not be made until such evidence has been received.

10.16 If, in the judgment of the Trustees, the Pensioner is unable to care for his affairs because of illness, accident, or incapacity, either mental or physical; then, any payment due, unless claim shall have been made therefor by a duly appointed legal representative, may be paid to the spouse or other person or party deemed by the Trustees to have incurred expense for the Pensioner. Any such payment shall be a payment for the account of the Pensioner, and shall be a complete discharge of the liability therefor under the Plan.

10.17 A copy of the Plan and other documents under which the Plan was established or operated shall be made available for inspection at the office of the Plan Administrator to any Employee upon his request. The Trustees shall provide for each Participant to receive a booklet setting forth in layman's language a summary description of the essential features of the Plan. The Trustees shall also provide for each Participant to receive copies of each other document relating to the Plan and explanations of any material modification of or change in the Plan, Plan description, or summary description in accordance with applicable regulations.

ARTICLE 11. AMENDMENT OF THE PLAN

11.1 Subject to the terms and conditions of the Pension Agreement, the Trust Agreement, and any applicable laws or regulations, the Trustees may at any time or times amend or modify the Plan, retroactively or otherwise, in any respect consistent with the intent of the Plan and with the requirement that at all times the Plan will conform to the applicable requirements of the Labor Management Relations Act, 1947, as amended, the Employee Retirement Income Security Act of 1974, as amended, and to the Internal Revenue Code, and that Employer Contributions will be deductible as an item of expense by the Employer for income tax purposes. No amendment or modification of this

Plan may reduce any benefits payable to Pensioners who have retired prior to such amendment or modification. No amendment shall change the vesting schedule under the Plan unless each Vested Participant and each other Participant who is accruing Vesting Service Years as of the later of the date of adoption of or the effective date of such amendment shall have a nonforfeitable percentage of his accrued benefit at least as great as the nonforfeitable percentage determined under the vesting schedule in effect prior to such amendment. No such amendment or modification shall result in any portion of the funds to be recovered by any Employer or the Union, or cause or result in the expenditure of any portion of the funds for any purpose other than for the exclusive benefit of Participants, or beneficiaries, or for any payment or expenditure authorized under the Plan or the Trust Agreement. No amendment or modification of the Plan shall be adopted which will in any way impair the actuarial soundness of the Plan.

11.2   If the Trust Agreement or the Pension Agreement is amended by the insertion, modification, or deletion of any provisions relating to or affecting this Plan, the Trustees, to the extent legally permissible and in conformity with Article 11.1, shall amend the Plan to effectuate the intent of such amendment of the Trust Agreement or the Pension Agreement.

11.3   If this Plan is amended, the Trustees shall furnish a copy of such amendment promptly to the Union, the Employers, and the Plan Administrator.

11.4   It is intended that the Plan will constitute a qualified pension plan under the applicable provisions of the U.S. Internal Revenue Code, as now in effect or hereafter amended. Any modification or amendment of the Plan may be made retroactively, if necessary or appropriate, to qualify or maintain the Plan as a plan meeting the requirements of the applicable provisions of the U.S. federal tax laws, as now in effect or hereafter amended or adopted, and the regulations issued thereunder.

ARTICLE 12. TERMINATION OF PLAN

12.1   It is expected that the Plan will be continued in effect indefinitely and that each Employer will continue to make
contributions required by the applicable Pension Agreement. Subject to Article 12.2 and the Trust Agreement, the
Trustees reserve the right to institute proceedings to effect
a partial or total termination of the Plan.

   In the event of a partial or total termination of the Plan
or a complete discontinuance of Employer Contributions,
the Normal Pension Benefit, to the extent funded as of the
date of termination or discontinuance, credited to each Participant will be nonforfeitable.

12.2   The Trustees shall file, prior to the effective date of the
termination, a notice with the Pension Benefit Guaranty
Corporation that the Plan is to be terminated on the proposed termination date. The termination may not be earlier
than ten days after the filing of such notice. The Trustees
will pay no amount pursuant to this Article 12 unless they
receive notice, within 90 days subsequent to the proposed
termination date, from the Pension Benefit Guaranty Corporation that the assets held under the Plan are sufficient to
discharge the obligations of the Plan as determined by the
Pension Benefit Guaranty Corporation. In this event the
Trustees may distribute the assets of the Plan in the manner
described in Article 12.4.

12.3   The Pension Benefit Guaranty Corporation, a nonprofit
corporation, has been established within the Department of
Labor by the Employee Retirement Income Security Act of
1974 to insure that Participants and beneficiaries covered
under the Plan do not incur a loss of benefits caused by a
termination of the Plan before sufficient funds have been
accumulated to pay all benefits.

   Under certain conditions specified in applicable federal
laws and regulations, the Pension Benefit Guaranty Corporation may institute proceedings to terminate the Plan. In
this event, the Pension Benefit Guaranty Corporation will
be responsible for determining the degree of insurance

coverage, the priority of claims, and the distribution of assets and insurance proceeds to all claimants.

If, within the 90-day period described in Article 12.2, the Pension Benefit Guaranty Corporation is unable to determine, pursuant to a "notice of termination" as described in Article 12.2, that the assets held under the Plan are sufficient to discharge, when due, the obligations of the Plan, the Pension Benefit Guaranty Corporation will notify the Trustees of that finding within the 90-day period and may institute proceedings to terminate the Plan as described in the preceding paragraph.

12.4   A Participant's benefit, determined to be payable under Article 12.2, will be equal to the Normal Pension Benefit to which he is entitled under Article 12.1. Plan assets shall be allocated to provide benefits on the basis of an actuarial study and report by a qualified actuary to be designated by the Trustees, in accordance with applicable laws and regulations. Benefits, with respect to a Participant who has then attained his Normal Retirement Date, will be distributed in the form of an immediate pension benefit. All other benefits will be in form of a paid-up deferred pension with payments commencing on each Participant's Normal Retirement Date. The form of the pension so distributed will be in accordance with Article 5.

12.5   Benefits, when determined as described above, will remain fixed regardless of any person's employment status thereafter.

12.6   If, after the provisions of Article 12.4 have been applied, any balance remains in the Plan funds, such remaining balance shall be allocated among all Participants in accordance with a nondiscriminatory formula to be determined by the Trustees. Any amount to be allocated to a Participant may be in cash or in the form of a monthly benefit at the discretion of the Trustees. The determinations to be made under the provisions of this Article 12.6 shall be based on an actuarial study and report by a qualified actuary to be designated by the Trustees.

12.7   All other provisions of this Plan notwithstanding, no merger or consolidation with, or transfer of assets or liabilities to, any other plan shall be made unless each Participant in this Plan would receive a benefit, if the Plan then terminated immediately after the merger, consolidation, or transfer, which is equal to or greater than the benefit he would have been entitled to receive immediately before the merger, consolidation or transfer if the Plan had then terminated.

ARTICLE 13. ILLEGALITY OR INVALIDITY OF ANY PROVISION

13.1 If any provisions of the Plan are held to be illegal or invalid for any reason, such illegality or invalidity shall not affect the remaining parts of the Plan, but the Plan shall be construed and enforced as if such illegal and invalid provisions had never been inserted in the Plan.

13.2 The masculine gender shall include the feminine wherever applicable.

ARTICLE 14. SPECIAL PROVISIONS

14.1 The provisions of Article 14 shall apply only to Participants who were covered under this Plan on December 31, 1975.

14.2 *Retirement Date.* The Normal Retirement Date for said Participant shall be the earlier of (*a*) or (*b*) as follows:

    a. The Normal Retirement Date determined pursuant to Article 3 of this Plan, or

    b. The Normal Retirement Date determined under the Plan as it existed on December 31, 1975.

The Early Retirement Date for said Participant shall be the earlier of (*c*) or (*d*) as follows:

    c. The Early Retirement Date as determined under Article 3 of this Plan, or

    d. The Early Retirement Date as determined under the Plan as it existed on December 31, 1975.

14.3 *Normal Pension Benefit.* The Normal Pension Benefit for said Participant shall be the greater of (*a*) or (*b*), as follows:

> *a.* The Normal Pension Benefit as determined under this Plan, or
>
> *b.* The Normal Pension Benefit accrued through December 31, 1975, under the Plan as it existed on that date.

14.4   *Vested Benefit on Termination of Coverage*

> *a.* The vested rights at any time after December 31, 1975, of said Participant, who was a Covered Employee on December 31, 1975, shall be the greater of (1) or (2) as follows:
>
> > (1)   His vested rights as determined under Article 6 of this Plan, or
> >
> > (2)   His vested rights as determined under the vesting provisions of the Plan as it existed on December 31, 1975.
>
> *b.* The vested rights of said Participant, who was a Vested Employee on December 31, 1975, and who does not become an Active Participant under this Plan after December 31, 1975, shall continue to be the same vested rights he had as of December 31, 1975.
>
> *c.* The vested rights of said Participant, who was a Vested Employee on December 31, 1975, and who does become an Active Participant under this Plan shall be computed according to Article 6 of this Plan. In no event, however, shall his future vested benefit be less than the vested benefits he had as of December 31, 1975.

APPENDIX C

SPECIMEN SUBSCRIPTION AGREEMENT

XYZ WORKERS PENSION PLAN

Subscription Agreement

WHEREAS:

A. Effective January 1, 1966, the Board of Trustees established the XYZ Workers Pension Plan, herein called the Plan, pursuant to a Trust Agreement, known as the XYZ Workers Pension Fund Agreement and Declaration of Trust, wherein it is provided that an Employer who is not a signatory Employer may become a party to this Trust Agreement by executing a written agreement whereby said Employer accepts and agrees to be bound by the terms of the Trust Agreement.

B. The undersigned Employer desires to become a party to this Trust Agreement.

NOW THEREFORE, the undersigned Employer agrees as follows:

1. Effective as of _____, Employer agrees to commence making contributions for its employees and to be bound by all of the terms, provisions, conditions, and limitations of the Plan and Trust Agreement and all lawful amendments thereto. Employer hereby appoints as Employer

Trustees those presently serving in that capacity and their duly appointed successors provided, however, that if the Employer signing this Subscriber's Agreement is a Union which is not signatory, as an Employer, to a collective bargaining agreement with a XYZ Workers International Association Local Union covering the employees for whom contributions will be made under this Agreement, then the said Employer hereby waives any and all rights which it may otherwise have to participate in the selection and appointment of Employer Trustees.

2. Employer further agrees to comply with all rules, resolutions, and regulations heretofore or hereafter promulgated by the Board of Trustees in accordance with the Plan and Trust Agreement.

3. Employer shall make contributions on behalf of its employees at the contribution rate applicable to the pertinent employee group as provided in the Employer's collective bargaining agreement, or, if Employer is a Union which is not subject to a collective bargaining agreement covering its employees, at a rate of $x.xx per hour.

4. The rates of Employer contributions into this Pension Trust Fund shall be governed by rules and regulations adopted from time to time by the Trustees governing the conditions applicable to the acceptability of employer contributions pusuant to the recommendations of the actuary and legal counsel. The Employer will supply the Board of Trustees with all data required for the effective administration of this Plan.

Signed at _____ on _____, 19___.

(EMPLOYER)   ABCD Corporation _____

By _____

Title _____

Accepted on _____, 19___, on behalf of the Board of Trustees of XYZ Workers Pension Plan.

By _____   By _____
   Employer Trustee   Union Trustee

APPENDIX D

SPECIMEN PENSION CLAUSE IN A COLLECTIVE BARGAINING AGREEMENT

COLLECTIVE BARGAINING AGREEMENT
between
ABCD CORPORATION
and the
XYZ WORKERS UNION,
LOCAL NO. 2
Adopted _____, 1966

PENSION PLAN

I. CONTRIBUTIONS

The company will contribute at the following cents per hour rates, for each covered employee, to the XYZ Workers Pension Trust Fund to provide benefits in accordance with the XYZ Workers Pension Plan:

Effective _____, 1966 . . . . . . 20¢ per hour

Effective _____, 1967 . . . . . . 25¢ per hour

Effective _____, 1966 . . . . . . 30¢ per hour

Covered employees will be all of the company's employees represented by the Union.

Contributions will be made only on straight-time hours worked including paid vacations, sabbatical leaves, and paid holidays up to a maximum of 173 ⅓ hours per month. Contributions for new covered employees shall begin on the first hour worked under this Agreement.

II. TERMINATION OF EXISTING COMPANY PLANS

The benefit to which each employee now participating under an existing plan shall be entitled shall be determined as the benefit to which the employee would be entitled under the existing plan as now constituted, if no further credits accrue for the employee thereunder after March 1, 1966, but the employee is considered to have a fully vested right only if this person has completed ten (10) years of service and only if this person remains in the service of the company until retirement in accordance with the terms of the existing plan or meets the age and service requirements for vesting of company-purchased benefits.

As soon as possible, the company will review with the Union the situation of any persons now participating in an existing plan who are age sixty-three (63) or over, for the purpose of making proper arrangements to prevent such persons being prejudiced by reason of the termination of the existing plan.

All contributions under existing plans for and by employees subject to this Agreement shall be terminated as of March 1, 1966.

III. CONTRACTUAL RETIREMENT AGE

The contractual retirement age for all employees is sixty-five (65). However, if an individual employee does not qualify for the minimum pension, that employee shall be permitted to continue working for the length of time necessary to qualify for a pension up to a maximum of two (2) years.

APPENDIX E

SPECIMEN ADMINISTRATIVE FORMS

This appendix includes:

Section A. A detailed outline of the plan administrator's responsibilities under ERISA for reporting and disclosure.

Section B. Specimen retirement information and application forms.

Section C. Specimen forms which explain—

a. The preretirement benefit to spouse option;

b. The automatic joint and survivor pension required for certain married participants at retirement; and

c. The normal pension form and other optional forms of pension which may be available under a plan.

Section D. A specimen employer remittance form used by the administrator for billing and accounting for employer contributions.

Section E. An outline of participant census data required by the plan actuary to perform periodic actuarial valuations.

SECTION A
REPORTING AND DISCLOSURE REQUIREMENTS
FOR MULTIEMPLOYER PLANS

I. ITEMS TO BE FILED WITH THE DEPARTMENT OF LABOR

A. *Plan Description.* The Plan Description must be filed with Secretary of Labor on Form EBS-1 within 120 days after a new plan comes into existence. An updated plan description is required to be filed no more frequently than once every five years.

B. *Summary Description of Plan Modification and Information Changes.* A summary description of any "material" plan modification or information change as distributed to the participants must be filed by the plan administrator with the Secretary of Labor within 210 days after the end of the plan year in which such modification or change is adopted or occurs.

C. *Summary Plan Description.* A Summary Plan Description must be filed with the Secretary of Labor within 120 days after a new plan comes into existence. The Summary Plan Description must be filed every five years after the first filing to incorporate amendments made during the period, unless no amendments have occurred. In any event, the Summary Plan Description must be refiled every tenth year after the plan is subject to these requirements.

D. *Terminal Reports.* The administrator of a pension plan that is "winding up its affairs" (without regard to the number of participants remaining in the plan) will be required to file a terminal report and possible supplemental reports with the Secretary of Labor. This report will be filed with the annual report unless regulations specify otherwise.

II. ITEMS TO BE FURNISHED TO PLAN PARTICIPANTS AND BENEFICIARIES

A. *Summary Plan Description.* A Summary Plan Description must be furnished to participants and beneficiaries. It must be furnished by the later of (*a*) 90 days after they enter the plan (or in the case of beneficiaries, begin receiving benefits) or (*b*) 120 days after a new plan comes into existence.

B. *Summary Description of Plan Modification and Information Changes.* A summary of any material modification to the plan must be furnished within 210 days after the end of the plan year in which such modification or change is adopted. Additionally, every fifth year a new updated Summary Plan Description which integrates all plan amendments made within that period must be furnished. In the absence of any amendments, a new Summary Plan Description must be furnished every ten years.

C. *Summary Annual Report.* For disclosure purposes, a summary of the Annual Report must be furnished to each participant and beneficiary within nine months after the close of the fiscal year of the plan.

D. *Statement of Vested Benefits.* Plan administrators are also required to furnish a statement of vested benefits to any participant who separates from service during the year with a right to a deferred vested benefit, but does not begin receiving benefits during the year. This statement must indicate the nature, amount, and form of the deferred vested benefit to which the participant is entitled and be sufficient to inform the employee of his accrued benefits under the plan and the percentage of such benefits that are nonforfeitable. This statement must be furnished on or before the date the Annual Report is filed with the Secretary of the Treasury.[1]

E. *Statement of Benefit Rights.* A statement setting forth a participant's or beneficiary's benefits under an employee benefit plan must be furnished if so requested in writing. The plan administrator must furnish this statement within 30 days and it must include (1) the total benefits accrued, and (2) the nonforfeitable pension benefits, if any, which have accrued or the earliest date on which benefits will become nonforfeitable. Such a request, however, need not be honored more

---

[1] For administrative details, see New Administrative Duties Imposed by ERISA in Chapter 7.

than once during any one 12-month period. This requirement will apply to plans to which more than one unaffiliated employer contributes only to the extent provided in regulations that will be issued.

F. *Explanation of Joint and Survivor Annuity.* The plan administrator must furnish an explanation of the joint and survivor annuity benefit prior to the time the participant becomes eligible to submit a pension application.[2]

G. *Plan Documents.* Copies of all documents under which a plan is established or operated must be made available for examination by participants and beneficiaries in the same manner as the Plan Description and Annual Report. This will generally include all collective bargaining agreements, trust agreements, and contracts. Copies of these documents must also be furnished upon written request for a reasonable charge, not to exceed $0.25 a page.

H. *Statement of Reasons for Denying Claim.* Participants and beneficiaries of employee benefit plans subject to ERISA must be given a written statement of reasons in the event a claim for benefits is denied. This statement must be written in a manner calculated to be understood by the participant and must include:

1. The specific reason or reasons for the denial;

2. Specific reference to pertinent plan provisions on which the denial is based;

3. A description of any additional material or information necessary for the claimant to perfect the claim and an explanation of why such material or information is necessary; and

4. An explanation of the plan's claim review procedure.

This review procedure must be reasonable and is required to be set forth in the Summary Plan Description.

The claimant must be allowed at least 60 days from

---

[2] For administrative details, see Qualified Joint and Survivor Annuity Benefits in Chapter 7.

the notice of denial in which to appeal. Like the notification denying the claim, the decision on an appeal must be in writing with specific reasons for the decision, must be written in a manner calculated to be understood by the claimant, and must contain specific references to the plan provisions on which the decision is based.

III. ITEMS TO BE FILED WITH THE SECRETARY OF TREASURY

A. *Annual Registration and Reports to the Secretary of the Treasury.* Administrators of employee benefit plans subject to the vesting standards of ERISA are required to file an annual registration statement with the Internal Revenue Service.

This registration statement must be filed with the Annual Report on Schedule SSA to Form 5500. This registration statement must contain the following information:

1. The name of the plan;
2. The name and address of the plan administrator;
3. The name and taxpayer identifying number of each participant who was separated from service during the year and is entitled to a deferred vested benefit at the end of the year;
4. The nature, amount, and form of the deferred vested benefit to which each separated participant is entitled; and
5. Such other information as the IRS may require.

At the time this statement is filed, the plan administrator must also include evidence that he has sent each separated participant, entitled to a deferred vested benefit, a statement containing the same information as the registration statement.

The information contained in this registration statement will be forwarded to the Secretary of Health, Education, and Welfare and made available to the participant when he becomes eligible for social security benefits.

B. *Notification of Change in Status.* Any change in the name of the plan, or in the name or address of the plan administrator, must be reported to the IRS, as well as the termination, merger, or consolidation of the plan with any other plan or its division into two or more plans.

This requirement will apply to plans to which more than one unaffiliated employer contributes only to the extent set forth in regulations to be issued.

C. *Annual Reports and Actuarial Reports.* In addition to the annual registration statement, the plan administrator must file a copy of the Annual Report with the Internal Revenue Service within seven months after the end of each plan year. This report is made on Form 5500 (for plans with 100 or more participants) or Form 5500-C (for plans with fewer than 100 participants), together with any required schedules. Also, actuarial reports are required at periodic intervals and in the event of a merger, consolidation, or transfer of assets.

IV. ITEMS TO BE FILED WITH THE PENSION BENEFIT GUARANTY CORPORATION

A. *Payment of Premium.* The premium payments to the PBGC must be submitted with Form PBGC-1 within 7 months after the beginning of the plan year unless an extension is granted by the PBGC.

B. *Terminal Reports.* The administrator of a pension plan that is "winding up its affairs" (without regard to the number of participants remaining in the plan) will be required to file a terminal report and possible supplemental reports with the PBGC.

C. *Notice of Termination.* This notice must be filed ten days prior to termination of plan. No special form is required, but contents should include the fact that the plan is being terminated and should indicate the proposed date of termination.

D. *Reportable Events.* If any of the following events occur, the plan administrator is required to notify the PBGC, presumably by letter, within 30 days after he knows or has reason to know of its occurrence.

1. A tax disqualification;
2. A benefit decrease by plan amendment;
3. A decrease in active participants to eighty percent (80%) of the number at the beginning of the plan year, or seventy-five percent (75%) of the number at the beginning of the previous plan year;
4. An IRS determination that there has been a plan termination or partial termination for tax purposes;
5. A failure to meet the minimum funding standards;
6. Inability to pay benefits when due;
7. A distribution of $10,000 or more in a 24-month period to a "substantial owner," if the plan has unfunded nonforfeitable benefits after the distribution (unless the distribution was made on account of death);
8. A merger, consolidation, or transfer of assets or liabilities.
9. The occurrence of any other event which the PBGC determines may be indicative of a need to terminate the plan.

Also any contributing employer who has knowledge of any of the foregoing "reportable events" is required to report it to the plan administrator.

E. *Other Notices.* In addition, administrators of defined benefit employee pension plans are required to (1) notify each contributing employer within six months after the close of each plan year if he is a "substantial employer" for that year; and (2) notify the PBGC within 60 days of the withdrawal of a "substantial employer."

SECTION B

This section contains the following sample forms:

1. Request for Retirement Benefit Information and illustration of the amounts of benefit creditable under various options.
2. Pension Application.

XYZ WORKERS PENSION TRUST FUND
50 Best Road, Los Angeles, California 99999

REQUEST FOR RETIREMENT BENEFIT INFORMATION

The requested information will be taken from Trust Fund Office records. Formal application for retirement must be submitted furnishing information and proof as required by the rules of the Plan. The Board of Trustees must approve the application before any benefits will be paid.

Election of an optional pension form must be made prior to the commencement of any pension payments. Written notice of such election shall be made in accordance with the rules and regulations established by the Trustees. The election of a form of pension shall, in any event, be subject to any conditions imposed by the Trustees with respect to the granting of such form of pension.

Personal Information (to be completed by member)

1. Participant Information:

   Name: _____ Date of Birth: _____

   Social Security Number: _____ Local No.: _____

2. Spouse Information (for calculation of Joint and Survivor Pension only)

   Name: _____ Date of Birth: _____

   Social Security Number: _____

Calculation of Pension Amounts (to be completed by Trust Fund Office)

Notice: These pension examples have been calculated using information available to the Trust Fund Office at this time. Upon your actual retirement, a final pension benefit determination will be made when all required information has been received.

REQUEST FOR RETIREMENT BENEFIT INFORMATION
(continued)

1. Date of Retirement:
   - ☐ Normal: _____ ☐ Postponed: _____
   - ☐ Early: _____
2. Normal Pension Benefit:
   a. Past Service:

   From _____, 19__ , to _____ , 19__

   Past Service Benefit = $10 × ____ Years = $ _____

   b. Future Service:

   From _____, 19__ , to _____ , 19__

   (1) Number of Covered Hours   _____

   (2) Number of Years of Credited Future
   Service [= (1) ÷ 1,500]   _____

   (3) Future Service Benefit
   [= (2) × $10] = $ _____

   Accrued Normal Pension Benefit [= $a + b$ (3)] $ _____

   c. Early Retirement: If member retires directly from service, Retirement Benefit will be reduced 0.5 percent for each of the first 60 months his retirement precedes age 65 plus 0.3 percent for each additional month prior to age 60.

   Total Percent Reductions _____ = $ _____

   Accrued Early Pension Benefit $ _____

Note: Pensions payable to you at date of retirement under the various forms of pension available under the Plan are described on the reverse side of this form.

By: _____ Date: _____

REQUEST FOR RETIREMENT BENEFIT INFORMATION
(concluded)

Illustration of Pension Forms (to be completed by Trust Fund Office)

Following are examples of the pensions payable to you under the various pension forms available under the Plan:

	Monthly Benefit for Your Lifetime	*Monthly Benefit to Surviving Spouse*
Automatic Joint and Survivor Pension	$_____	$_____
Normal Form of Pension (payable as long as Pensioner lives—remaining guaranteed payments to beneficiary if Pensioner dies before receiving 36 monthly pension payments)	$_____	Not applicable
Joint and Two-thirds Survivor Pension	$_____	$_____
Joint and 100 Percent Survivor Pension	$_____	$_____

XYZ WORKERS PENSION PLAN
50 Best Road, Los Angeles, California 99999

PENSION APPLICATION

Instructions

1. Please read each question carefully.
2. Print all information required.
3. Be sure to answer all questions to avoid delays in processing your pension application.
4. Attach additional sheets if you need more space to answer any questions.
5. Be sure you have completed the application where required, and attach the following:
   a. Proof of age.
   b. Authorization to obtain earnings data from the Social Security Administration (the form is enclosed).
   c. If married:
      1. Proof of age of spouse.
      2. Copy of marriage certificate.
6. Sign and date this application.
7. Mail completed application and attachments to Trust Fund Office.
8. You should receive an acknowledgement of receipt of this application from the Trust Fund Office. If you do not receive an acknowledgement within five business days from the day you mail the application, please notify the Trust Fund Office.

   The Trust Fund Office will prepare an illustration of your pension benefits under each of the available types of pension and will send this illustration to you along with the ELECTION OF OPTION form which you must complete to specify the type of pension you wish to receive.

Proof of Age

In order to be eligible for retirement benefits, you are required to produce proof of your age. The following is a list of the documents which may serve as proof of your age. The list is arranged starting with the best type of proof and going down to the less desirable types of documents. You are required to furnish the best type of proof which is available, and the Trustees may require additional proofs of age if the documents you submit do not constitute convincing proof of your age. The original of any document you submit will be returned to you. Please check below which documents you have submitted with this Pension Application.

PENSION APPLICATION INSTRUCTIONS *(continued)*

Employee   Spouse   (if applicable)

☐ ☐ Birth Certificate.

☐ ☐ Baptismal Certificate or a statement as to the date of birth shown by a church record certified by the custodian of such record.

☐ ☐ Notification of Registration of Birth in a public registry of vital statistics.

☐ ☐ Hospital Birth Records, certified by the custodian of such records.

☐ ☐ Physician's statement or midwife who was in attendance at birth, as to the date of birth shown on their record.

☐ ☐ Document showing approval of federal or state social security pension.

☐ ☐ Certification of Age by the United States Census Bureau.

☐ ☐ Naturalization Record (photostat not permitted; submit original).

☐ ☐ Immigration paper (photostat not permitted; submit original).

☐ ☐ Military record—Certificate of Discharge, etc.

☐ ☐ Passport (United States passport may not be photostated; submit original).

☐ ☐ School record, certified by the custodian of such record.

☐ ☐ An Insurance Policy with application at least five years old.

☐ ☐ Marriage record (application for marriage license or church record, certified by the custodian of such record) or marriage certificate.

☐ ☐ Confirmation record.

☐ ☐ Other evidence, such as voting or registration records. Family Bible, newspaper clipping, or signed statements from persons who have knowledge of the date of birth.

PENSION APPLICATION

A. Participant Information

1. Name _____
              (Last)   (Middle)   (First)

2. Address _____

              (City)   (State)   (Zip)

3. Telephone Number _____

4. Address to which pension checks are to be sent, if other than above:

   _____

              (City)   (State)   (Zip)

5. Social Security Number _____

6. Local Union Number _____

7. Date you retired or plan to retire _____
                               (Month)   (Year)

8. Date of Birth _____
             (Month)   (Day)   (Year)

9. Sex   ☐ Male   ☐ Female

10. *Health Benefits*—You may be eligible to continue Health Care benefits, as described in your Health Care Plan booklet, on a self-pay basis, following retirement. If eligible, do you wish to continue these benefits? (A "No" answer may not be changed at a later date.)   ☐ Yes   ☐ No

11. Are you married?   ☐ Yes   ☐ No

    If you are married (even if you are separated) supply the following information:

    a. Name of Spouse _____
                         (Last)   (First)   (Middle)

    b. Spouse's Date of Birth_____
                             (Month)   (Day)   (Year)

    c. Spouse's Social Security Number _____

    d. Date of Marriage _____
                      (Month)   (Day)   (Year)

    If you are married, the Trust Fund Office cannot prepare an illustration of the amount of your monthly pension under each of the types of pension available to you unless you complete items (*a*) through (*d*) above.

PENSION APPLICATION *(continued)*

B. Service Information

1. Supply the following information for your most recent Covered Employment.

    a. Employer _____

    b. Date of Hire _____
                         (Month)   (Day)   (Year)

    c. Date of Termination, if any _____
                                       (Month)   (Day)   (Year)

2. List below all jobs held prior to retirement, subject to a Collective Bargaining Agreement in the XYZ Industry in California, and before you began to work for a contributing employer under this Pension Plan.

Name of Employer	Address	Dates of Employment			
		From		To	
		Month	Year	Month	Year

(Attach additional sheets if more space is needed)

ANSWER ALL APPLICABLE QUESTIONS

3. If you served in the Armed Forces of the United States (submit photocopy of discharge papers).

    Date Entered _____ Branch _____ Date Discharged _____

4. List below any periods during which you were totally disabled and thereby prevented from engaging in any employment.

From			To			Nature of Disability
Month	Day	Year	Month	Day	Year	

PENSION APPLICATION *(continued)*

5. List below any periods during which you received Workmen's Compensation Disability Benefits.

From			To			
Month	Day	Year	Month	Day	Year	Nature of Disability

6. Have you worked as a XYZ Employee in the Western States in an area not covered by this Pension Plan?

   ☐ Yes   ☐ No   If yes, list dates, Local Union Numbers

From			To			Local Union Number	City	State
Month	Day	Year	Month	Day	Year			

C. Designation of Beneficiary

Note: You may name any person of your choice, or your own estate, to receive any death benefit payable under the Plan. However, if you are married when you die and your spouse has not consented in writing to the form you filed, then one half of your death benefit will be paid to your surviving spouse and the form you filed will apply only to the other half.

I hereby designate the following beneficiary to receive any payments under the XYZ Workers Pension Plan, other than those payable to my spouse under the terms of the Plan, which may due in the event of my death and revoke any prior beneficiary designated. I reserve the right to change the beneficiary in the future by giving the Pension Plan written notification. (Instructions: Give full name of beneficiary, for example, Mary Lou Jones, not Mrs. Harry Jones.)

Name _____
　　　　　　　(Last)　　　　　　(First)　　　　　(Middle)

Relationship _____

Address _____

If the beneficiary is not your spouse, complete either item 1 or item 2 below:

1. ☐ I am not married.

PENSION APPLICATION *(concluded)*

2. ☐ I am married, and my spouse has signed below to indicate her consent to this designation. (The spouse's signature must be witnessed.)

Date _____

Spouse's Signature _____

Signature of Witness _____

D. Certification

I hereby apply for a pension from the XYZ Workers Pension Trust Fund. I have read the Instructions for Application for the Pension, and agree to be bound by all the Rules and Regulations of the Pension Plan. I understand that I must notify the Trust Fund Office if I become reemployed in the XYZ industry or any other building craft trade, and must abide by the rules concerning Loss of Pension, as contained in the Plan.

I certify under perjury that all of the foregoing is true and correct. I understand that the Trustees have the right to recover any payments made to me in error because of a false statement.

Signature _____

Name of Witness (print) _____

Date _____

Signature of Witness _____

SECTION C

This section contains the following forms:

1. Information concerning the Preretirement Benefit to Spouse Option, Preretirement Benefit to Spouse Option Election Form, and Revocation Form for the Preretirement Benefit to Spouse Option.
2. Information for Employees concerning Options.
3. Election of Option.

XYZ WORKERS PENSION PLAN
50 Best Road, Los Angeles, California 99999

INFORMATION CONCERNING THE PRERETIREMENT BENEFIT TO SPOUSE OPTION

If you are married and at least age 54, you may elect the Preretirement Benefit to Spouse Option providing you are in covered employment at the time of your election. This Option provides, should you die before you retire, a lifetime income payable to your spouse. The following paragraphs describe when the Option becomes effective, the period of coverage, the amount of spouse income payable in the event of your death, and the reduction in your future retirement income if you make the election.

Effective Date. If you wish to have this Option, you must complete the attached election form and submit it to the Trust Fund Office. When elected, the Option becomes effective after all three of the following occur:

a. After you become eligible to retire (but not before your 55th birthday).
b. After you have been married for at least one year.
c. After a waiting period of six months following receipt of your election by the Trust Fund Office. The six months waiting period does not apply if death is caused by an accident that occurs after the date you elect this option.

Note: This Option *automatically* becomes effective (1) on your Normal Retirement Date, (2) at the time you terminate covered employment if you are eligible to retire early at that time, or (3) the time you become eligible to retire early if you have terminated covered employment prior to that time by transferring to a job, with the same employer, which is not covered by the plan, and you continue to work for the same employer. In any of the above cases, the Option will only become effective after you have been married for one year.

Your Normal Retirement Date depends on your service under the plan but it cannot be before your 65th birthday. Termination of covered employment occurs at the end of a "grace period" which is a period of two consecutive calendar years during which you fail to work at least 435 covered hours per year.

If you are or become married and do not wish spouse coverage, you should contact the Trust Fund Office *before* the date on which the option automatically becomes effective.

Coverage Period. Coverage will begin when the Option becomes effective and will cease on the *first* to occur of:

a. The date of your retirement,
b. The date six months after the date you revoke the option, or
c. The date your spouse dies or you are divorced. (If you remarry and want coverage for your new spouse, you should request a new election form.)

INFORMATION CONCERNING THE PRERETIREMENT BENEFIT TO SPOUSE OPTION (continued)

Amount of the Spouse Pension. The amount of the spouse pension is equal to a percentage of the benefit you would have received had you retired on the day before your death. The amount of reduced benefit depends on the ages of both you and your spouse on your date of death. As an example, assume you had elected this Option and died at age 60 and your wife was then age 55. If your early retirement monthly benefit would have been $300 had you retired at age 60, your wife would be entitled to a benefit of $126 per month for her remaining lifetime. This amount is determined by multiplying the $300 by the percentage from the following table (41.9 percent in the example):

Percentage of Benefit Payable to Your Spouse

Spouse's Age as Compared to Pensioner's Age	Male Pensioner Age of Pensioner on Date of Death				Female Pensioner Age of Pensioner on Date of Death			
	55	60	62	65	55	60	62	65
Ten years younger	41.7	40.3	39.7	38.7	45.1	44.4	44.1	43.6
Five years younger	43.0	41.9	41.5	40.7	46.2	45.7	45.5	45.2
Same age	44.4	43.6	43.2	42.7	47.2	46.9	46.8	46.7
Five years older	45.7	45.2	45.0	44.7	48.1	47.9	47.9	47.9
Ten years older	46.9	46.7	46.6	46.5	48.7	48.7	48.7	48.8

Reduction in Your Future Retirement Income. Election of this Option is a cost item and must be charged against your retirement benefit when you begin receiving payments. The charge will be made by reducing your pension payments after you retire. The reduction will be based on the length of time the Option was in effect (the Coverage Period) and the difference in ages between you and your spouse.

The reduction in your retirement pension is illustrated in the following table. As an example, if you retire at age 65, your wife is five years younger and the Option became effective ten years ago—the reduction in your retirement benefit would be 10.5 percent (1.050 times ten years). If a benefit of $400 were payable, this would result in your $400 monthly benefit reducing to $358.

Reduction for Each Year Option Was in Effect

Spouse's Age Compared to Your Age	Your Sex	
	Male	Female
Ten years younger	1.100%	0.770%
Five years younger	1.050	0.735
Same age	1.000	0.700
Five years older	0.952	0.666
Ten years older	0.909	0.636

INFORMATION CONCERNING THE PRERETIREMENT BENEFIT TO SPOUSE OPTION *(concluded)*

Election/Revocation. If you wish to provide your spouse with a monthly pension upon your death as described above, please fill in the attached election form.

You may, at any time, revoke your election to provide this coverage. Any revocation should be in writing to the plan administrator and it will become effective six months after the date it is received or on your retirement date, if sooner. However, the monthly amount of pension payable to you upon your retirement will still be reduced to reflect the period of time during which the coverage was in effect.

The preceding description deals with Benefit to Spouse coverage in the event of your death before your Normal Retirement Date. Your Normal Retirement Age is based on your Plan participation but can not be before age 65. After your Normal Retirement Date, similar coverage will automatically be in effect *UNLESS* you elect otherwise.

The Trust Fund Office will be happy to assist you in estimating the effect of the Option on your benefits. Whether or not you choose this option, you should contact the Trust Fund Office around the time of your 64th birthday.

XYZ WORKERS PENSION TRUST FUND
50 Best Road, Los Angeles, California 99999

PRERETIREMENT BENEFIT TO SPOUSE OPTION ELECTION FORM

Social Security Number _____

Employee's Name _____
                      (Last)   (First)   (Middle)

Local Union Number _____

    I have read the attached information and I wish to elect the preretirement Benefit to Spouse Option to become effective on the earliest possible date. I understand that this date cannot occur for *at least six months* and before *I become eligible to retire* under the Plan. I further understand that any future retirement benefits payable to me will be reduced to provide this benefit.

Name of Spouse _____
                    (First)   (Middle Initial)   (Last)

Spouse
Date of Birth _____ Spouse Social Security No. _____

Date of   Your   Date of Union
Marriage _____ Date of Birth _____ Membership _____

Your Home
Address (please print) _____

_____

My most recent Employer is:

                                    Date of
                      Date of   Termination,
Name _____ Hire _____ if any _____

Employee's Signature _____ Date _____

Witness' Signature _____

After receipt and processing by the Trust Fund Office, a signed copy of this application will be returned to you. If you do not receive a copy within 60 days please contact the Trust Fund Office.

☐   Your Effective Date for this Option is _____

☐   We are unable to determine your Effective Date at this time. It will be determined by examination of your work records at the time of your death or retirement under the Plan. You may request an earlier determination by writing the Trust Fund Office any time after

_____ .

Trust Fund Office—by _____
                           (Signature)   (Date)

XYZ WORKERS PENSION TRUST FUND

50 Best Road, Los Angeles, California 99999

REVOCATION FORM FOR THE PRERETIREMENT BENEFIT TO SPOUSE OPTION

Please read the attached information concerning the Preretirement Benefit to Spouse Option.

A. If you had previously elected this Option and now wish to revoke such election, please complete the box at the bottom of this form. The cancellation will take effect *six months* after the date this Form is received by the Trust Fund Office or on your effective retirement date, if sooner.

B. This Option *automatically* becomes effective (1) on your Normal Retirement Date, (2) at the time you terminate covered employment if you are eligible to retire early at that time, or (3) the time you become eligible to retire early if you have terminated covered employment prior to that time by transferring to a job, with the same employer, which is not covered by the plan, and you continue to work for the same employer. In any of the above cases, the Option will only become effective after you have been married for one year.

If you *do not* wish to have this Option, you must complete the box at the bottom of this form. This revocation will prevent the Option from becoming effective, or cancel it if it is effective, at any time up to your actual retirement under the Plan.

I do not wish the Preretirement Benefit to Spouse Option and hereby revoke any automatic or previously written election. I understand that the monthly amount of pension which may become payable to me on my retirement will be reduced to pay for any coverage I may have had under the Option.

Social Security No.	Employee's Name	(First)	$\left(\begin{array}{c}\text{Middle}\\\text{Initial}\end{array}\right)$ (Last)	Local Union Number

Employee's Signature _____ Date _____

Spouse's Signature _____ Date _____

Witness's Signature _____ Date _____

Trust Fund Office—by _____

(Signature)　　　　　　　　　　　　　(Date)

_____

(Date Received by Trust Fund Office)

XYZ WORKERS PENSION TRUST FUND
50 Best Road, Los Angeles, California 99999

INFORMATION FOR EMPLOYEES
CONCERNING OPTIONS

You have the choice of one of several forms of pension when you retire. The various pension forms are available to you under the following conditions:

IF YOU ARE MARRIED and have been married for at least one year on your retirement date, your monthly pension will be paid under the Automatic Joint and Survivor Pension Form unless you and your spouse elect one of the other available forms. You may elect the Normal Form of Pension, the Joint and Two-Thirds Survivor Pension, or the Joint and 100 Percent Survivor Pension.

IF YOU ARE NOT MARRIED or have not been married on your retirement date for at least one year, your monthly pension will be paid under the Normal Form of Pension (Life Pension with Payments Guaranteed for 36 Months) unless you elect otherwise.

For your information, the available pension forms are described below:

Automatic Joint and Survivor Pension Form

As a Participant eligible for age retirement in the XYZ Workers Pension Plan you will, if you are married and have been married at least one year on your retirement date, receive your monthly pension payments under the Automatic Joint and Survivor Pension Form unless you and your spouse elect otherwise. If you are married, but have been married less than one year, you may elect the Automatic Joint and Survivor Pension Form.

Under this form of pension your monthly benefits are *reduced* so that if you die after the date your pension begins and your spouse survives you, a monthly benefit will be continued to your spouse for your spouse's remaining lifetime in the amount of one half of the benefit which you were receiving at the time of your death. If your spouse dies before the date your pension begins, this pension form will be canceled and no reduction will be made in your monthly pension. If your spouse dies after the date your pension begins but during your lifetime, monthly pension benefits will continue to you in the same amount as was in effect immediately prior to the death of your spouse.

You may elect, at any time prior to your effective retirement date, *not* to have the Automatic Joint and Survivor Pension Form. You may then elect one of the following forms of pension.

Normal Form of Pension

If (1) you are not married, or have been married less than one year, or (2) if you have been married at least one year and you and your spouse so elect, benefits will be payable to you with the Normal Pension Form. Under this form of pension your monthly benefits will *not be reduced* and will continue as long as you live. Under this pension form a death benefit will be

INFORMATION FOR EMPLOYEES
CONCERNING OPTIONS *(continued)*

payable to your designated beneficiary if you have not received 36 monthly pension payments at the time of your death. In such event, the single sum value of the remaining payments shall be paid to your designated beneficiary.

Joint and Two-Thirds Survivor Pension

This pension form is similar to the Automatic Joint and Survivor Pension Form, except that a greater benefit is payable to your surviving spouse. If you are married, you and your spouse may elect this form.

Under this form of pension your monthly benefits are *reduced* on the effective date of the pension form so that if you die after the date your pension begins and your spouse survives you, a monthly benefit will be continued to your spouse for your spouse's remaining lifetime in the amount of *two thirds* of the benefit which you were receiving at the time of your death. If your spouse dies before the date your pension begins, the Option will be canceled and no reduction will be made in your monthly pension. If your spouse dies after the date your pension begins but during your lifetime, monthly pension benefits will continue to you in the same amount as was in effect immediately prior to the death of your spouse.

The amount of the reduction in your pension will be greater than the amount of the reduction under the Automatic Joint and Survivor Pension Form, since under this Joint and Two-Thirds Survivor Pension, a larger monthly benefit will be continued to your spouse if your spouse survives you.

Joint and 100 Percent Survivor Pension

This pension form is similar to the Automatic Joint and Survivor Pension Form, except that a greater benefit is payable to your surviving spouse than that provided under the Automatic Joint and Survivor or Joint and Two-Thirds Survivor Pension Forms. If you are married, you and your spouse may elect this form.

Under this form of pension your monthly benefits are *reduced* when your pension begins so that if you die after the date your pension begins and your spouse survives you, a monthly benefit will be continued to your spouse for your spouse's remaining lifetime in the amount of 100 percent of the benefit which you were receiving at the time of your death. If your spouse dies before the date your pension begins, the Option will be canceled and no reduction will be made in your monthly pension. If your spouse dies after the date your pension begins but during your lifetime, monthly pension benefits will continue to you in the same amount as was in effect immediately prior to the death of your spouse.

The amount of the reduction in your pension will be greater than the amount of the reduction under the Automatic Joint and Survivor Pension Form or the Joint and Two-Thirds Survivor Pension Form, since under this Joint and 100 Percent Survivor Pension, a larger monthly benefit will be continued to your spouse if your spouse survives you.

XYZ WORKERS PENSION TRUST FUND
50 Best Road, Los Angeles, California 99999

ELECTION OF OPTION

Important Notice: Please read th enclosed explanation of your benefits before completing this form. Your signature below indicates that you have read and understand the benefit explanation. Your benefit election cannot be changed once benefit payments have begun.

Social Security Number _____

Employee's Name _____
                    (Last)   (First)   (Middle)

Local Union Number _____

Please complete Section A, B, or C below:

A. ☐ I AM NOT MARRIED. (I AM SINGLE, DIVORCED, OR A WIDOW[ER]). I UNDERSTAND THAT THE NORMAL FORM OF PENSION IS PAYABLE.

    Date _____

    Employee's Signature _____

B. ☐ I AM MARRIED (OR LEGALLY SEPARATED) AND HAVE BEEN MARRIED FOR AT LEAST ONE YEAR. I UNDERSTAND THAT THE AUTOMATIC JOINT AND SURVIVOR PENSION FORM IS IN EFFECT FOR ME UPON MY RETIREMENT.

    1. Name of Spouse _____
                       (Last)   (First)   (Middle)

    2. Spouse's Date of Birth _____
                          (Month)   (Day)   (Year)

    3. Spouse's Social Security Number _____

    4. Date of Marriage _____

    Date _____

    Employee's Signature _____

C. ☐ I AM MARRIED (OR LEGALLY SEPARATED) AND HAVE BEEN MARRIED LESS THAN ONE YEAR. I UNDERSTAND THAT THE NORMAL FORM OF PENSION IS IN EFFECT FOR ME UPON MY RETIREMENT.

    1. Name of Spouse _____
                       (Last)   (First)   (Middle)

    2. Date of Marriage _____

    Date _____

    Employee's Signature _____

ELECTION OF OPTION *(continued)*

D. ☐ I AM MARRIED (OR LEGALLY SEPARATED) AND HAVE BEEN MARRIED AT LEAST ONE YEAR. MY SPOUSE AND I ELECT THAT THAT AUTOMATIC JOINT AND SURVIVOR PENSION FORM NOT BECOME EFFECTIVE. (SIGNATURE OF EMPLOYEE, SPOUSE, AND WITNESS ARE REQUIRED.)

    1. ☐ I wish to elect the Normal Form of Pension.

    2. ☐ I wish to elect the Joint and Two-Thirds Survivor Pension. (Complete items (*a*) through (*d*) below.)

    3. ☐ I wish to elect the Joint and 100 Percent Survivor Pension. (Complete items (*a*) through (*d*) below.)

        a. Name of Spouse _____
                          (Last)   (First)   (Middle)

        b. Spouse's Date of Birth _____
                          (Month)   (Day)   (Year)

        c. Spouse's Social Security Number _____

        d. Date of Marriage _____
                          (Month)   (Day)   (Year)

Date _____

Employee's Signature _____

Spouse's Signature _____

Witness _____

E. ☐ I AM MARRIED AND HAVE BEEN MARRIED LESS THAN ONE YEAR. I ELECT THAT THE NORMAL PENSION FORM NOT BECOME EFFECTIVE.

    1. ☐ I wish to elect the Automatic Joint and Survivor Pension.

    2. ☐ I wish to elect the Joint and Two-Thirds Survivor Pension.

    3. ☐ I wish to elect the Joint and 100 Percent Survivor Pension.

        a. Name of Spouse _____
                          (Last)   (First)   (Middle)

        b. Spouse's Date of Birth _____
                          (Month)   (Day)   (Year)

        c. Spouse's Social Security Number _____

        d. Date of Marriage _____

        e. Date _____

        f. Employee's Signature _____

SECTION D
SPECIMEN EMPLOYER REMITTANCE FORM

XYZ EMPLOYER REMITTANCE FORM

Employer's Monthly Report

1. *Important:* Include social security numbers for all employees
2. Make check payable to: XYZ Workers Pension Plan
3. *Mail check* with original and first two carbons to: XYZ Workers Pension Plan 50 Best Road, Los Angeles, California 99999

Total contributions due for month $ _____
Collection costs, if applicable, adjustments, etc. (explain below) $ _____
Amount of check $ _____

Twelve percent liquidated damages plus reasonable attorneys fees will be assessed on all delinquencies.

Report for _____ *Date Due* _____ *Employer No.*

I certify that the Employees listed hereon are covered under a written Pension Agreement or Labor Contract calling for contributions on their behalf, and that this list includes all such employees and NO OTHERS.

Authorized Signature _____

Date _____ Title _____

	Social Security Account Number	Employee's Name		Local Union Number	Date of		Total Due for Month
		Last Name	Initials		Hire Mo. Day	Term Mo. Day	
1							
2							
3							
4							
5							
6							
7							
8							
9							
10							
11							
12							
13							
14							
15							
16							
17							

By submitting this document, we agree to be bound by the above Trust and the Plan and actions of its trustees.

XYZ WORKERS PENSION PLAN
Actuarial Data Base—Nonretired Participants

Reference Number	Field Description	Comments
1.	Record code	"0" Complete "1" Basic Data Complete "2" Incomplete
2.	Current contribution rate	Provide totals by rate for balancing
3.	Date of birth a. Year b. Month	
4.	Industry employment date a. Year b. Month	Should be reassigned after return from "parity" break for nonvested participants only
5.	Years of service a. Contributory b. Noncontributory c. Total service	
6.	Contribution start date a. Year b. Month	Should be reassigned after return from "parity" break for nonvested participants only
7.	Participant's last status	Provide totals by status for balancing
8.	Accrued benefit	
9.	Vesting code	
10.	Break in service a. Indicator c. Month b. Year	
11.	Sex code	"0" if not available
12.	Record key a. Social security number b. Control name	
13.	Date of death a. Year b. Month	
14.	Employment history (last 5 years worked) a. Year b. Number of covered hours c. Total employer contributions	
15.	Date of last contribution	Required for all records

Note: This data request is oriented to our actuarial valuation requirements only. If this file is to be used for other purposes, additional data may be required. For example, another Break-in-Service Indicator will be needed for "parity" breaks.

XYZ WORKERS PENSION PLAN

Actuarial Data Base—Participants Receiving Benefits

Reference Number	Field Description	Comments
1.	Record code	"0"—data is complete "1"—data is incomplete
2.	Benefit type	Disability, early, normal, postponed, beneficiary
3.	Social security number	
4.	Control name	
5.	Sex code	"0" if not available
6.	Pensioner birthdate a. Year b. Month	"0" if not available
7.	Retirement date a. Year b. Month	"0" if not available
8.	Form of pension	Automatic J & S, normal, J & ⅔ S, J & 100% S
9.	Spouse birthday a. Year b. Month	If applicable
10.	Date of death	If applicable
11.	Date of benefit suspension	If applicable
12.	Date of benefit reinstatement	If applicable

Note: This data request is oriented to our actuarial valuation requirements only. The computer record used for benefit payments would contain additional data (such as the employee's address).

APPENDIX F

SPECIMEN ACTUARIAL REPORT

ACTUARIAL REPORT
AS OF JANUARY 1, 1977
FOR THE
XYZ WORKERS PENSION PLAN

Contents

Actuarial Certification, 325

SECTION

TABLE

ACTUARIAL CERTIFICATION

This report has been prepared in accordance with generally accepted actuarial principles and practices relating to pension plans and, to the best of my knowledge, fairly reflects the actuarial condition of the XYZ Workers Pension Plan as of January 1, 1977.

In my opinion, the assumptions used in preparing the actuarial report, to which this certification is attached, for the XYZ Workers Pension Plan, (a) are in the aggregate reasonably related to the experience under the plan and to reasonable expectations, and (b) represent my best estimate as of the valuation date of anticipated experience under the plan. The report and accompanying tables (which describe the actuarial assumptions and methods employed and summarize the principal eligibility and benefit provisions upon which the valuation was based) are complete and accurate to the best of my knowledge.

In preparing the report, I have relied upon information on plan participants provided by the plan's Administrative Office and information regarding plan assets supplied by the auditors for the plan. Further, we have made such tests of the reasonable accuracy of the nonretired employee data as we considered necessary and proper under the circumstances and as are in accordance with generally accepted actuarial principles and practices.

Certified By:

_____

Daniel F. McGinn
Fellow of the Society of Actuaries
Enrolled Actuary, Enrollment No. 649

_____

Date

SECTION A. INTRODUCTION AND PURPOSE

We have completed the actuarial valuation of your plan as of January 1, 1977, and the results are presented in this report. The main purposes of this report are:

1. To show the financial status of the plan as of January 1, 1977;
2. To determine whether or not the anticipated employer contributions will be adequate to maintain the actuarial funding of the plan;
3. To provide a statement of the Funding Standard Account for 1976 (as required by ERISA) and also an estimated Funding Standard Account for 1977;
4. To provide contribution and disclosure information generally required for accounting purposes;
5. To study the experience under the plan to evaluate the rates of turnover, death, and retirement used in the actuarial valuation.

SECTION B. COMMENTS

1. *Actuarial Valuation Results.* The actuarial valuation results show that the amortization period for the Unfunded Supplemental Present Value is 12.3 years. The 12.3-year amortization period developed in this report demonstrates that the benefits provided by your plan are being very rapidly funded by the current level of employer contributions.

   The primary reason for the decrease in the amortization period from the 27.5 years developed in the January 1, 1976, actuarial valuation was the change in the assumed rates of employee turnover. Experience turnover exceeded assumed turnover to a great extent, at the younger ages, and, as a result, the actuarial assumptions were changed to more closely conform assumptions to actual experience. The gain from excess turnover in 1976 also contributed to the reduction in the amortization period. Actual turnover experience during the 1976 plan year is discussed more fully in Table 77–5A of Section F, "Actuarial Experience."

   The reduction in the amortization period would have been even greater if the employer contribution shortfall had not occurred in 1976. The effects of this contribution shortfall are discussed in more detail in Table 77-3 of this report.

2. *Funding Standard Account for 1976.* The Funding Standard Account (FSA) for 1976, which is required by ERISA, has been prepared and is shown in Table 77-3. This information must be filed with the Internal Revenue Service on Schedule B of Form 5500 by July 31, 1977. You will note that there is a credit balance in the Funding Standard Account at the end of 1976, so the federal minimum funding standards have been satisfied.

As pointed out in Table 77-3, the 1976 charges were based on the "shortfall method" of determining FSA charges, and the difference between these charges and the charges which are anticipated under the regular actuarial cost method will be treated as a shortfall loss to be amortized over a 16-year period commencing in 1981. The indicated commencement date reflects the fact that the "shortfall method" was adopted to amortize the temporary shortfall of employer contributions during 1976 for the funding standard account purposes. This "shortfall method" is allowed under rules and regulations published by the I.R.S.

3. *Estimated Funding Standard Account for 1977.* Table 77-4 presents an estimated Funding Standard Account for 1977. This estimate was prepared in order to determine whether the plan's experience during 1976 and contribution levels as of January 1, 1977, will tend to increase or decrease the balance in the Funding Standard Account.

Awareness of a developing trend in the balance prior to the actual establishment of that balance enhances confidence in the plan's funding status and allows the advance consideration of any necessary corrective steps if unfavorable experience were to cause a decline in the Funding Standard Account balance (surplus).

Table 77-4 shows that, assuming the anticipated contribution levels are met, the balance in the Funding Standard Account is expected to increase from $14,489 to $66,916. Therefore, no corrective steps are required at this time if the average number of hours worked per employee in the future is at or near the 1,500-hour assumption used in this actuarial valuation.

SECTION C.   FINANCIAL CONDITION OF THE PLAN

1. *Normal Cost for Benefits* .... $ 185,386

   The Normal Cost is the amount of the level annual contribution required to fully fund the plan over the average future service lives of the active participants if the Supplemental Present Value has been fully funded at the beginning of the plan year (see Table 77–2 for details).

2. *Supplemental Present Value* 1,994,619

   The Supplemental Present Value is the amount which would be required in addition to the Normal Cost payments to fully fund the plan at the beginning of the plan year (see Table 77–2 for details).

3. *Assets Available for Pensions and Benefits* 265,945

   This is the value of the assets available for pensions and benefits (see Table 77–1) for details). Equity assets have been valued using a five-year average of market values; all other assets have been valued at cost.

4. *Unfunded Supplemental Present Value* 1,728,674

   The Unfunded Supplemental Present Value is the excess of the Supplemental Present Value over the Assets.

   The Actuarial Basis and Method used to develop the figures above are summarized in Table 77–7 of this report.

5. *Present Value of Vested Benefits* 1,191,322

   This is the amount required if the plan terminated on January 1, 1977, to fully fund all benefits in which any employees or former employees have a vested interest, assuming retirement at normal retirement age, plus the present value of all benefits payable to currently retired or disabled lives. The cost of providing vested benefits to currently active employees who terminate prior to their retirement if the plan is continued is included in the Normal Cost and Supplemental Present Value shown in items 1 and 2 and is listed in Table 77–2.

SECTION D. CONTRIBUTION AND COSTS

The anticipated gross annual contribution to the plan is $337,500. This estimate is based on an anticipated average number of the hours to be worked in 1977 (1,500,000) multiplied by $0.225, the contribution rate as of January 1, 1977.

The anticipated contributions of $337,500 are broken down as follows:

1. Annual normal cost:
    a. Normal cost for benefits $185,386
    b. Estimated expenses   8,100

    c. Total normal cost $193,486
2. Payment toward the unfunded supplemental
    present value   144,014
3. Total anticipated contributions: 1 + 2   337,500

The anticipated level of contributions shown above would fund the Unfunded Supplemental Present Value in approximately 12.3 years from January 1, 1977.

SECTION E. EMPLOYEE DATA

Complete data were available for the entire 1,015 participants in the plan. The date of birth or date of employment was corrected for three participants who were included in the 1976 actuarial study. During 1976 the number of newly eligible employees equaled the combined number of 1976 deaths and voluntary terminations.

SECTION F. ACTUARIAL EXPERIENCE

The actuarial costs developed in this report are, by their very nature, "estimates" of the true costs of the plan. The true costs of the plan will not be known until the last participant has received the last benefit to be paid under the plan. The "estimates" are based on assumed future rates of investment income, mortality,

TABLE 77-1
Statement of Assets for the Plan Year Ending December 31, 1976*

	Auditor's Report Assets Valued at Market Value	Actuarial Asset Values Assets Valued at a Five-Year Average Market Value
1. Cash	$ 15,596	$ 15,956
2. Investments held by trust fund	210,400	223,393
3. Other assets	4,096	4,096
4. Net accruals	22,500	22,500
5. Total assets as of December 31, 1976 ...	$252,952	$265,945

* This statement is based on the auditor's report for the plan year ending on December 31, 1976.

TABLE 77-2
Summary of Valuation Results as of January 1, 1977

A. *Number of Participants*

   1. Active employees 1,000
   2. Vested inactive employees 15
   3. Pensioners .... None
   4. Total number of participants 1,015

B. *Supplemental Present Value*

   1. Active employees:
      a. Pension benefit $1,439,272
      b. Vested benefit on termination 479,758

      c. Total active $1,919,030
   2. Vested inactive employees 75,589
   3. Pensioners .... None

   4. Total supplemental present value $1,994,619

C. *Normal Cost*

   1. Normal cost for active employees:
      a. Pension benefit .... $ 101,963
      b. Vested benefit on termination 83,423

      c. Total normal cost .... $ 185,423
   2. There is no normal cost for inactive employees.

Note: The above figures are based on participant data provided by the Administrator's Office of XYZ Workers Pension Trust Fund as of December 31, 1976.
   See Table 77-6 for a Summary of Plan Provisions and Table 77-7 for a Summary of Actuarial Basis and Method.

turnover, and other appropriate factors. See Table 77–7 for a description of the actuarial basis and method.

Actuarial experience which is more favorable than that anticipated will produce a "gain" to the plan, whereas, experience

---

TABLE 77–3
Funding Standard Account for 1976

A. *Funding Standard Account Charges for 1976*

These are the amounts which are, according to ERISA, to be charged to the regular Funding Standard Account. Because of the long 1976 strike and the corresponding reduction in the number of hour worked, the charges for 1976 have been calculated by use of the "shortfall method." This method allows the difference between the anticipated actuarial charges under the regular actuarial cost method and the net FSA charges for the year to be amortized—commencing five years following the year when the shortfall occurred.

1.	Anticipated actuarial charges for 1976 are as follows:	
	a. Normal cost	$ 200,687
	b. Expected expenses	10,125
	c. Amortization of unfunded supplemental present value over 40 years	108,979
	d. Adjustment for interest to end of year	7,264
	e. Total anticipated 1976 charges	$ 327,055
2.	Estimated annual covered hours for 1976	1,500,000
3.	Estimated unit charge (= 1 ÷ 2)	$0.218037
4.	Actual 1976 covered hours	1,200,000
5.	Net funding standard account charges for 1976 (= 3 × 4)	$ 261,644

B. *Funding Standard Account Credits for 1976*

The Funding Standard Account credits for 1976 include actual employer contributions and an adjustment for interest, at the valuation rate, to the end of the year.

Actual amount of employer contributions	$ 270,000
Adjustment for interest to end of year	6,133
Total credits	$ 276,133

C. *December 31, 1976, Funding Standard Account Balance*
(total credits minus total charges) .... $ 14,489

Note: The shortfall loss during 1976 is equal to the difference between the anticipated 1976 charges shown on line A.1.*e.* and the net funding standard account charges for 1976 shown on line A.5. The amount of this shortfall loss is $327,055 minus $261,644, or $65,411. This loss is to be amortized over a 16-year period beginning in 1981.

332

which is less favorable than that anticipated will produce a "loss" to the plan. Gains decrease, and losses increase, future costs of the plan. Tables 77–5A through 77–5D, inclusive, set forth a detailed analysis with commentaries on the 1976 plan experience.

TABLE 77–4
Estimated Funding Standard Account for 1977

A. *Opening Balance* .... $ 14,489

B. *Anticipated Funding Standard Account Charges for 1977*

These are the amounts which are, according to ERISA, to be charged to the regular Funding Standard Account. The anticipated charges include the Normal Cost and estimated expenses, the continuing level annual payment needed to amortize the January 1, 1976, Unfunded Supplemental Present Value over the remaining 39 years of the original 40-year period, and an adjustment for interest, at the valuation rate, to the end of the year. These charges will be adjusted, using the shortfall method, to reflect actual covered hours during 1977.

Anticipated charges:
Normal cost $185,386
Expected expenses 8,100
Amortization of:
Unfunded supplemental present value 108,979
Actuarial losses 0
Adjustment for interest to end of year 6,870

Total charges $309,335

C. *Funding Standard Account Credits for 1977—Estimated*

The funding Standard Account Credits for 1977 will include the 1977 employer contributions, the amount required to amortize the net 1976 actuarial experience gain over a 20-year period, the amount required to amortize the decrease in the Unfunded Supplemental Present Value caused by the change in actuarial assumptions over a period of 30 years, and an adjustment for interest, at the valuation rate, to the end of the year.

Credits:
Estimated employer contributions $337,500
Amortization of:
Actuarial gains shown in Table 77–5E 8,056
Decrease in Unfunded Supplemental Present Value on account of the change in actuarial assumptions 7,463
Adjustment for interest on credits and opening balance to end of year 8,743

Total credits $361,762

TABLE 77–4 (continued)

D. *Estimated December 31, 1977, Funding Standard Account Balance*
   (= opening balance minus total charges plus total credits) .... $ 66,916

   If contributions are made to the plan as anticipated in our valuation, there will be a balance of $66,916 in the Funding Standard Account by the end of 1977.

TABLE 77–5A
Comparison of Actual and Expected Turnover

Age on 1/1/76	Number of Participants	Expected* Terminations	Actual Terminations
25	500	38.621	108
30	200	14.444	42
35	100	6.276	18
40	100	5.150	14
45	75	3.487	8
50	5	0.205	0
55	10	0.350	0
60	10	0.235	0
65	0	0.000	0
Total	1,000	68.768	190

* Based on 1976 actuarial assumption.

Comments: The above table compares the actual number of terminations with the number expected if the 1976 actuarial assumptions has been met.

One hundred ninety participants actually terminated instead of the 69 expected to terminate, and this experience produced a substantial gain which decreased the Unfunded Supplemental Present Value by $117,283. This gain occurred because a large number of the terminating participants had less than ten years of service and, therefore, were not vested in their accrued pension.

TABLE 77–5B
Comparison of Actual and Expected Retirements

Age on 1/1/76	Number of Participants	Expected Retirements	Actual Retirements
55	10	0.8	0
60	10	0.9	0
65	0	0.0	0
Total	20	1.7	0

TABLE 77–5B *(continued)*

Comments: Based on the assumed retirement rates, we would expect two participants to retire during 1976 and receive reduced early retirement pensions. Actually no one retired, and the plan suffered a loss which increased the Unfunded Supplemental Present Value by $3,349. When full actuarial reductions are applied to early retirement pensions and the Individual Level Cost Method with Supplemental Present Value is used, excess early retirements will generally produce a gain, and a lack of expected early retirement will produce a loss, as in this case. If the plan had provided for unreduced early retirement pensions, this experience would have produced a gain instead of a loss.

TABLE 77–5C
Comparison of Actual and Expected Deaths

Age on 1/1/76	Number of Participants	Expected Deaths	Actual Deaths
25	500	0.310	1
30	200	0.162	0
35	100	0.112	0
40	100	0.163	0
45	75	0.219	0
50	5	0.026	0
55	10	0.085	0
60	10	0.131	0
65	0	0.000	0
Total	1,000	1.208	1

Comments: This table illustrates the mortality experience under the plan. Note that it is not possible for the plan's experience to exactly to fit the mortality table during any one plan year, since only a fraction of the participants would be expected to die in any age group. The mortality under this plan produced a loss which increased the Unfunded Supplemental Present Value by $9,878, since the one participant who died was young and had not accrued a substantial pension.

TABLE 77–5D
Miscellaneous Gains and Losses—Comments

A number of other factors differed from the actuarial assumptions. The factor that had the greatest influence on actuarial results, other than the turnover experience which has previously been discussed, was the shortfall in the number of hours worked. The following comments discuss the several miscellaneous sources of gains and losses during calendar year 1976.

TABLE 77–5D (continued)

1. *Investment Income and Asset Value Changes.* The actual contributions to the plan during 1976 were $247,500. These contributions were made in 11 monthly payments of $22,500 at the end of each month from February through December. (The effect of these contributions being less than expected is discussed in item 2 below; here we are discussing investment performance.)

   If the investment earnings rate had been equal to the 5 percent rate assumed, the cash basis assets on January 1, 1977 (taking account of the actual expenses discussed in item 3), would have been $241,536. The actual assets on a cash accounting basis were $243,445, so favorable investment performance produced a gain, or decrease in the Unfunded Supplemental Present Value, of $1,909. (Since there was a $22,500 employer contribution "receivable," the real assets on an accrual accounting basis actually were $265,945.)

2. *Changes in the Number of Hours Worked.* In the January 1, 1976, valuation it was assumed that each participant would work 1,500 hours per year at a contribution rate of 22.5 cents per covered hour. Actually, in 1976, participants only worked an average of 1,200 hours, and this affected the plan in two ways. First, the participants did not earn as much pension credit as was expected, and this produced a gain which reduced the Unfunded Supplemental Present Value by $1,952. Second, the total contributions (actual contributions of $247,500 plus accrued contributions of $22,500, or a total of $270,000) were not as great as expected because of the smaller number of hours worked; and as a result, the payment to amortize the Unfunded Supplemental Present Value was $70,082 less than expected. The effects of this contribution shortfall are discussed in Table 77–3.

3. *Expenses.* The expected expenses were $10,125, but the actual expenses were $10,800. This, after adjustment for the loss of investment income due to the increase expenses, produced a loss which increased the Unfunded Supplemental Present Value by $692.

4. *Corrections to the Participant Data.* The employee data supplied to the actuary on January 1, 1977, indicated that the information for three of the participants was incorrect in the January 1, 1976, data. One of the 60-year-old participants and one of the 55-year-old participants had five more years of service than was previously reported, and one of the 50-year-old participants had less years of service than originally reported. The result of these data corrections was a loss which increased the Unfunded Supplemental Present Value by $4,539.

TABLE 77–5D *(concluded)*

5. *Change in Actuarial Assumptions.* In addition to the experience gains and losses described above, there was a decrease in the Unfunded Supplemental Present Value of $117,223 because of a change in the assumed rates of employee turnover. This "gain" is, for funding standard account purposes, considered as a separate item and is not aggregated with the experience gains and losses.

TABLE 77–5E
Summary of Gain and Loss Experience

The aggregate experience gain for 1976 was $102,686. This amount is determined as follows:

Source of Gain or Loss	Gain or (loss)
Investment income	$ 1,909
Turnover	117,283
Retirement	(3,349)
Hours worked	1,952
Expenses	(692)
Mortality	(9,878)
Data corrections	(4,539)
	$102,686

In addition there was a gain of $117,223 because of the change in actuarial assumptions. The total gain for the year was, therefore, $219,909. The effect of this gain is offset by the $70,082 contribution shortfall, so the Unfunded Supplemental Present Value was $149,827 smaller than expected.

Comments: During 1976, the total effect of experience on the Unfunded Supplemental Present Value of the component gains and losses was favorable. This will not always happen. For example, if there had been no gain because of turnover, and if no change had been made in the assumed turnover rates, the result would have been that the new Unfunded Supplemental Present Value would have been $84,679 greater than expected rather than $149,827 less than expected.

The *expected* Unfunded Supplemental Present Value on January 1, 1977, was $1,878,501. Because of the gains described above, the January 1, 1977, actuarial valuation produced an Unfunded Supplemental Present Value of $1,728,674 which was exactly $149,827 lower than expected, and this coincides with the amounts shown above.

Since this first year of experience under this plan has demonstrated such dramatically different turnover experience in comparison with expected results, the turnover factors for the plan have been changed. The actuarial assumptions are, under ERISA, supposed to reflect the actuary's best estimate of future experience, and for that reason the change has been made.

TABLE 77-6
Summary of Plan Provisions as of January 1, 1977

1. *Effective Date of Plan:* January 1, 1966.
2. *Pension Benefit*
   a. *Eligibility*
      (i) *Normal Retirement.* Participants shall reach their Normal Retirement Date upon the later of attainment of age 65 or the accumulation of ten years of total service, at least five of which are vesting service years, but in no event later than the tenth anniversary of the date contributions were first made on their behalf.
      (ii) *Early Retirement.* Participants who are at least age 55 and have completed ten years of vesting service, are eligible to retire early.
   b. *Monthly Pension Benefit.* The plan provides a monthly pension benefit credit of $10 for each year of service, payable at normal retirement age 65.
   c. *Credited Service.* Service credits to determine eligibility for plan benefits may be gained by future service and past service.
      (i) Future service is earned for employment under a bargaining agreement after an employer's contribution date, and is credited at the rate of one fifteen hundredth (1/1,500) of one year for each covered hour.
      (ii) Past service is earned for covered employment prior to the date specified in the plan. One quarter of a credit is given for each calendar quarter in which the participant earned at least $200 of wages in the industry.
   d. *Forms of Retirement Benefits*
      (i) *Normal Pension Form.* A plan participant, subject to the applicability of the Automatic Joint and Survivor Pension Form, can retire on a life pension with 36 monthly payments guaranteed.

TABLE 77–6 *(continued)*

    (ii) *Automatic Joint and Survivor Pension Form.* Participants who have been married at least one year on the date their pension commences and who have not elected the Normal Pension Form or any of the optional pension forms, receive this reduced joint and survivor pension. Under this Joint and Survivor Pension Form, in the event a participant dies, a life pension equal to 50 percent of the participant's reduced pension is continued to the surviving spouse.

    (iii) *Optional Pension Forms.* A plan participant can elect to receive his benefits in one of the following forms:

        a. Joint and two-thirds survivor pension.

        b. Joint and 100 percent survivor pension.

3. *Vested Pension Benefit.* Employees who have completed ten or more years of credited vesting service are fully vested in all accrued pension benefit credits.

4. *Preretirement Death Benefit.* An active participant may elect preretirement spouse pension protection. If this coverage is elected, the normal pension will be reduced, upon retirement, to reflect the cost of this benefit.

TABLE 77–7
Summary of Actuarial Basis and Method

A. *Valuation of Assets*

    The plan's actuarial asset values are based on the amortized values of bond securities and the five-year average market value of the equity investments.

B. *Actuarial Basis*

    1. *Investment Earnings Rate:*   5% per annum, compounded annually.

    2. *Mortality:*   Male 1971 Group Annuity Mortality Table (known as 1971 GAM) for all participants.

    Examples of the mortality rates are:

Age	Annual Probability of Death
25	0.062%
30	0.081
35	0.112
40	0.163

TABLE 77–7 *(continued)*

Age	Annual Probability of Death
45	0.292
50	0.529
55	0.852
60	1.312
65	2.126

3. *Turnover:*   Examples of the turnover rates used are:

Age	Annual Probability of Termination
25	15.44%
30	12.64
35	10.49
40	8.24
45	5.58
50	4.10
55	3.50
60	2.35
65	0.00

4. *Provision for Expenses:*   2.4 percent of gross employer contributions.

5. *Age Retirement Rates:*   Rates used for valuing the current plan:

Age	Annual Probability of Age Retirement
55	8.0%
56	8.0
57	8.0
58	8.0
59	9.0
60	9.0
61	35.0
62	35.0
63	35.0
64	50.0
65	100.0

6. *Projection of Pension Credits:*   Pension credits were projected on the assumption that all participants would work 1,500 covered hours per year at a contribution rate of 22.5 cents per hour worked.

TABLE 77–7 *(concluded)*

7. *Number of Covered Employees:* Actuarial calculations have been performed on the assumption that the number of active employees will remain stable, at the current level, indefinitely into the future.

C. *Actuarial Cost Method*

The Individual Level Cost Method with Supplemental Present Value was used. Under this method, the prospective pension benefits at normal retirement age are calculated for a cohort of new entrants with entry ages equal to the entry ages of the currently active participants. Level cost factors payable from entry age to normal retirement age are developed based upon the actuarial assumptions described above. The normal cost is found by applying these level cost factors to the prospective benefits. The present value of the future benefits payable to currently active participants is also calculated.

The supplemental present value for the benefits for active lives is the excess of the present value of the future benefits of currently active lives over the present value of future normal costs. The supplemental present value for the benefits for terminated employees with vested benefits are found by applying present value factors to these benefits.

The normal costs and supplemental present values for the termination benefits are calculated in a similar manner.

APPENDIX G

SPECIMEN RECIPROCAL AGREEMENT

RECIPROCAL AGREEMENT

This Agreement is made and entered into by and between the XYZ Workers Pension Plan (referred to herein as "XYZ Plan") and the XYZ Workers Pension Plan of Nevada (referred to herein as "West Coast Plan").

WITNESSETH:

WHEREAS, the XYZ Plan and the West Coast Plan desire to provide reciprocal benefits to the respective beneficiaries of each Plan when said beneficiaries are employed in the area of the other, and,

WHEREAS, each Plan is a qualified pension plan under Section 401 of the Internal Revenue Code and is exempt from income tax under the regulations of the Internal Revenue Service, and,

WHEREAS, the XYZ Plan has been created in the State of California and the West Coast Plan has been created in the State of Nevada as a result of agreements between local unions of the International Brotherhood of XYZ Workers and employers and said agreements require contributions to be made by the employers to the respective pension plans, and, therefore, each Plan is subject to applicable state and federal laws, and,

WHEREAS, the Boards of Trustees of the XYZ Plan and the West Coast Plan have been duly authorized to enter into this Reciprocal Agreement,

NOW THEREFORE, in consideration of the foregoing and of the mutual undertakings herein, the XYZ Plan and the West Coast Plan agree as follows:

1. No beneficiary of either the XYZ Plan or the West Coast Plan shall suffer any disqualification from benefits or any loss of years of credited service under his Plan by reason of any period of employment in the area of the other Plan.

2. Each Plan will retain its own Plan year and will apply its own rules for determining years of credited service, vesting service, break in service or eligibility for benefits; provided, however, that in applying these rules, each Plan shall calculate periods of employment in the area of the other Plan (referred to herein as the "Related Plan") for the purpose of determining eligibility for benefits pursuant to the following rules and regulations:

   a. The term "Plan," as used in these rules and regulations, means either the XYZ Plan or the West Coast Plan. The term "Related Plan" means the West Coast Plan whenever "Plan" refers to the XYZ Plan and "Related Plan" means the XYZ Plan whenever "Plan" refers to the West Coast Plan.

   b. The term "Related Hours" means hours of employment which are creditable under the Related Plan.

   c. The term "Related Credit" means years of vesting service, or portions thereof, creditable to a Participant under the Related Plan.

   d. The term "Combined Pension Credit" means a Participant's Total Service accumulated under the Plan plus the total of a Participant's Related Credit.

   e. It is specifically recognized that a Participant may have Past Service employment that would have been creditable under the Plan except for his failure to be entitled to Past Service Credit as set forth in the Past Service provisions of the Plan. However, such past employment may be creditable:

      (i) If the Participant had Related Hours, which, in combination with his Covered Hours under the Plan, would have satisfied the Past Service provisions; and

      (ii) If his Past Service employment that would have been

covered by the Plan, except for his failure to be entitled to Past Service Credit as set forth in the Past Service provisions, were continuous (as defined by the Plan or the Related Plan) with creditable employment in the area of the Related Plan.

f. A Participant shall not receive double credit for the same period of past employment. No more than one year of Pension Credit or Related Credit shall be given for all employment in any given calendar year.

g. A Participant who, because of his Combined Pension Credits, is eligible to retire in accordance with the retirement eligibility provisions of the Plan shall be eligible for Reciprocal Benefits if he meets the following requirements:

    (i) He would be eligible for a benefit under the Plan were his Combined Pension Credits treated as Pension Credits under the Plan; and

    (ii) He has accumulated at least one year of Past Service Credit or one year of Vesting Service, as defined by the Plan and determined without regard to this Reciprocal Agreement.

h. Related Hours shall be considered in determining whether a Participant has failed to accumulate sufficient Vesting Service Years to avoid a forfeiture of Credited Vesting Service Years and consequent loss of Pension Credits which had been credited to him pursuant to the conditions of the Plan.

i. The amount of the Reciprocal Benefit payable by the Plan, for a Participant retiring for age, shall be determined based on the Credited Past Service and Credited Future Service earned under the Plan, as modified by Section 2(*e*) of this Agreement, excluding any years of Credited Service forfeited pursuant to the provisions of the Plan.

j. The amount of Reciprocal Benefit, if any, payable by the Plan to the spouse or beneficiary of a Participant as defined in the Plan, shall be determined by the applicable provisions of the Plan, based on the Participant's years of Credited Service under the Plan.

k. Payment of a Reciprocal Benefit shall be subject to all of the conditions applicable to the other types of benefits under the Plan.

3. It shall be the responsibility of each beneficiary to make application for benefits under this Reciprocal Agreement and to supply all information required by each Plan necessary to the calculation of eligibility for benefits and amount of benefit payments. Neither Plan shall incur liability because of the failure of a Related Plan to provide data or to make payment of benefits related to credits earned in the area of the Related Plan. The obligation to determine and report credits earned in the area of the Related Plan shall rest on the Related Plan of the Participant.

4. Upon receipt of an application, the XYZ Plan and the West Coast Plan shall engage in such investigation and exchange of information as may be necessary to determine the applicant's eligibility for benefits pursuant to the rules of each Plan.

5. If an applicant fails to meet the eligibility requirements of either Plan, after application of the terms of this Agreement, the Plan to which he applied shall notify the applicant of that fact in writing and shall include therein the reasons for the applicant's disqualification.

6. There will be no duplicate payment of benefits for the same period of credited service as a result of this Agreement. If either Plan is required to pay benefits for a particular period of credited service without the application of this Agreement, that Plan will pay those benefits, and the other Plan will pay benefits for such period as a result of this Agreement.

   If neither Plan would be required to pay benefits with respect to a particular period of credited service, in the absence of this Agreement, but both Plans would pay such benefits as a result hereof, then each Plan shall compute and pay benefits based on service earned in the jurisdiction of such Plan, subject to the provisions of Section 2(f) of this Agreement.

7. Each Plan shall pay its benefits on its own normal form or actuarially equivalent form, if applicable, as determined by the respective plan. Any election of an optional form of pension shall be effective with respect to a particular Plan only if properly elected in accordance with the rules of that Plan.

8. This Agreement shall become effective upon the date when the Trustees of each Plan shall have executed the same and shall continue indefinitely so long as both Plans are in existence; provided, however, that either party may terminate the same upon giving at least one year's prior notice in writing to the other party. It is the understanding of the parties that during the one-year notice period, the representatives of both Plans will attempt to resolve the rights of the employees concerned, including the matter of allocations of benefits accrued by employees during the life of this Reciprocal Agreement. In the event the parties are unable to agree on any issue, prior to 60 days before the contemplated termination of the Agreement, such unresolved issues shall be submitted to impartial arbitration before an arbitrator selected by the parties and the decision of the arbitrator shall be final and binding on all concerned.

9. This Agreement may be amended upon the mutual agreement of the Boards of Trustees of both Plans at any time provided that any such amendment does not decrease the benefits previously earned by the beneficiaries covered by said Plans.

IN WITNESS WHEREOF, the parties have executed this Agreement by the signatures below, at the dates shown, of the Board of Trustees of each Plan.

DATED: _____   DATED: _____

XYZ WORKERS PENSION PLAN   XYZ WORKERS PENSION PLAN
OF NEVADA

INDEX